Luís Pereira Coutinho
Editor

Political Representation and Constitutional Adjudication

Springer

Editor
Luís Pereira Coutinho
Faculty of Law
University of Lisbon
Lisbon, Portugal

ISSN 1534-6781 ISSN 2214-9902 (electronic)
Ius Gentium: Comparative Perspectives on Law and Justice
ISBN 978-3-031-85985-4 ISBN 978-3-031-85983-0 (eBook)
https://doi.org/10.1007/978-3-031-85983-0

This Springer imprint is published by the registered company Springer Nature Switzerland AG
The registered company address is: Gewerbestrasse 11, 6330 Cham, Switzerland

Ius Gentium: Comparative Perspectives on Law and Justice 124

Ius Gentium is a book series which discusses the central questions of law and justice from a comparative perspective. The books in this series collect the contrasting and overlapping perspectives of lawyers, judges, philosophers and scholars of law from the world's many different jurisdictions for the purposes of comparison, harmonisation, and the progressive development of law and legal institutions. Each volume makes a new comparative study of an important area of law. This book series continues the work of the well-known journal of the same name and provides the basis for a better understanding of all areas of legal science.

The *Ius Gentium* series provides a valuable resource for lawyers, judges, legislators, scholars, and both graduate students and researchers in globalisation, comparative law, legal theory and legal practice. The series has a special focus on the development of international legal standards and transnational legal cooperation.

Introduction

Constitutional courts claim to act "in the name of the people" and, moreover, are supposed to do so in the express terms of many constitutional texts. This raises the question of knowing whether they can be deemed as proper representatives of the people in theoretical terms. From the outset, the only certainty that exists is admittedly not reassuring. We are not speaking of electoral representation, the most obvious candidate—at least in present times—when we refer to political representation.

From a theoretical perspective, the apparent paradox residing in a non-electoral representation of the people is not unsolvable. In fact, political representation may mean different things and take different forms. The basic insight justifying this volume was that a quest for a meaning which is relevant for our case is not fruitless. In fact, while searching for it, one is trying to make sense of a language and practice of claimed representation. The effort implies the determination and comparison of different paths to conceive the legitimacy of constitutional courts and the rationality presiding over their action. That, while keeping in mind that in a constitutional democracy not all forms of legitimacy are electoral and not all public rationalities are straightforwardly democratic (in the sense of involving the casting and counting of votes by the citizens and their elected representatives), remaining nevertheless attributable to "the people" in some sense.

It is therefore relevant to take stock of different proposals allowing for that attribution while defining its terms. There are different theoretical possibilities discussed in this volume. The first to be explored is that which was advanced within a continental tradition still developing under the influence of the general theory of the state. According to the corresponding concept of political representation—explored by Pierre-Marie Raynal and Luís Pereira Coutinho—, constitutional courts are to be deemed representatives of the people alongside other constitutional organs composing the constitutional person of the state. That is, as organs foreseen by the Constitution which act according to its terms, thus articulating the rationality of constitutional law, constitutional courts are expressing the political rationality of "the people" as a body which cannot be confused with the majority of the citizens composing it—the former rationality necessarily corresponding to the latter.

For some contributors to this volume, it would be hasty to reject the discourse of political representation on the basis of a simplistic denunciation of its "conceptualism", or on the grounds that it endorses a fiction in some sense. Rather, it is more fruitful to analyze the character of that discourse and to clarify its inherent rationality. In this vein, Raynal concludes that the rationality of liberal constitutionalism is at stake in "judicial representation". Also exploring the rationality implied in modern constitutional law,

Pereira Coutinho takes stock of different theories—from Kelsen's to Alexy's—concluding that they conceive the constitutional jurisdiction as an institutional expression of a commonality of citizens, even if the latter is conceived in different terms by each of those theories. Additionally, addressing the constitutional discourse on political representation, Nogueira de Brito considers that there is no way out of it, "even if (or because) representation is a fiction".

To the extent that it expresses the rationality of constitutional law, non-electoral political representation is understood in different terms—by those who accept it—depending on the way in which the same rationality is conceived. Most prominently, a highly moralized discourse on constitutional law such as that advanced by Robert Alexy—according to which constitutional courts vindicate law's "claim to correctness" when taking decisions based on "sound and correct arguments"—considers that at stake is the "argumentative representation" of the people conceived as a body of "constitutional persons". The unparalleled diffusion of Alexy's conception justifies its critical treatment by Pereira Coutinho, Pierre Brunet, Dimitrios Kyritsis, and Bojan Spaic[1].

The question placed by Nogueira de Brito is not whether constitutional courts represent the people—for him, they do so as participants in a "joint representational practice"—but whether the rationality of constitutional law animating them is dualistic or monistic. For Nogueira de Brito, political representation must be understood in monistic terms—with no political unity "preceding and conditioning an order of legal acts"—, that resulting from a phenomenological reconstruction of collective action. Moreover, this is a beneficial result if compared with those which deceptively assume a "people" that pre-exists its joint representation by the organs composing the constitutional state.

Other theoretical possibilities are available to make sense of constitutional courts as "representatives". Brunet's contribution mainly focuses on whether political representation by the constitutional courts can be taken as a form of democratic representation, even if that possibility depends on exploring institutional alternatives to the present *status quo* which would make constitutional review more expressive of shared values in society and more dialogical in character. Differently from Brunet, Pedro Lomba rejects an "overexpansion" of the concept of political representation into the sphere of the courts—if by that concept one means that the power of courts is still derived from the people directly. Lomba nonetheless believes that constitutional courts cannot be conceived as indifferent to the "representative device". Rather, they should be conceived as "representative trustees", thus charged with the preservation of the citizen's trust in "representative balance", the latter implied in a logic of representation demanding the coexistence of the independent condition of citizens with the dependency inherent in the representative framework.

One may also be speaking in this context of political representation in an "empirical" or "realist" sense, that depending on the observation that constitutional judges, even if not elected, resound—either legitimately or not—the political conceptions of majorities[2]

[1] See in this volume Pereira Coutinho, Sect. 2; Brunet, Sect. 2; Kyritsis, Sect. 3; Spaic, Sect. 4.

[2] See Brunet's discussion of "an American concept of representation by the judges", *infra*, Sect. 1.3. See also Kyritsis' discussion of Christopher Eisgruber's conception of the American Supreme Court as "representative", *infra*, Sect. 3.

or those of elected representatives[3]. Yet another proposal, also discussed in this volume, is radically different both in its non-empiricism and in the non-vicarious nature of the form of political representation expected—from a normative perspective, in this case—from constitutional courts. In the latter case, constitutional courts are to be conceived as representatives precisely because they may stand against elected representatives, who cannot make a monopolistic claim to represent the people, then abusively seizing or capturing an uncapturable "general will"[4].

Many of the contributors to this volume are skeptical regarding both the accuracy and the possible benefits of a language of political representation by the constitutional courts. Pasquale Pasquino claims that to speak of "representation" in this context really means to "play with the semantics of the term", one which can only be properly used when we are speaking of "the authority authorized and accountable via popular elections". Michel Troper also claims that one should resist "the temptation" of conceiving constitutional courts as representatives, at least if one wants to avoid the risk of falling into a sort of "idolatry" by assuming the existence of a "perpetual people" or "general will" which is different from that of the actual people.

One should note that the skeptical arguments developed in this volume are not—at least not all of them—dismissive of the legitimacy of constitutional review, either normative or actual. The point, rather, is that legitimacy should not be understood in terms of "political representation". Pasquino considers that constitutional review stands as an essential element of the contemporary constitutional structure of divided power, whose legitimacy is not to be understood in "monocratic" terms (i.e., exclusively "democratic" or "representative"). Also refusing the idea of the contemporary constitutional state as being uniformly democratic (with all powers needing to be deemed representative to be legitimate), Troper considers that "ours is a mixed government", in which an aristocratic element competes with a democratic element.

Not committing to the idea of an aristocratic element in the structure of the contemporary constitutional government, Kyritsis believes nevertheless that it is shaped by "different moral forces—not all of which refer back to the people's will". Kyritsis defends that the benefit of taking the courts as representatives is not demonstrated, and it must be so, considering that—under the terms of his moralized constitutional theory—a given constitutional language on powers and their legitimacy should be construed in terms that enhance the legitimacy of the relevant political order. Far from achieving that result, a "unitary legitimation thesis"—according to which the decisions of all organs of the state, also constitutional courts, must be traced back to the people—would stand in opposition to "the moral appeal of polyphonic legal orders", which "lies precisely in that they seek to combine the distinctive political virtues of different institutions", not all of them "representative of the people".

Within a discussion about the politicization of the constitutional jurisdiction and the judicialization of politics, Spaic addresses in particular an empirical sense of political representation by constitutional courts, asking whether it determines constitutional adjudication and does so justifiably. Spaic concludes that, rather than explaining the legitimacy of constitutional courts in terms of representation, one should opt for a "piecemeal

[3] See Spaic's discussion, *infra*.

[4] See the theories on the "representation of representation" discussed in Troper, *infra*, Sect. 3.1.

approach" evaluating different strategies that may or may not contribute to it. Under this spirit, Spaic focuses in particular on a strategy of "dialogization" that relies on the virtue of judicial candor. That strategy would increase the likelihood of popular legitimacy of constitutional adjudication while remaining in accordance with its "dual–political and legal–nature".

Luís Pereira Coutinho

Contents

Introduction

Luís Pereira Coutinho(✉)

University of Lisbon's School of Law, LPL Lisbon Public Law Research Centre, Lisbon, Portugal
lpcoutinho@fd.ulisboa.pt

Constitutional courts claim to act "in the name of the people" and, moreover, are supposed to do so in the express terms of many constitutional texts. This raises the question of knowing whether they can be deemed as proper representatives of the people in theoretical terms. From the outset, the only certainty that exists is admittedly not reassuring. We are not speaking of electoral representation, the most obvious candidate – at least in present times – when we refer to political representation.

From a theoretical perspective, the apparent paradox residing in a non-electoral representation of the people is not unsolvable. In fact, political representation may mean different things and take different forms. The basic insight justifying this volume was that a quest for a meaning which is relevant for our case is not fruitless. In fact, while searching for it, one is trying to make sense of a language and practice of claimed representation. The effort implies the determination and comparison of different paths to conceive the legitimacy of constitutional courts and the rationality presiding over their action. That, while keeping in mind that in a constitutional democracy not all forms of legitimacy are electoral and not all public rationalities are straightforwardly democratic (in the sense of involving the casting and counting of votes by the citizens and their elected representatives), remaining nevertheless attributable to "the people" in some sense.

It is therefore relevant to take stock of different proposals allowing for that attribution while defining its terms. There are different theoretical possibilities discussed in this volume. The first to be explored is that which was advanced within a continental tradition still developing under the influence of the general theory of the state. According to the corresponding concept of political representation – explored by Pierre-Marie Raynal and Luís Pereira Coutinho –, constitutional courts are to be deemed representatives of the people alongside other constitutional organs composing the constitutional person of the state. That is, as organs foreseen by the Constitution which act according to its terms, thus articulating the rationality of constitutional law, constitutional courts are expressing the political rationality of "the people" as a body which cannot be confused with the majority of the citizens composing it – the former rationality necessarily corresponding to the latter.

For some contributors to this volume, it would be hasty to reject the discourse of political representation on the basis of a simplistic denunciation of its "conceptualism", or on the grounds that it endorses a fiction in some sense. Rather, it is more fruitful to analyze the character of that discourse and to clarify its inherent rationality. In this vein, Raynal concludes that the rationality of liberal constitutionalism is at stake in "judicial

L. Pereira Coutinho (Ed.): ICPRCR 2022, IUSGENT 124, pp. 1–4, 2025.
https://doi.org/10.1007/978-3-031-85983-0_1

representation". Also exploring the rationality implied in modern constitutional law, Pereira Coutinho takes stock of different theories – from Kelsen's to Alexy's – concluding that they conceive the constitutional jurisdiction as an institutional expression of a commonality of citizens, even if the latter is conceived in different terms by each of those theories. Additionally, addressing the constitutional discourse on political representation, Nogueira de Brito considers that there is no way out of it, "even if (or because) representation is a fiction".

To the extent that it expresses the rationality of constitutional law, non-electoral political representation is understood in different terms – by those who accept it – depending on the way in which the same rationality is conceived. Most prominently, a highly moralized discourse on constitutional law such as that advanced by Robert Alexy – according to which constitutional courts vindicate law's "claim to correctness" when taking decisions based on "sound and correct arguments" – considers that at stake is the "argumentative representation" of the people conceived as a body of "constitutional persons". The unparalleled diffusion of Alexy's conception justifies its critical treatment by Pereira Coutinho, Pierre Brunet, Dimitrios Kyritsis, and Bojan Spaic.

The question placed by Nogueira de Brito is not whether constitutional courts represent the people – for him, they do so as participants in a "joint representational practice" – but whether the rationality of constitutional law animating them is dualistic or monistic. For Nogueira de Brito, political representation must be understood in monistic terms – with no political unity "preceding and conditioning an order of legal acts" –, that resulting from a phenomenological reconstruction of collective action. Moreover, this is a beneficial result if compared with those which deceptively assume a "people" that pre-exists its joint representation by the organs composing the constitutional state.

Other theoretical possibilities are available to make sense of constitutional courts as "representatives". Brunet's contribution mainly focuses on whether political representation by the constitutional courts can be taken as a form of democratic representation, even if that possibility depends on exploring institutional alternatives to the present *status quo* which would make constitutional review more expressive of shared values in society and more dialogical in character. Differently from Brunet, Pedro Lomba rejects an "overexpansion" of the concept of political representation into the sphere of the courts – if by that concept one means that the power of courts is still derived from the people directly. Lomba nonetheless believes that constitutional courts cannot be conceived as indifferent to the "representative device". Rather, they should be conceived as "representative trustees", thus charged with the preservation of the citizen's trust in "representative balance", the latter implied in a logic of representation demanding the coexistence of the independent condition of citizens with the dependency inherent in the representative framework.

One may also be speaking in this context of political representation in an "empirical" or "realist" sense, that depending on the observation that constitutional judges, even if not elected, resound – either legitimately or not – the political conceptions of majorities[1]

[1] See Brunet's discussion of "an American concept of representation by the judges", *infra*, Sect. 1.3. See also Kyritsis' discussion of Christopher Eisgruber's conception of the American Supreme Court as "representative", *infra*, Sect. 3.

or those of elected representatives[2]. Yet another proposal, also discussed in this volume, is radically different both in its non-empiricism and in the non-vicarious nature of the form of political representation expected – from a normative perspective, in this case – from constitutional courts. In the latter case, constitutional courts are to be conceived as representatives precisely because they may stand against elected representatives, who cannot make a monopolistic claim to represent the people, then abusively seizing or capturing an uncapturable "general will"[3].

2. Many of the contributors to this volume are sceptical regarding both the accuracy and the possible benefits of a language of political representation by the constitutional courts. Pasquale Pasquino claims that to speak of "representation" in this context really means to "play with the semantics of the term", one which can only be properly used when we are speaking of "the authority authorized and accountable via popular elections". Michel Troper also claims that one should resist "the temptation" of conceiving constitutional courts as representatives, at least if one wants to avoid the risk of falling into a sort of "idolatry" by assuming the existence of a "perpetual people" or "general will" which is different from that of the actual people.

One should note that the sceptical arguments developed in this volume, are not – at least not all of them – dismissive of the legitimacy of constitutional review, either normative or actual. The point, rather, is that that legitimacy should not be understood in terms of "political representation". Pasquino considers that constitutional review stands as an essential element of the contemporary constitutional structure of divided power, whose legitimacy is not to be understood in "monocratic" terms (i.e., exclusively "democratic" or "representative"). Also refusing the idea of the contemporary constitutional state as being uniformly democratic (with all powers needing to be deemed representative to be legitimate), Troper considers that "ours is a mixed government", in which an aristocratic element competes with a democratic element.

Not committing to the idea of an aristocratic element in the structure of the contemporary constitutional government, Kyritsis believes nevertheless that it is shaped by "different moral forces – not all of which refer back to the people's will". Kyritsis defends that the benefit of taking the courts as representatives is not demonstrated, and it must be so, considering that – under the terms of his moralized constitutional theory – a given constitutional language on powers and their legitimacy should be construed in terms that enhance the legitimacy of the relevant political order. Far from achieving that result, a "unitary legitimation thesis" – according to which the decisions of all organs of the state, also constitutional courts, must be traced back to the people – would stand in opposition to "the moral appeal of polyphonic legal orders", which "lies precisely in that they seek to combine the distinctive political virtues of different institutions", not all of them "representative of the people".

Within a discussion about the politicization of the constitutional jurisdiction and the judicialization of politics, Spaic addresses in particular an empirical sense of political representation by constitutional courts, asking whether it determines constitutional adjudication and does so justifiably. Spaic concludes that, rather than explaining the legitimacy of constitutional courts in terms of representation, one should opt for a "piecemeal

[2] See Spaic's discussion, *infra.*

[3] See the theories on the "representation of representation" discussed in Troper, *infra*, Sect. 3.1.

approach" evaluating different strategies that may or may not contribute to it. Under this spirit, Spaic focuses in particular on a strategy of "dialogization" that relies on the virtue of judicial candor. That strategy would increase the likelihood of popular legitimacy of constitutional adjudication while remaining in accordance with its "dual – political and legal – nature".

Theoretical Possibilities

Is Judicial Representation a Democratic Myth?

Pierre-Marie Raynal(✉)

CY's Faculty of Law, CY Cergy Paris University, Cergy, France
pierre-marie.raynal@cyu.fr

Abstract. This chapter analyses political representation as a fictional rhetoric. The aim of this rhetoric is to obtain, from its audience, a recognition of law as the expression of the sovereign will of the political community; whereas it is, in actual fact, only the work of persons who have effectively participated in its making. That which I call "judicial representation" appears as a variant of political representation, whose specific purpose is to legitimize constitutional review. Considering judicial representation as fictional rhetoric can raise two questions. Firstly, to which category of false discourse does it belong: fiction in the strict sense, lie, or myth? Secondly, to what extend can it be understood as a form of democratic discourse? The hypothesis put forward is that judicial representation is a myth that can be qualified as democratic, but only if we limit the understanding of this term to its contemporary liberal sense.

1 Introduction

This chapter seeks to clarify the fiction of the constitutional judge as a representative[1]. The demonstration relies on two core assumptions: firstly, political representation is a fictional rhetoric; secondly, the constitutional judge is a representative.

1.1 A First Assumption: Political Representation as Fictional Rhetoric

The object of political representation as fictional rhetoric is to persuade an audience to recognize positive law as the work of an abstract entity which, by definition, has no will to exercise and is thus incapable of making any rule.

This abstract entity, the "represented", is believed in some way to be authentic, but exists only through the term which designates it. Different terms may be mobilized according to the contexts: "Republic", "Crown", "State", "Nation", "People", or even "European Union". The intention is in each case to evoke the existence, unanimity, and permanence of an otherwise intangible political community, and to invoke its will in order to legitimize political power.

---

[1] The present article started out, at Professor Luís Pereira Coutinho's invitation, as a conference paper delivered in Lisbon on November 2022. I thank Luís for this invitation. I also thank my friend Gregory Bligh for his invaluable help.

L. Pereira Coutinho (Ed.): ICPRCR 2022, IUSGENT 124, pp. 7–24, 2025.
https://doi.org/10.1007/978-3-031-85983-0_2

In this sense, the rhetoric of political representation characterizes multiple types of justificatory discourses. Their common feature is to invoke this sovereign will, which is both politically majestic and legally supreme. And this is what explains the empirically false and therefore fictional character of this rhetoric: it asserts *against empirical experience* that legal rules ultimately express the will of the political community, not the multiple effective wills that are their cause *in fact*. This fictional rhetoric is at work in the assertion that the author of positive law is the political community, not the various individuals who have *effectively* made decisions enacted into law.

This is no trivial concern. Beyond its methodological implications[2], the fictional character of political representation deserves our attention because it is an official rhetoric, mobilized by the legal system itself. Let us mention a double illustration where the enterprise of persuasion is particularly intense: the famous opening of the American Constitution: "We, the people of the United States"; and the preamble of the Portuguese Constitution proclaimed as "the decision of the Portuguese people". These justificatory statements are typical of political representation. Despite their central importance in terms of legitimacy, they don't tally with the facts. In reality, any constitutional text is the result of multiple debated and disputed political choices – whether in the phases of drafting, adoption, revision or finally interpretation. There is thus a strong tension between the central legitimizing role of such justificatory statements, and their obvious lack of correspondence with the facts. It is this sense that this official justification, which turns out to be empirically false, belongs to the fictional register: *in fact* the Constitution isn't the work of the political community, but *in law* we act as if it were so.

I readily admit that such observation is iconoclastic and politically sensitive, since by taking a factual point of view, it disturbs the legal narrative. According to the unanimist imaginary which is the backdrop of this story, positive law would find its final cause in the harmonious will of a political community certain of its values, and not in the tumult of a political reality from which it nevertheless does originate. By the way, it seems customary for constitutionalists to endorse this account by substituting the legal viewpoint for the factual one. In this way, it is quite consistent to support the idea that this general will, although absent in fact, is present in law[3].

It is easy to grasp the influence of this usage by mentioning the professional call of order made against Léon Duguit's "realist" theory of the State, according to which "the

[2] For a general presentation of the doctrinal debates relating to the definition of fiction in law, please refer to my work (2020b, pp. 17–53).

[3] In a classic work of French legal culture, the jurist Raymond Carré de Malberg (1931, p. 151) put it this way: "*encore que la loi ne soit, en fait, que l'œuvre d'une majorité, elle se présente, en droit, comme le produit de la volonté générale, et cela non pas seulement en un sens idéal ou fictif, mais par des raisons tirées de réalités juridiques, à savoir pour ce motif réel que le législateur de qui elle émane, est, par définition juridique, l'organe d'une collectivité qui n'est pas autre chose que la totalité des citoyens eux-mêmes*".However, this legal vision disappears in the Rousseauist conclusion of the book. In it, Carré de Malberg (p. 215 ff.) criticizes the "mystification" spread by the rhetoric of political representation when it supports "the parliamentary expression of the general will": "*tout homme qui n'est pas résigné à se payer de mots [ne saurait] se contenter de l'argument qui consiste à prétendre que tous les citoyens sont présents dans le Parlement à l'instant de la création de la loi: car un tel argument est emprunté à un genre de vision mystique qui manque manifestement de toute base réelle*".

national will […] is a pure illusion" (Duguit 1928, p. 14). He was rapidly saddled with the title of "anarchist of the chair" by his colleague and friend Maurice Hauriou (1912, p. 409), another of the great names of this felicitous era of French legal culture, who was critical of Duguit's "iconoclastic zeal". This title was not only claimed immediately by other influential publicists of the time[4], but, incidentally, by Duguit himself[5].

Unlike Duguit, however, it is important for me to point out that by emphasizing the fictional dimension of the rhetoric of political representation, my objective is not to discredit or to unweave the narrative thread of constitutional law[6]. Quite the contrary: I mean to take it seriously, because it constitutes a privileged vector for the legitimization of political power. And only its contemplation matters to me here.

1.2 A Second Assumption: The Constitutional Judge as Representative

It is therefore from the perspective of an observer that I approach my second assumption, according to which the constitutional judge must be considered as a representative. This can be understood in two distinct ways, depending on the conception of political representation adopted.

According to the broad conception, political representation is an important component of the State, the function of which is to justify all positive law. Indeed, in accordance with the two pillars of the general theory of the State, the power of the State is a political power which is both sovereign – it entails a centralization and monopoly of the authority to make law – and institutionalized – law-making power is not owned, as a matter of private property, by those who exercise powers of government. As a result, within a given territory, law-making power is ascribed exclusively to an abstract entity. It is only in the name of, and on behalf of, the abstract entity that one governs. Official authority is thus a question of "willing for the State", the only will to which the population owes obedience, which is invoked, playing a definite role in legal justification, although it is not empirically effective – i.e. it is a fiction. A clear illustration of this political system can be found in the writings of Georges Burdeau (1970, p. 16), a remarkable French jurist of the last century:

---

[4] Referring to the writings of Adhémar Esmein, Léon Michoud, Etienne-Ferdinand Larnaud, Joseph Barthélemy and, last but not least, Maurice Hauriou, Carré de Malberg (1920 p. 203) notes that: "*l'appréciation très dominante et très nette qui a été émise par les maîtres actuels de la science française du droit public touchant la valeur de la doctrine de M. Duguit, se résume dans cette objection capitale: une telle doctrine conduirait à l'anarchie*".

[5] Duguit (1927, pp. 653–654) gave indeed a clear answer: "*On m'a accusé d'être un anarchiste. Hauriou m'appelle anarchiste de la chaire.* […] *Anarchiste si l'on veut; je n'ai pas peur des mots. Anarchiste ma doctrine; j'accepte l'épithète et je maintiens la doctrine si elle peut contribuer à débarrasser une fois pour toutes la science juridique des concepts métaphysiques qui l'encombrent encore*".

[6] For Duguit (1928, p. 97), this discredit was part of an implicit jusnaturalist approach, aimed essentially at a better limitation of political power: "*Je persiste à penser que* […] *les gouvernés ne seront protégés efficacement contre l'arbitraire des gouvernants* […] *que si le législateur est bien pénétré de cette idée que les lois ne s'imposent à l'obéissance des citoyens que si elles sont conformes au droit supérieur qui s'impose à lui législateur*".

"When I obey the policeman, who enjoins me to use the crosswalk, it's not irrelevant for the appreciation of my discipline, to know that I'm bowing not to his whistle, but to the authority he represents. It is not the will of the man (whom I know because he is the husband of my concierge) that determines my behaviour, it is the power of the State, itself the guarantor of an order that in this case I respect, and for which the agent is only a modest but effective tool. If, by chance, I convert my money into Treasury bonds, it is not the cashier at the Banque de France that I trust, it is an entity, the State, which I have never seen, and which I will nevertheless regard as a thief if, in a year, it repays me in depreciated currency. And when I accuse a minister of frivolity or deputies of incompetence, it is obvious that my judgement worsens as soon as a human weakness is added to the breach of duty: the bad exercise of their authority is especially guilty because they are not the owners of their Power".

However, there is a stricter conception of political representation underlying a understanding of the assumption that the constitutional judge is a representative. In any case, it is this commonly accepted conception that gives full meaning to the debate. Unlike the broad conception, which covers the whole range of law-making powers, the stricter conception focuses on law-making at the summit of the State, that is the legislative function. This focus is found in classic authors such as Hobbes and Sieyès, or Locke and Rousseau. It is mainly explained by the idea that governing involves legislating[7]. This is why political representation in the strict sense has the specific purpose of legitimizing the legislation, the status of "representative" being reserved only to the portion of the governing group actually participating in its enactment. In this sense, asserting that the constitutional judge acts as a representative in exercising judicial review, implies that he does also have a say in the making of legislation, and therefore that he claims to "will for the Nation"[8].

Within the contemporary liberal systems in which constitutional courts operate, representative arguments are mobilized and disputed by distinct institutions. This inevitably leads to a central question: who is the best representative? Which institution is the most credible to best express the will of the political community? Obviously, the answer gives rise to many controversies, which influence the balance of power in legislative matters. For example, to get to the point, some support the Parliament, others favor the constitutional judge. In each case, the answer is still in the category of fiction: in the absence of political unanimity, legislation can never be the concrete expression of the general will. It can but remain the expression of the particular will of either a small number of elected parliamentarians – this is parliamentary representation –, or of a handful of constitutional judges – this is judicial representation.

In that sense, that which I call "judicial representation" appears as another variant of political representation *stricto sensu*. Its purpose is to legitimize constitutional review

[7] This can be explained by the fact that all these authors use the notion of sovereignty as originally theorised by Jean Bodin (1993, p. 162): "*puissance de donner et casser la loi*".

[8] The constitutional judge is involved in the legislative function, since, on condition it has been referred to, its consent is required to enact a law that has been adopted (*a priori* control) and/or to maintain in force a law already enacted (*a posteriori* control).

through the following argument: the law validated by the judge is the best expression of the will of the political community. In other words, the judicial expression of the general will is better than its parliamentary expression. However, this justificatory statement finds no confirmation in tangible reality. Whatever its merits, constitutional review cannot guarantee a better realization of the general will, because this will be not effective but merely invoked. In reality, the exercise of constitutional review involves nothing more than the particular will of the judge, which may or may not confirm the legislator's.

As I mentioned previously, I do not intend to question the merits of the fictional character of judicial representation. Firstly, because all variants of political representation belong to a same register. Secondly, because it is not obvious in any case that the representative argument is the best way to support constitutionality review anyway; even on the hypothesis that constitutional review ought to be promoted.

Rather, my purpose is to improve the examination of judicial representation, by subjecting it to two questions which seem to me to be inevitable. These are the questions which, I hope, will provoke reflection. Firstly, to which category of counterfactual discourse does this rhetoric belong – fiction in the strict sense, lie, or myth? Secondly, can this rhetoric be linked to the question of democracy?

2 The Discursive Register of Judicial Representation: Fiction in the Strict Sense, Lie or Myth?

In order to answer the first question, the three discursive categories mentioned must be briefly exposed.

First of all, fiction in the strict sense characterizes a communication in which the speaker and the audience share knowledge of the falseness of the speech, which presupposes that they both know what is true. This explicitly false character is found in the linguistic form of the "as if" which, according to the neo-Kantian philosopher Hans Vaihinger (1935, p. 93), is distinctive of fiction: "this formula [...] states that reality as given, the particular, is compared with something whose impossibility and unreality is as the same time admitted"[9].

A lie, on the other hand, is a statement given to be true to an audience by a speaker who knows it to be false, or vice versa. Unlike in fictional speech, therefore, the latter does not pass on his knowledge to the former, or at least knowledge is not shared. This means, however, that the liar must be able to differentiate between what is true and what

[9] This work, in which Vaihinger exhorts science to take fiction seriously, has had a significant influence on most legal theorists who have studied legal fiction. This is particularly the case of Hans Kelsen (1986 & 2014). A first article dating from 1919, part of the wave of reflection opened up by Vaihinger's work, is largely critical, whereas a second dating form 1964 is laudatory, because Kelsen proposes for the first time to reclassify the fundamental norm as a fiction in Vaihinger's sense.Lon L. Fuller (1967, p. 7) and Alf Ross (1969, p. 221) also relied on Vaihinger to define fiction as a kind of calculated error: "A fiction is generally distinguished from an erroneous conclusion (or in scientific fields, from a false hypothesis) by the fact that it is adopted by its author with knowledge of its falsity"; "The starting point is that fiction is an untrue assumption [...] Further, the assumption must be made with a full realization of its untruth. In this respect fiction differs from mistake".

is false. Hence Hannah Arendt's remark on this subject (1972, p. 31): "the trouble with lying and deceiving is that their efficiency depends entirely upon a clear notion of the truth which the liar and deceiver wishes to hide. In this sense, truth, even if it does not prevail in public, possesses an ineradicable primacy over all falsehoods". Truth as a stake thus remains an issue in here.

This allow us, finally, to distinguish the myth as a communicational context in which the speaker and the audience do not consider whether its content is true or false. Firstly, because the speaker does not typically claim to be the author of the speech, as is admitted by the audience. And secondly, because it simply doesn't make sense to test it against the facts. As the French historian Paul Veyne nicely notes (1983, p. 34 & p. 73), myth is an "anonymous story" that calls for "proof by poetry". In other words, myth essentially aims for aesthetic assent, not empirical relevance, in the sense that its threshold of acceptances relates to its beauty rather than its truthfulness.

But in what intelligible sense, then, can myth be considered as a category of false speech? It is a typically modern critical reflex to seek to characterize myth as false rather than true[10]. It implies a decisive attachment to rational evaluation. It is important, however, not to neglect the influence, as Burdeau notes (1980, p. 157), of the "fantasizing power of the mind when it thinks about politics". If we agree with him that "authority is a mystery" (2013, p. 353), then the imaginary prevails in the political world, and consequently the key to legitimacy is a matter of belief rather than experience. Hence my hypothesis that political representation, in general – not only judicial –, is to be classified within the enchanted category of myth.

2.1 The Mythical Register of Political Representation

It seems to me that the remarkable degree of persuasion achieved by the rhetoric of political representation, is essentially explained by the fact that it plays on emotion rather than reason. This is captured in this aphorism of the French philosopher Lucien Jaume (2003, p. 1338): "*To represent is to make believe*". Indeed, political representation requires belief in the unanimist imaginary mentioned above. This imaginary corresponds to the fundamental myth of the general will, which is no doubt the political ideal of the Modern Age.

The fundamental importance attached to unanimity can be explained by the conception of ethics of the Moderns, derived in particular from Hobbes' *Leviathan*. This

[10] As Veyne (1972, p. 72 ff.) shows with profundity, this was not the way of looking at things in the "ancient world". Using a historical method inspired by the work of Michel Foucault, the historian reveals that, according to the Greeks' own "programme of truth", myth was neither fiction nor a lie: "*À rationaliste, rationaliste et demi: peut-on sérieusement croire que les poètes ont forgé la mythologie pour le plaisir ? L'imagination pourrait-elle être futile ? C'est trop peu de dire, avec Platon, que les mythes peuvent être éducatifs, s'ils sont bien choisis: Strabon estime que tout mythe a une intention instructive et que le poète n'écrivait pas l'Odyssée pour s'amuser, mais pour enseigner la géographie. A la condamnation rationaliste de l'imaginaire comme faux, réplique l'apologie de l'imaginaire comme conforme à une raison cachée. Car on ne saurait mentir. Il est donc impossible qu'un mythe soit entièrement mythique. Les Grecs ont pu critiquer les fables dans le détail, mais non les négliger. Le seul débat était de décider si la mythologie n'était véridique qu'en partie ou si elle l'était entièrement*".

conception recognizes the full autonomy of humanity in the ethical sphere. This principle of autonomy differs from the Ancients' principle of heteronomy, according to which the source of all justice lies in a cosmic or divine, at any rate superhuman, necessity. From this point of view, humanity is not autonomous in ethical matters, since it is bound by a transcendental order, which must be contemplated to discover the values[11].

In contrast, in accordance with the principle of ethical autonomy that characterizes the Modern view, values manifest themselves and have meaning only inside the human sphere and not beyond it. In a way, they are not pre-existing, they do not exist independently of the language used to formulate them. Humanity is thus placed at the center of the world, and the starting point for moral reflection is no longer a supra-human demand, but the demand of humanity itself. It is up to humanity, then, to determine what is good and bad, either from the requirements of individual (ethical individualism) or from the requirements of society (ethical holism)[12]. In both cases, the unanimous will of the political community appears from this perspective as the most sublime and powerful basis for legitimacy.

Of course, such political unanimity doesn't exist as empirical fact. Nonetheless, it remains aesthetically relevant, and for this reason emotionally convincing, to imagine positive law as a torrent of rules that finds its primary source in the general will. It is false, but beautiful, and that is precisely why the charm works.

That said, we know that according to the sophists, those masters of rhetoric who taught their art of persuasion to the golden youth of the Greek world, emotional argumentation is more effective than rational argumentation. The first strikes the sensitive chord, while the second encounters the filter of critical reflection. A simple illustration of this can be found in contemporary marketing: it is through the dreams presented him that the consumer is lead to buy the lottery tickets – "imagine all the things you can do if you win the jackpot" – rather than through information about the product – "statistically you have one chance in a million of winning". The question to be asked, then, is whether the myth of the general will isn't really an instrument of mystification. In this case, political representation would have to be included in the sulfurous category of lie.

This leads us to be in accordance with the long tradition of the "noble lie" initiated by Plato. Its logic has been perfectly summarized by Alessandro Passerin d'Entrêves (1969, p. 16): "Men are not all capable of seeing the truth, nor is it always a good thing for them to know it. In order to prompt them to obey it is necessary to know how to stir their heart and their imagination much more than their intellect". According to Plato in *The Republic*, this is precisely the utility of myth in political matters, which shows impressive persuasive effectiveness in manipulating feelings. Converted into an instrument of government, myth becomes mystification: in the shade of the fantasy it spreads, it is in fact nothing more than a lie that is necessary for the common good; hence precisely its nobility, i.e. its moral justification. In the aristocratic city model proposed by Plato, the right to govern reserved to the rare philosophers therefore implies a right

[11] Political power and law are thus conceived in a monumental sense, in that their primary source and ultimate purpose respond to a supra-human order.

[12] Political power and the law are conceived in an instrumental rather than monumental way, in that they are placed entirely under man's control and therefore only have to respond to his command.

to lie. This right consists of deluding the people in order to serve their "true" interests, which they are nevertheless unaware of. And because of this general ignorance, writes Plato (2000, 459c, p. 157), "the probability is that our rulers will need to employ a good deal of falsehood and deception for the benefit of those they are ruling"[13].

In a way, the contemporary phenomenon of the crisis of representation seems to be a reaction to the "noble lie". Indeed, this crisis is essentially a political criticism that can be formulated in these terms: "Whether legislators or judges, representatives officially claim to represent the political community, but in reality, they only serve particulars interests". Never mind, for my purpose, the merits of this criticism. I would rather point out that it confirms, more than it refutes, the profundity of the myth of the general will. Indeed, it is important to note that this criticism only makes sense on the condition of believing in this myth. Why blame representatives for representing "badly", if we consider that the will they are required to realize was a pure illusion in the first place? Let's admit then that it would be better to have a popular expression of the general will, by means of a referendum. But even in this case, the mechanism of representation remains. From a strictly factual point of view, the law enacted by referendum is not, to use the formula of the French Constitutional Council, "the direct expression of national sovereignty"[14]. It is the decision of the majority of the citizens who turned up to vote, and did so validly. Even in this limiting case, therefore, the will of the "people" as a political community remains imaginary.

It is possible, however, to take a disenchanted look at this imagined will, considering it as a pure artifice that needs no adhesion. Such was the view of Thomas Hobbes, who conceived political representation in the register of fiction rather than myth[15]. The reader of *Leviathan*, indeed, is not invited to believe in the staging of government – its formation and exercise –, but rather to rationally understand the utility of the performance for the securing of civil peace. In this sense, it doesn't matter what term is used to signify the abstract entity to which the fiction lends a will: "State", "Nation", "chair", "cat" or even "Tû-Tû". In any case, it's simply a matter of pretending that enacted legislation is the expression of the unanimous will of its recipients[16], and not that of its actual authors, a

[13] Thus, the love of the city is justified by the noble lie of autochthony and the rigid division of functions by the one of metals. Concerning the eugenics that Plato (2000, 459d-460a, p. 157–158) encouraged in the field of marriage and the birth rate, "all this has to happen with no one apart from the actual rulers realising it [...] In that case we must legislate for some festivals, at which we shall bring together the brides and their grooms. We must have sacrifices, and our poets must compose hymns appropriate to the unions which are taking place. [...] We must have lotteries, I think – and pretty ingenious one – so that every time there is a marriage the inferior type we want to exclude will blame chance rather than the rulers".

[14] Cons. Const., n°62–20 DC, 6 novembre 1962, *Loi relative à l'élection du Président de la République au suffrage universel direct, adoptée par le référendum du 28 octobre 1962.*

[15] It would be too tedious to develop the Hobbesian theory of representation here. For further details, I refer you to the chapter of my book devoted to it (2020b, pp. 305–342).

[16] The "norm-population" in the language of Joseph Raz, *The Concept of a Legal System*, 2nd ed., Oxford, Clarendon Press, 1980, p. 199.

purported "sovereign representative"[17]. Admittedly, Hobbes advocates an absolute representation aiming to prevent any crisis of representation: no one has the right to question in public the official link between the effective will of the "sovereign representative" and the invoked will of the "Commonwealth"[18]. But this absolute representation may well take the form of a public sham, because no one is obliged, privately or inwardly, to sincerely or seriously recognize in the legislation the will of the Republic. If that is the case, so much the better. But if not, then in the public sphere one must act "as if". In short, representation in the Hobbesian sense is not a question of being hoodwinked, or of a willing suspension of disbelief, but of giving the appearance of belief in public for the sake of civil peace.

Nevertheless, I think that would be wrong to rationally reduce political representation as mere theatre. Two reasons lead me to dismiss the disenchanted category of fiction.

Firstly, as Leo Strauss (1952, p. 152) has correctly identified, the decisive motive of Hobbes' demonstration is a negative emotional argument: the fear of "(violent) death"[19]. It is this fear that presides over the rational calculation to which Hobbes (1909, p. 92 ff.) invites the reader: the situation without the absolute power of the Leviathan to guarantee public order would descend into "the war of every man against every man". By evoking the "state of nature", his aim is to make an impression upon the reader's imagination, through fear, since he considers, following Machiavelli, that "of all passions, that which incline men least to break the laws is fear" (p. 229). Hobbes certainly concedes that it is natural for every citizen to be inclined to disobey laws, or at the very least to criticize them in public, since the function of these laws is precisely to restrict "his original right to do what he please" (p. 115). But, if each citizen considers his situation correctly, it is in his best interest to constantly restrain this inclination and submit to the authority of the "sovereign representative". Because "though of so unlimited a power, men may fancy many evil consequences, yet the consequences of the want of it, which is perpetual war of every man against his neighboor, are much worse" (p. 160). The mortal peril of this imaginary world, then, is the backdrop of the theory of political representation as put forth by the Malmesbury philosopher.

A second reason, which leads us beyond Hobbesian considerations, leads me to dismiss the disenchanted category of fiction. Most contemporary political regimes cultivate

[17] According to Hobbes (1909, p. 204): "that none can make laws but the Commonwealth, because our subjection is to the Commonwealth only [...] But the Commonwealth is no person, nor has capacity to do anything but by the representative, that is, the sovereign; and therefore the sovereign is the sole legislator.".

[18] Reasoning on the basis of the classical classification of political regimes, Hobbes (1909, p. 142) considers that the legislator can be either a monarch or an assembly with a closed or open right of entry: "When the representative is one man, then is the Commonwealth a monarchy; when an assembly of all that will come together, then it is a democracy, or popular Commonwealth; when an assembly of a part only, then it is called an aristocracy". We also know that the necessity for an assembly to resort to the expedient of majority is one of the main pragmatic reasons why Hobbes (p. 145) is in favor of monarchy: "a monarch cannot disagree with himself, out of envy or interest; but an assembly may; and that to such a height as may produce a civil war".

[19] "The aim of the State is for him as a matter of course peace, i.e. peace at any price. The underlying presupposition is that (violent) death is the first and greatest and supreme evil. This presupposition does not seem to him to require criticism, debate, or discussion".

a certain amount of patriotism. Far from implying cold reason, patriotism embellishes the abstract entity whose will is invoked to legitimize political power. This is done through various devices such as the elaboration, and diffusion of a national narrative in which the Nation becomes the heroine of History[20], or even international sports competitions where it is symbolically the Nations who compete, lose and win. Such diverse institutional approaches have in common the tendency to arouse and cultivate an intimate affective bond, which encourages the belief in (indeed, the cherishing of) in the idea of legislation as ultimately expressing the sublime will of the homeland. This is the heart of Rousseau's intuition (1964, p. 252) that "the greatest support of public authority is in the hearts of the citizens".

In sum, everything indicates that political representation is a mythical rhetoric. Its different variants all belong to this enchanted register, in that they are based on the fundamental myth of the general will.

2.2 The Mythical Register of Judicial Representation

The judicial representation, which claims the merits of the judicial expression of the general will, therefore manifests itself by an argumentation that is essentially emotional, in order to justify constitutional review. For a better understanding of the feelings generated, it is appropriate to consider the political doctrine behind it, namely liberal constitutionalism. As we know, this doctrine promotes the limitation of state power to guarantee fundamental rights. Considered from a rhetorical angle, it appears that the necessity of the limitation is justified by the negative emotional argument of fear, while the validity of the guarantee is based on the positive emotional argument of hope.

A clear illustration of this can be found in the writings of John Locke. Galvanized by a revolutionary context, the author of the *Second Treatise* uses a particularly biting tone to defend his political views[21]. As Locke argues, not all individuals are able to decide reasonably for themselves how to act. Consequently, the prescriptive and coercive authority of "the legislative" is necessary to guarantee public order. But the crucial thing for Locke (1947, p. 196) is that they do not "act contrary to the trust reposed in them", by deciding "to lay and carry on designs against the liberties and properties of the subject". Unless of course, Locke notes mockingly (p. 237), we hope for "a peace [...] maintained only for the benefit of robbers and oppressors. Who would not think it an admirable peace betwix the mighty and the mean, when the lamb, without resistance, yielded his throat to be torn by the imperious wolf?". Through this derisory tone, Locke intends to scare his reader in order to undermine the very idea of absolutism. Indeed, absolutism implies placing blind faith in a monarch or aristocratic or democratic assembly. It amounts "to

[20] According to Ernest Gellner (1983, p. 34), State is characterized by "the monopole of legitimate education", which he thinks since the industrial age "more important, more central than is the monopoly of legitimate violence", due to its superior utility in the construction and propagation of the "homogenizing" idea of nation.

[21] When he was writing *The Second Treatise of Government*, between 1681 and 1683, Locke took a radical position on the events that would precipitate, in accordance with his wishes, the "Glorious Revolution" of 1688. For this reason, as Dunn (1969, p. 120) noted, "the entire project for which his book was [...] the justification of revolutionary action or at least the threat of such action under certain circumstances".

think[ing], that men are so foolish, that they take care to avoid what mischiefs may be done them by polecats, or foxes; but are content, nay, think it safety, to be devoured by lions" (p. 167). This picture is certainly striking: if rulers are potential lions, it is not only necessary to be suspicious of them on principle, but also and above all to put them in a cage or in other words subject them to rules. For this reason, it is then reasonable to hope for the establishment of a fair representation – that is to say, in the liberal perspective outlined by Locke, a political representation conditioned on the respect by "the legislative" for the "life, liberty and estate" of each individual (p. 163).

Fear and hope therefore, each of these two emotions are stimulated by judicial representation. The liberal fear feeds the criticism of parliamentary representation, which is, for its part, based on the myth that the voted law is the best expression of the general will. Schematically, this criticism is carried out in three steps. The first step is to reveal the illusion of the myth in order to discredit Parliament and the executive that leads it: in reality, the parliamentary legislation only reflects the decision of a partisan majority. On the basis of this observation, the first step leads to a second, which is to stigmatize the liberticidal potential of a majority will, summoning the threatening theme of the "tyranny of the majority". The anxiety aroused by this theme – the original content of which is easily forgotten[22] – aims in particular to persuade people of the inadequacy of the initial mechanisms forged by constitutionalism to limit the legislator, such as the separation of powers and the constituent power (written and rigid Constitution). In a third and final step, constitutional review is revealed as the salutary mechanism, in the hands of the judge, providing a better guarantee of rights. And from the point of view of the liberal hope, this guarantee is the essential point.

Of course, it would be dangerous to fall into the illusion of a judge as a "*mouthpiece of the Constitution*", since it conceals a power in presence of which it is essential to remain wary. Hence, the importance of protecting against it in various ways; as for example the American impeachment procedure. Because it is human, it is also subject to the corrupting effect of power, and simply counting on the "ethics of the judge" or self-restraint is insufficient and, above all, dangerous. In accordance with the liberal fear, therefore, the confidence granted to the judge must be limited. But if constitutional review is truly the best mechanism for the protection of rights, then it is reasonable to believe that the judge is, at least, an excellent "representative". All that is needed is to weave liberal hope in the fundamental myth of political representation, for it to follow, as a matter of course, that the political community desires the protection of rights. The figure of the judge can then come out of the wings and take center stage as the main protagonist.

[22] Indeed, it is very obvious to Tocqueville (2004, p. 208 & p. 234) that the tyranny of the majority means the tyranny of the poor: "*Est-ce la majorité ou la minorité qui fait la loi ? La majorité sans doute; et si je prouve que les pauvres composent toujours la majorité, n'aurai-je pas raison d'ajouter que dans les pays où ils sont appelés à voter, les pauvres font seuls la loi ? Or, il est certain que jusqu'ici, chez toutes les nations du monde, le plus grand nombre a toujours été composé de ceux qui n'avaient pas de propriété, ou de ceux dont la propriété était trop restreinte pour qu'ils pussent vivre dans l'aisance sans travailler. Le vote universel donne donc réellement le gouvernement de la société aux pauvres.* [...] *En Amérique, l'échelle européenne des pouvoirs étant renversée, les riches se trouvent dans une position analogue à celle des pauvres en Europe; ce sont eux qui souvent se défient de la loi.* [...] *Aux États-Unis, où le pauvre gouverne, les riches ont toujours à craindre qu'il n'abuse contre eux de son pouvoir*".

In other words, according to this specific perspective of contemporary constitutionalism, "willing for the Nation" is equivalent to "willing for the guarantee of rights". Validated law only appears to be the best expression of the general will as long as it has been checked by the constitutional judge.

Thus, judicial representation appears as a rhetoric which legitimates the constitutional review and thus supports the institutional influence of the judge in legislative matters. This rhetoric relies heavily on the liberal myth of "human rightism" as the will of the political community. It remains to be examined whether this rhetoric is democratic.

3 The Political Register of Judicial Representation: Democratic or Not?

Questioning the democratic quality of judicial representation, and therefore of the process of constitutional review it promotes, presupposes an answer to that age-old question: What is democracy? As George Orwell (1957, p. 149) rightly observed, any answer is bound to be controversial:

> "In the case of a word like *democracy*, not only is there no agreed definition, but the attempt to make one is resisted from all sides. It is almost universally felt that when we call a country democratic we are praising it: consequently, the defenders of every kind of regime claim that it is a democracy, and fear that they might have to stop using that word if it were tied down to any one meaning".

Since the mid-nineteenth century, democracy has gradually become a key word in civic language[23]. Its influence generates an imperative for legitimacy that can be summarized as follows: to describe a regime as democratic is equivalent to giving it credit, and, conversely, to withhold the title is equivalent to discrediting it. Under these conditions, the definition of democracy is a major political issue, since it determines the award of this persuasive label, which is particularly effective in terms of rhetoric. This explains the internal semantic conflict at play within doctrines of constitutional review: support for judicial review requires a definition of democracy that is able to include it, while rejecting definitions that would keep judicial review outside the scope of the concept of democracy properly speaking. In contemporary French doctrine, for example, much work is being done to redefine the term "democracy" in such a way as to include constitutional review and thus justify it[24]. In contrast, this support is excluded by those who are worried about the increasing role of an unelected judge in the field of legislation, claiming its incompatibility with another "true" definition of democracy[25].

[23] On this see F. Dupuis-Déri (2013, p. 13 ff.).

[24] The work of Dominique Rousseau (2015, p. 117 ff.) is particularly illustrative here.

[25] Focusing on election by universal suffrage, Michel Troper (2011, p. 132 & p. 137) for instance denies the democratic quality of the constitutional judge: "*une objection* [...] *vient immédiatement à l'esprit: dans une démocratie, les décisions sont prises par une majorité du peuple ou par les représentants du peuple, élus pour un temps limité, tandis que les cours sont composées de juges non élus et qu'elles ont le pouvoir de s'opposer à des décisions adoptées par les élus du peuple. Il s'agit donc d'une institution antidémocratique.* [...] *Or l'analyse du droit*

My position on this subject may not satisfy either of these two positions. I propose to use two distinct definitions of democracy in order to deepen the analysis of the delicate relation between judicial representation and democracy. The main reason for this difficulty, in my opinion, is not that this rhetoric promotes the participation in the legislative function of judges who are not elected by universal suffrage. Rather, I think the deeper explanation resides in its liberal inspiration, which leads it to require the limitation of legislative power, rather than popular participation in it. The two definitions of democracy mentioned previously allow us for a different understanding of this claim.

3.1 An Aristocratic Register in the Classical Sense

The first definition derives from the classical classification of political regimes, initially theorized by Aristotle and still found, with remarkable continuity in the long history of Western political thought, in the writings of Madison and Sieyes[26].

In a nutshell, this classification is based on two basic criteria. The first is a quantitative criterion. Its purpose is to count the number of people entitled by textual, conventional or customary rules to take part in the legislative function, in order to determine if those rules designate a single person, a few or the many. The second is a qualitative criterion. Its purpose is to evaluate the merits of the legislation with reference to the civic idea of the common good, in order to determine if the legislator and consequently the regime are good or evil. Ultimately, the aim is to examine a particular political regime through the prism of a twofold question: how many participate in the enactment of legislation, and is that legislation consistent with, or conducive to, the common good?

This investigation leads to the classification of six types of regime, which correspond to the following summary definitions. Where legislation is the work of a single one like a providential person, the regime is a *monarchy* if he pursues the common good, otherwise it is a *tyranny*. If legislation is made by a few, in other words an elite, the regime is an *aristocracy* if this elite pursues the common good, otherwise it is an oligarchy. Finally, if legislation is made by the many – i.e. by the people, understood here in the concrete sense which does not refer to the political community –, the regime is a *democracy* if the common good is pursued, otherwise it is an *ochlocracy*, i.e. the government of the mob.

Following this classification, what is commonly known as "representative democracy" is actually an elective aristocracy. This is because in this regime, the legislative function is the reserved province of a Parliament which, though certainly elected by universal suffrage for a temporary mandate, remains composed of a few hundred members. Similarly, the establishment of a constitutional court to review parliamentary law does not characterize a "constitutional democracy", but a judicial aristocracy. Indeed, the

positif conduit à une conclusion simple: les cours constitutionnelles disposent d'un pouvoir discrétionnaire important et participent, conjointement avec les élus, à l'exercice du pouvoir législatif. Un gouvernement dans lequel le pouvoir législatif est partagé entre des autorités élues ou démocratiques et des autorités non élues ou aristocratiques est un gouvernement mixte".

[26] It is a commonplace in the history of ideas that the origins of this classification hark back to Herodotus' *Histories* in the mid-fifth century BC, leading all the way up to Hegel in the first half of the nineteenth century, who considered it outdated with the modern age of the State. See G. W. F. HEGEL (2001, p. 219).

members of this court (usually appointed) are at most a dozen. The mode of designation has no influence on the aristocratic nature of the regime, since its specificity is that "the many" have no say in the enactment of legislation.

For this reason, judicial representation is aristocratic and not democratic in the classical meaning of the word. What, then, of the rhetoric of political representation? Its purpose is to persuade that a handful of constitutional judges are better representatives than elected parliamentarians. In other words, it aims to convince that one elite is superior to another.

It seems to me that the core of the controversy concerns the claim to political knowledge: of the parliamentarian or the constitutional judge, who has the best knowledge of the common good? This is clearly a thorny question because it raises the central issue of legitimacy. The fact is that the credibility of an institution, and therefore its influence in the exercise of power, largely depends on the confidence that people have in its political knowledge[27]. This is why each of the two competing rhetorics claims the superiority of the political knowledge of the institution it defends.

Thus, parliamentary representation, the first to appear historically, strives to defend Parliament's political knowledge. In its view, parliamentary knowledge has two main merits. On the one hand, this knowledge is in the hands of a small number of citizens elected by universal suffrage, which mechanically entails that they are somehow considered more capable of understanding the common good than the vast number of voters. Election is indeed an aristocratic procedure of designation, insofar as, unlike the sortition, its own mechanics prevents that the elected is anybody[28]. On the other hand, this knowledge is the result of sustained and public deliberation, i.e. a contradictory debate in search of compromise and subject to the critical review of public opinion. Ultimately, according to parliamentary representation, the people have every reason to trust in Parliament as the best representative, it being a forum within which political knowledge, first made available, is then *debated*.

Of course, this is not the position of the advocates of judicial representation, who would rather convince us to distrust parliamentary knowledge. They claim that this knowledge is seriously inadequate not only because of its partisan nature, but also and above all because of *its weakness in legal matters*. Neither universal suffrage nor political professionalization offers any guarantee that parliamentarians are equipped with the necessary skills in this field. Moreover, anyone untrained in the legal language will be quite unable to understand what is really at stake when it comes to protecting fundamental rights. As a result of this ignorance, the parliamentary majority would be unable to respect the "life, liberty and estate" of each individual, and consequently to express the general will in the best possible way. Therefore, just as the patient looks for advice and

[27] For a more detailed analysis of this notion, please refer to my study (2020a).

[28] As Bernard Manin wrote (pp. 156–160): "one thing […] still be ruled out by the elective procedure, namely that representatives be similar to their constituents. Elected representatives must of necessity have a positively valued trait that distinguishes them from, and makes them superior to, those who elect them. The democratic ideal of similarity between rulers and ruled has demonstrated, since the end of the eighteenth century, such a powerful appeal that it may not be unimportant to show that it is incompatible in principle with the elective procedure, however amended".

prescriptions from the doctor, the parliamentarian ought reasonably to consult, and defer to, the Constitutional Court possessing the *juridical knowledge* that ought to be recognized as truly distinctive of a political elite. One can significantly point to the expression currently used in France to designate the member of the Constitutional Council: "*Les Sages*" – which means "The Wise Men"[29].

Just like its parliamentary counterpart, judicial representation is therefore not democratic in the classical sense of the term. However, it can be brought in line with a second, more contemporary, definition of democracy.

3.2 A Democratic Register in the Contemporary Sense

This second definition is derived from the contemporary classification of political regimes, which gradually substituted for the previous one in the aftermath of World War II and now found in many political science textbooks. Synthetically, this classification distinguishes three regimes on the basis of a criterion that is clearly liberal, since it concerns the status attributed to free speech.

In a *democratic regime*, speech is free, and consequently everything is done to enable and guarantee the confrontation of political opinions in the public sphere. In an *authoritarian regime*, this freedom is prohibited or at least severely curtailed, so as to prevent any public criticism of the government in power. In the totalitarian regime, finally, this freedom is annihilated, in the sense that it aspires to eliminate all political dissent both in the public and in the private sphere itself. The freedom of speech is therefore not only illegal, it is also and above all immoral: the citizen ought to feel ashamed for his critical opinion towards the regime and its leader.

Contemporary classification can also be based on the status accorded to the political opposition. In a democracy, this opposition is legitimized. By virtue of the principle of political alternation and the related principle of competitive elections, it is a standing possibility that the faction in opposition may govern in case of electoral victory. Hence Adam Przeworski's famous aphorism (1991, p. 10): "Democracy is a system in which parties lose elections". However, this is not the case in an authoritarian regime, where the opposition is muzzled and all appearance of political life is effectively locked down. Thus, the authoritarian ruler maintains a position of power that is not submitted to the hazards of open and pluralist elections. Finally, in the totalitarian regime, voicing opposition is akin to alienation – it ought not to cross one's mind. Carl Schmitt brings this demand for devotion to the foreground in his critique of what he sees as a major blindspot of Hobbesian authoritarianism. In one of the main works of his Nazi period, Schmitt (1996, p. 57) considers that the preservation of "the right of private freedom of thought and belief in the political system [is] the seed of death that destroyed the mighty Leviathan from within and brought about the end of the mortal god".

If one is to proceed from this classification, then judicial representation may be considered to have a democratic aspect. In accordance with its liberal inspiration, this rhetoric aims to convince people of the necessity of the constitutional judge for the

[29] The use of this key word of the aristocratic register goes back mainly to Plato (2000, 412c-414a, pp. 205–208 & 540c-540e, p. 399), who envisaged for his ideal City an extremely selective and particularly long education to appoint the rare and precious philosopher kings.

protection of fundamental rights, starting with freedom of thought and freedom of speech. It is particularly in the face of the dangers of authoritarianism and totalitarianism that the praise for constitutional review as an indispensable shield takes on its full meaning.

It is important to stress, once again, that the fact that the Constitutional Court is not elected by universal suffrage is but secondary. The main point is that the Court contributes to the public debate, and consequently increases the seeking of political compromise. Certainly, the technical nature of his juridical knowledge makes public debate more complex. As a result, we might, along with like Jennifer Nedelsky (2011, p. 246), question the place taken by the expertise and ultimately esoteric language of the constitutional judge:

> "There is broader question of whether judicial review, like any judge-made decision, fosters informed public deliberation on the issues. Of course, sometimes controversial constitutional issues, like same-sex marriage, attract a lot of public attention. But part of the issue is whether judges are, or should be, seen to be, uniquely qualified to resolve constitutional disputes. To the extent that they are held out to be so, or that formal legal expertise is required to understand the issues, the public capacity for democratic deliberation on core values is undermined".

It's important to note, however, that doubts about judicial representation do not depreciate its democratic value. In fact, it is precisely the opposite. The Constitutional Court, like any democratic institutions in the contemporary meaning, is in any case subject to the critical examination of public opinion; including scholarly opinion. And, unless we follow Hobbes (1909, p. 249) in considering that such a debate is in itself a "poison" because it weakens the State[30], this must surely give us reason rejoice.

References

Arendt H (1972) Lying in politics: reflections on the pentagon papers (1971). In: Crises of the Republic. Mariner Books, New York

Bodin J (1993) Les Six livres de la République (1576). Librairie générale française, Paris

Burdeau G (1970) L'État. Editions du Seuil, Paris

Burdeau G (1980) Traité de science politique (tome I, vol. I), 3e ed. LGDJ, Paris

Burdeau G (2011) Le sociologue et le mystère de l'autorité (1962). In: Denquin J-M (ed) Écrits de Droit constitutionnel et de Science politique. Editions Panthéon-Assas, Paris

Carré de Malberg R (1984) La Loi, expression de la volonté générale. Étude sur le concept de loi dans la Constitution de 1875 (1931). Economica, Paris

Carré de Malberg R (1920) Contribution à la théorie générale de l'État, vol I. Recueil Sirey, Paris

Duguit L (1901) L'État, le droit objectif et la loi positive. Librairie Albert Fontemoing, Paris

Duguit L (1927) Traité de droit constitutionnel, vol. I, 3e edn. Ancienne Librairie Fontemoing, Paris

30 According to Hobbes' authoritarian perspective, the culture of public debate is based on one of those "seditious doctrines" that lead « men [...] to debate with themselves, and dispute the commands of [the Representative of] the Commonwealth; and afterwards to obey, or disobey them, as in their private judgements they shall think fit. Whereby the Commonwealth is distracted and Weakened".

Duguit L (1928) Traité de droit constitutionnel, vol. II, 3e edn. Ancienne Librairie Fontemoing, Paris
Dunn J (1969) The political thought of john locke. an historical account of the argument of the "Two Treatises of Government". Cambridge University Press, Cambridge
Dupuis-Déri F (2013) Démocratie. Histoire politique d'un mot aux Etats-Unis et en France. Lux Éditeur, Montréal
Fuller LL (1967) Legal fictions (1930). Stanford University Press, Stanford
Gellner E (1983) Nations and nationalism. Cornell University Press, Ithaca
Hauriou M (1912) Les deux réalismes. Recueil de Législation 8:405–410
Hegel GWF (2001) The Philosophy of Rights (Grundlinien der Philosophie des Rechts (1821), S. W. Dyde Trans.). Batoche Books, Ontario
Hobbes T (1909) Leviathan. Or the matter, forme and power of a commonwealth ecclesiasticall and civil (1651). Clarendon Press, Oxford
Jaume L (2003) Représentation. In: Aland, D., Rials, S. (eds.) Dictionnaire de la culture juridique. PUF, Paris
Kelsen H (1986) The function of a constitution (Die Funktion der Verfassung (1964), I. Stewart, Trans.). In: Tur R, Twining WL (eds) Essays on Kelsen. Clarendon Press, Oxford
Kelsen H (2014) On the Theory of Juridic Fictions. With Special Consideration of Vaihinger's Philosophy of the As-If (Zur Theorie der juristischen Fiktionen. Mit besonderer Berücksichtigung von Vahingers Philosophie des Als Ob (1919), C. Kletzer, Trans.). In: Del Mar M, Twining WL (eds) Legal Fictions in Theory and Practice. Springer International Publishing, Switzerland (2014)
Locke J (1947) Two treatise of government (1690). Hafner Publishing Company, New York
Manin B (1997) The principles of representative government. Cambridge University Press, Cambridge
Orwell G (1957) Politics and the english language (1946). In: Selected Essays. Penguin Books, London
Nedelsky J (2011) Law's relations. a relational theory of self, autonomy, and law. Oxford University Press, New York
Passerin d'Entrêves A (1967) The notion of the state. An introduction to political theory. Oxford University Press, London
Plato. The Republic (Perì politeías (-315), T. Griffith, Trans.). Cambridge University Press, Cambridge (2000)
Przeworski A (1991) Democracy and the market: political and economic reforms in eastern europe and latin america. Cambridge University Press, Cambridge
Raynal P-M (2020) Les enjeux institutionnels du savoir politique sous la Ve République. Jus Politicum. Revue internationale de droit politique 24:181–206
Raynal P-M (2020) De la fiction constituante. Contribution à la théorie du droit politique. L'Harmattan, Paris
Schur R (2009) Legal Fictions. In: King L, Schur R (eds) African American Culture and Legal Discourse. Palgrave Macmillan US, New York, pp 191–207. https://doi.org/10.1057/9780230101722_12
Rousseau D (2015) Radicaliser la démocratie, propositions pour une refondation. Seuil, Paris
Rousseau J-J (1964) Discours sur l'économie politique (1755). In Œuvres complètes, vol. III. Paris: Bibliothèque de la Pléiade (1964)
Schmitt C (1996) The Leviathan in the state theory of Thomas Hobbes (Leviathan in der Staatslehre des Thomas Hobbes (1938), G. Schwab, Trans.). University of Chicago Press, Chicago
Strauss L (1952) The political philosophy of hobbes: its basis and its genesis. University of Chicago Press, Chicago
Tocqueville de A (2004) De la démocratie en Amérique (1835) (vol. I). In Œuvres. Paris: Éditions Robert Laffont

Troper M (2011) La logique de la justification du contrôle de la constitutionnalité des lois (2003). In Le droit et la nécessité. PUF, Paris
Vaihinger H (1935) The Philosophy of as if (Die Philosophie des Als Ob (1911), C. K. Ogden, Trans.). Kegan Paul, London
Veyne P (1983) Les Grecs ont-ils cru à leur mythe ? Essai sur l'imagination constituante. Éditions du Seuil, Paris

In Search of what is Common: Political Representation by the Constitutional Jurisdiction

Luís Pereira Coutinho(✉)

University of Lisbon's School of Law, LPL Lisbon Public Law Research Centre, Lisbon, Portugal
lpcoutinho@fd.ulisboa.pt

Abstract. The most important theories of constitutional jurisdiction can be reconstructed as attempts to conceive the terms in which the decisions of constitutional courts can legitimately be attributed to "the people". The classic concept of political representation – which does not reduce it to electoral representation or representativeness – still resonates in those theories. Considering that the said attribution can only be made if, by "the people", one understands a commonality of citizens, this chapter defends that constitutional courts should be understood in contemporary constitutionalism – as a "constitutionalism of fear" – as representatives of a commonality of fear.

Keywords: Political representation · constitutional jurisdiction · constitutionalism of fear

1 The Constitutional Concept of Political Representation

The unitary structure of the modern constitutional state – i.e., its construal in terms that reflect a single principle of legitimacy, that of "national sovereignty" or the sovereignty of "We the People" – implies that all its organs act "in the name of the people", including those which are not elected. Granted, non-electoral representation can only be conceived at the level of political language – the constitutional language structuring the state – but that does not make it arbitrary. Rather, the point is that the power of the state only exists in the terms of a constitutional language – which expresses the said principle of legitimacy – defining it both as a limited power and as bound by a bond of representation of the people. In this sense, the state, in all its corresponding organs, is as limited as it is representative of the people.

The idea that the state definitionally – constitutionally – represents the people is already present in Hobbes, who precisely introduced the concept of political representation at issue in these lines. In Hobbes, the sovereign – as instituted by the original contract – makes present the unity of the people and is authorized to act in its name

I thank Dimitrios Kyritsis, Lars Vinx, and Miguel Nogueira de Brito for helpful comments on previous versions.

L. Pereira Coutinho (Ed.): ICPRCR 2022, IUSGENT 124, pp. 25–37, 2025.
https://doi.org/10.1007/978-3-031-85983-0_3

(1998 [1651]: 101 ff.). The endorsement of the constitutional language of the contract by the citizens – the corresponding acceptance of the sovereign as their representative – is not irrational. Rather, at stake is the self-representation of citizens as such, i.e., of citizens in their commonality of interests, precisely those which the sovereign is to advance if the bond of representation is not to be broken, i.e., if a relation between protection and obedience is to be preserved[1].

This same logic persists in the language of French revolutionary constitutionalism. The sovereign nation that is personified by the constitutional state – and thus represented by the constitutional organs of the state, both the elected and the non-elected – implies a commonality of citizens, i.e., the establishment of common interests, now named as "rights", as those which must be represented (Carré de Malberg 1920: 11 ff.; 1922: 283 ff.). In Sieyès's words (2003 [1789]: 156), "those interests by which citizens resemble one another", making the citizen "someone who can be represented", are those which must be addressed in the "formation of the social law".

If political representation in a constitutional sense expresses a commonality of citizens – that which the constitutional state is bound to make present –, elected representation (or representativeness) is a democratic ambition which may assume the inexistence of that commonality, concerning instead the expression of differences and thus not excluding the legitimacy of partisanship. It is by no means an accident that such an ambition gained force precisely at the moment a Revolutionary language of common rights was denounced as a bourgeois fiction, i.e., as a false commonality which in truth advanced the interests of a certain class against those of other classes. With political representation in a constitutional sense being thus framed as a form of "false consciousness", political representativeness increasingly gained space as the true political ideal to be pursued.

This created a dilemma. An unrestricted advancement of political representativeness in detriment of political representation endangered the former. Indeed, if political representativeness was to be understood as involving the acknowledgement and expression of both majorities and minorities, it depended on the preservation of those political rights that are common to all, and inherently of those constitutional structures – organs and procedures – that channel their different interests and values. Political representativeness thus demanded the preservation of political representation, i.e., it demanded the preservation of a commonality of citizens which was not to be endangered by the results of the representative process.

This is the point from which it becomes possible to understand the persisting relevance of the constitutional concept of political representation, also in the case – particularly in the case – of a constitutional state that grants political representativeness to its citizens. If the latter is to persist, the said commonality must be represented against circumstantial majorities, namely by a constitutional jurisdiction. As I will try to demonstrate, some notable theories of constitutional jurisdiction can be reconstructed in this light, i.e., as theoretical explanations of *what is common*, being therefore representable by the same jurisdiction.

[1] For further developments, see Coutinho 2020: 66 ff.

2 Theories of the Constitutional Jurisdiction as Theories of Political Representation

I will begin my exploration by two restrictive – so-called "representation-reinforcing" – theories of constitutional jurisdiction, those of Hans Kelsen and John Hart Ely.

Apparently, Kelsen does not present his theory of constitutional jurisdiction as a theory of political representation but as a corollary of his theory of law as a hierarchical structure of norms – the constitutional jurisdiction being therefore a mere consequence of the supremacy of constitutional norms over legislative norms. The appearance is deceiving, however. In fact, Kelsen's understanding of the constitutional jurisdiction, and indeed of constitutional supremacy, can only be understood as involving the prevalence of the political representation of all citizens over the representativeness of some groups by the legislator. Being well aware of the multiple ambitions of political representativeness in a pluralist democracy, Kelsen was also aware that these ultimately depended on constitutional law, and thus on a constitutional jurisdiction representing all groups, both majoritarian and minoritarian, its purpose being the preservation of their common democracy as a necessarily constitutional democracy.

If Kelsen did not formulate that understanding in positive terms, he unmistakably advanced it in negative terms. He made clear that mere group interests cannot contaminate constitutional adjudication, which must therefore stand above them. This is clarified in his refusal to consider as proper constitutional principles those which "express only the interests of certain groups" and whose application cannot therefore have "the character of an application of law". Amongst these principles are "equity, liberty, equality, justice, morality, etc.". Since, for Kelsen, any objective concretization of these is impossible, their meaning would inevitably amount to a projection of the interests of certain groups over others. Consequently, even if included in constitutional texts, those principles should still be taken as "postulates which are not legally binding" and that are therefore exclusively directed at the legislator, the constitutional jurisdiction lacking the authority to invalidate any law on their basis (Kelsen 1928).

These lines can be read as implying a negative theory of political representation by the constitutional jurisdiction – one which excludes the mere expression of group interests, developing instead in accordance with "a regulative ideal of legal objectivity" (Vinx 2008: 175). However, Kelsen may be read as going beyond a merely negative theory. Indeed, at issue is a conception of *common legal citizenship* – of "common membership in a jural community" in Dyzenhaus's words (2022: 161 ff.) – to be primarily represented by the legal practice, in particular that of the constitutional court. It is that common citizenship that grants authority to constitutional law and to the institution that expresses it – that authority being implied in the presupposition of the basic norm, considering the prescriptive dimension that Kelsen acknowledges it to have.

That is, legal citizens are assumed to acknowledge the authority of constitutional law as a common language of citizenship and thus to be represented by the jurisdiction that expresses it. This means, in Lars Vinx's words (2007: 174), that citizens are assumed by Kelsen to have a "shared understanding…of the meaning of the distinction between the [constitutional] conditions of legal legitimacy and matters of substantive justice". Regarding the latter, citizens cannot claim representation by the constitutional jurisdiction but must instead aim their efforts at achieving political representativeness of their inevitably partisan conceptions. Contrarily, regarding conditions of legal legitimacy, representation of a commonality of citizens is in order, those conditions primarily having to do with the preservation of constitutional structures and the inherent rights of minorities.

At least regarding its consequences, Kelsen's theory is remarkably similar to that which was to be defended by John Hart Ely in the American context. In both Kelsen and Ely – using the latter's words –, "the Court should keep its hands off the legislature's value judgments", "the definition and imposition of values" being outside the boundaries of what is admissible to a constitutional jurisdiction. That is, "substantive decisions are to be made democratically and constitutional decisions are generally to be limited to policing the mechanisms of decision and distribution" (Ely 1980: 72, 181).

Certainly, Ely does not make it explicit that he is developing a theory on the common features of citizenship in defense of which the constitutional jurisdiction is required to represent all citizens, eventually against majoritarian decisions. Still, his theory actually means a clarification of the basic requirements of political participation – including those basic rights and immunities that protect minorities – without which no common citizenship could persist.

In this sense, both Kelsen's and Ely's theories may be understood as restricting the extent in which the constitutional jurisdiction may represent a commonality of citizens against the possibly partisan decisions of their own representatives. This does not mean to completely prevent the representative process from producing partisan results. On the contrary, for both Kelsen and Ely, it is inevitable that the results of the representative process may be partisan, that not necessarily meaning that they should be invalidated by judicial review. The idea, therefore, is not to ensure the nonpartisanship of state action in all cases; it is only to ensure that partisanship does not reach the point of blocking or compromising an inclusive representative process, thus preventing it from possibly generating yet other partisan results. The point is also that there is a stronghold of impartiality – of political representation of *all* citizens – corresponding to constitutional law and the jurisdiction that expresses it. Its authority over representative institutions will depend therefore on remaining faithful to political representation in the proper sense. In Lars Vinx's words, referred to Kelsen, in a constitutional state, judges must "vicariously exhibit the virtues that would otherwise be required of every citizen. By accepting the regulative ideal of legal objectivity [i.e., of political representation] as their guidepost, reviewing judges allow the rest of us to be partisans" (2007: 175).

Considering the above, so-called "representation-reinforcing" theories of constitutional review may, therefore, be understood as continuous with the foundational theories of political representation. As seen above, both Hobbes and Sieyès understood political representation as implying a common language of citizenship, precisely that which could be represented by the political authority, the boundaries of the political being restricted in accordance.

This continuity must be qualified, of course. I have no intention to deny that, as developed from Hobbes to Sieyès, political representation was the utmost expression of "Enlightenment politics", i.e., of a "politics to end all politics", pluralism being completely outside of the equation (Shklar 1957: 8). What is being proposed instead is that, in its new Kelsenian life, political representation was paradoxically susceptible of being converted into the utmost expression of a "politics to allow all politics". By legitimating the constitutional jurisdiction to express a common language of citizenship – and also by restricting it in accordance –, political representation allows for a pluralist democracy, both in the sense of preventing it from self-destruction and in the sense of not allowing it to be overcome by what is not common. Again, in Kelsen, the latter purpose is achieved by not allowing constitutional norms to be interpreted (or interpretable) as mere expressions of group interests. In Ely, the same purpose is achieved by restricting judicial review to the structures of decision and distribution inherent to an inclusive representative process.

What remained constant, in the paradoxical history of political representation, was the preservation of its Janus-faced nature as a both legitimating and limiting basis of political authority, namely of constitutional authority. It remained true from Hobbes to Kelsen, that political representation both requires the representing authority to express what is common, and demands that it restricts itself to what is common.

Both Kelsen and Ely condemned the constitutional practice of the American Supreme Court. Kelsen focused on the Lochner Era, finding in its decisions – namely those referred to "due process" as "substantive due process" – a paramount example of the capture of constitutional adjudication by group interests, his remedy being not to conceive certain "constitutional principles" as interpretable by the courts. Decades later, Ely focused on the practice of the same Court during the tenures of Chief Justices Warren and Burger, finding in it a condemnable, since inevitably partisan, "discovery of fundamental values" illegitimately imposed on the representative process.

Starting also from the practice of the Warren and Burger Courts, Dworkin reached very different results, proposing a theory of adjudication that fundamentally aimed, both at fitting that practice, and at constituting its best possible interpretation from a moral perspective (1986). Dworkin's "integrity" precisely means that constitutional adjudication should fit the past practice (dimension of fit) as read in its best moral light (dimension of "political morality").

Dworkin's theory is much more explicit as a theory of representation than those of Kelsen and Ely. At issue in integrity precisely is to understand the legal practice as a "common enterprise" of the political community. The latter is understood as a "community of principle" – or "community of moral members" – which is thus taken to be represented whenever constitutional matters are adjudicated as "matters of principle". In this light, when deciding in accordance with integrity, the constitutional authority is to be considered the most perfect expression of the "general will" in a renewed – or not so renewed – understanding of it. It should be mentioned that Dworkin is not afraid to summon the notion (1996: 20 ff.).

Thus, like other theories of constitutional adjudication, Dworkin's theory assumes a commonality of citizens. However, unlike those other theories, it frames that commonality in very demanding terms as implying an endorsement of "principle" in the terms he believes to be concordant with a best moral light. Dworkin thus runs the risk of abstracting too much from the actual differences that exist among citizens. In fact, in this context, the point of the constitutional jurisdiction will not be to allow the citizens to be partisan. That point may very well be instead to prevent citizens from being partisan in the pursuit of their interests and values, with the overarching political structure of the constitutional state being replaced by an "underarching" umbrella of "moral membership".

It is true that Dworkin does not insulate the judicial practice from public deliberation, considering it instead as a "superior kind of republican deliberation", one correspondingly open to continuous participation (taking place, first of all, in the very form of legal claims) and "public discussion" (1996: 30). Nonetheless, deliberation in this context will still be framed by an assumed notion of commonality that cannot be challenged, with claimants, defendants or respondents, or any other participants in this form of "republican deliberation" (from *amici curiae* to newspaper columnists) being themselves expected to use "arguments of principle" or risk being excluded from the debate for their lack of "public spirit". In fact, from Dworkin's perspective, "republican deliberation" cannot be "plagued" by "militant" sensibilities which challenge the requirements of "moral membership" (2006: 258). The common boundaries of deliberation are therefore defined from the start, something that Dworkin explicitly acknowledges when he considers it to be "result-driven", also admitting that his own endorsement is tied to an observation of the American constitutional practice that "shows" that its judges "understand the Bill of Rights as a constitution of principle" (1996: 34-5). Considering this, only a very limited pluralism can be accommodated by Dworkin's integrity.

In addition to undermining pluralism, Dworkin's proposal appears to contradict the fundamentally *political* intent of the concept of political representation as designed by Sieyès and later redesigned in the Kelsenian moment of constitutionalism. That intent resided in a definition of (limited) authority and (corresponding) legitimacy in terms that narrowed its claim to represent the citizenry: to affirm that only the common interests of citizens deserve political representation meant to restrict it to the pursuit of those interests that can actually be framed as common. In fact, even if Dworkin's theoretical equation may be similar to Sieyès's, the intent is very different, no longer being *negative* but positive regarding the extent of the power susceptible of being exercised in the name of the political community. Unlike the "sovereign nation" (or "We the People", for that matter), Dworkin's "community of principle" is a commonality which serves as the legitimating axis of a potentially unlimited, not totally constituted, power. Legal authority and corresponding political legitimacy are now replaced by *moral* authority and *moral* legitimacy, the latter being potentially unlimited by nature, for who can possibly stand in the way of what is both politically and morally "right"?

It should be acknowledged that Dworkin, in spite of his moralization of political representation, paradoxically attempts to preserve the distinctive character of legal reasoning – as the only form of reasoning exercisable by the courts. He restricts that reasoning to the adjudication of "matters of principle", clearly distinguishing "arguments of principle" from "arguments of policy". However, the autonomy of legal reasoning from political considerations is aimed, not at liberating the political process from any "unbearable" rule, be it majoritarian or counter-majoritarian – as it was the case in Kelsen –, but at ensuring it remains an uncorrupted form of *moral* reasoning to be pursued whatever the extent of the judicial authority therefore exercised and regardless of its political impacts. Judges are therefore to pursue their reasoning inflexibly, determining to its full extent the meaning of every single constitutional principle. In this vein, Dworkin acknowledges that judicial decisions will inevitably interfere directly on "comprehensive issues". For him, that simply must be accepted as a fact of legal life, constitutional interpretation implying the ascription of "controversial conceptions" to "contested concepts" (1978: 134, 290; 2006: 176 ff, 253).

By rigidly considering the demands he attributes to integrity (and thus to the representation of a "community of moral members"), Dworkin thus defends an unquestionable prevalence of what is "right" (both *legally* and *morally* right), not only over what is convenient or expedient, but also over another form of "right". That other form of right, which deserves due attention when *constitutional* law is at stake, is *political right in a constitutionalist sense*, one in which considerations of pluralism – and inherently of (limited) authority and overarching political legitimacy – are crucial. It is precisely the latter notion of right that is inextricably attached to political representation as properly *political*.

In Robert Alexy (2022: 135–136), Dworkin's "community of principle" is replaced by a community of "constitutional persons". As "rational persons", constitutional persons both "accept the constitution" and "are able and willing to accept sound and correct arguments for the reason that they are sound and correct". They are therefore assumed to be "argumentatively represented" by the constitutional jurisdiction.

If constitutional persons are both rational and accepting of the constitution, then the constitution they accept is by definition a rational constitution. Alexy's conception of "argumentative representation" thus raises the question of knowing what is it that makes a constitution rational, i.e., it demands for a clarification of the rationality inherent to constitutionalism.

As seen above, the rationality of constitutionalism, and inherently of political representation, was distinctively political, both in its foundational and in its Kelsenian moments. Again, the point was always to legitimate and also to limit the power of the state (or that of its constitutional jurisdiction). In Sieyès, that meant restricting the state to the representation of narrowly defined interests. In Kelsen, that meant restricting its constitutional jurisdiction to the defense of those requirements on which the exercise of a common political citizenship depends. In these terms, the constitutional state – as structured by the political representation of a *narrowly* defined commonality – became capable of navigating pluralism. It even became capable, when completed by Kelsen, of allowing its citizens to be partisan while preserving their political unity.

It is very unclear whether Alexy's notion of "discursive constitutionalism" has the same virtuality. In fact, instead of marking the political unity of plural citizens, a constitutional personhood represented by the constitutional jurisdiction, appears to be a demanding form of moral personhood. It is demanding since it must raise to the level of acceptance of the results discursively reached by the constitutional jurisdiction, however challenging they may be (i.e., however contrary they may be of those different interests and values actually endorsed by citizens). In other words, citizens will be expected to live up to their constitutional personhood as it inevitably runs against their own political citizenship (they will be "forced to be free" if one uses Rousseau's ominous expression).

Thus, as Dworkin's theory of integrity, Alexy's discursive theory appears to be strange to the fundamentally *political* intentionality of the language of constitutionalism as it was designed in its foundational moments. This does not mean, of course, that one should take these moments as sacrosanct. I admit that present-day constitutionalism is not necessarily to be conceived in the same terms it was designed by Sieyès and later redesigned by Kelsen. In fact, those foundational formulations may neither fit our practices nor mirror the values we see reflected in them.

Still, a feature remains without which we would no longer be speaking of constitutionalism proper, past, or present. In fact, one can hardly be speaking of constitutionalism if one fails to conceive it as a language aimed at both legitimating and limiting the power of the state (also that of its constitutional jurisdiction) before its citizens (Kyritsis 2017: 7 ff.; 2022: 216 ff.). That flaw becomes inevitable in case one dismisses political representation as making present that which may be assumed to be common. In that case, one will be conceiving the state – or its constitutional jurisdiction – as an uncompromising agent which curtails the political participation of its citizens while reaching results which cannot possibly be assumed to be endorsed by them.

I believe this flaw is present in Alexy's discursive theory. Remember that, besides constitutional review (as inherently rational since based on "sound and correct" arguments) and representation (of constitutional persons conceived as inherently rational), Alexy's theory stems from the connection of yet three other concepts: constitutional rights, balancing, and discourse (2022: 129 ff.). This essentially means that a rational constitution contains rights understood as "optimization requirements" to be balanced against one another. Through "sound and correct arguments", the constitutional jurisdiction will be able to determine which of those rights prevails in each case.

In light of the above, Alexy's theory – if it is to be accepted as theory of constitutionalism – will depend on whether balancing is able to produce results one may assume to be commonly accepted, or at least acceptable, by citizens with different interests and worldviews. More precisely, the same theory will depend on whether citizens can be assumed to endorse the "sound and correct arguments" on which those results depend.

I'm sceptical. Beginning with some examples, the results of the balancing between property rights and social rights (in case a property tax is at issue), or between the autonomy of the mother and the life of the fetus (in case abortion is at issue) will be radically different in light of different perspectives. Moreover, what is a sound and correct argument from one perspective may not even be a proper argument from another. With this I'm not necessarily denying that there may be formal characteristics that make some arguments, and not others, as sound and correct. What I'm saying is that those formal characteristics are not the ones leading to the prevalence of property over social rights, autonomy over life, or privacy over public security, to use yet another example.

In fact, the soundness and correctness of arguments on which balancing actually depends will necessarily be substantive and not strictly formal, i.e., it will depend on assumptions that cannot possibly assumed to be shared by the many participants in a constitutional democracy. Correspondingly, the rationality on which Alexy's "discursive constitutionalism" – and corresponding balancing – depends will not be one that limits the constitutional jurisdiction to the expression of what is common. On the contrary, such a theory, with all the credits bestowed on it by a formal theory of argumentation – and by a highly idealized conception of constitutional personhood –, will allow the constitutional jurisdiction to express what is not common.

Finally, it should be added that balancing does not really address the most fundamental conflicts that cross our constitutional democracies. These do not concern the weighing between different principles but the previous determination of the latter. In fact, some principles are divisive in themselves either because there is no consensus on whether they should be admitted as constitutional principles, or because their meaning – also their *prima facie* meaning – is up for grabs. This clearly is the case of human dignity: what is it in it that must be "optimized", autonomy in the Kantian sense, or "common humanity" in Ratzinger's sense (2005)? The conflicts around human dignity will therefore necessarily depend on assumptions which cannot possibly be adjudicated through balancing. What is said about human dignity, could also be said about "life", or about the protection of "marriage" and "family".

3 A Commonality of Fear

The above appears to lead us to a process-centered or "representation-reinforcing" theory of constitutional review. However, one shouldn't be so hasty, as it is still necessary to attend to other considerations.

When debating process-centered theories of judicial review, Michael Perry (1978) claimed that the same are "very difficult to defend in this post-Holocaustal age". We know that Ely tried to defend his theory against that claim. He did it by clarifying that "a representation-reinforcing theory of judicial review" effectively prevents "the victimization of a discrete and insular minority" in the terms that quintessentially characterized the Holocaust (1980: 135 ff.; 181–2).

However successful Ely's argument is, there is still something to Perry's objection that deserves attention. In fact, at issue is to apprehend a feature of our common citizenship as a somehow traumatized citizenship, one which consequently is not satisfied by remaining characterized in fundamentally procedural terms. At issue is also to apprehend features of contemporary constitutionalism that probably may only be successfully described as reflective of that trauma – of an ingrained common fear of tyranny. Those features can hardly be described by a theory strictly focused on correcting the failures of the representative process with disregard for its results.

In other words, a successful account of present-day Western constitutionalism and the practice of corresponding jurisdictions must frame the latter as representing a commonality of fear. In this conclusion, I am approaching the notion of "constitutionalism of fear", recently introduced by Dimitrios Kyritsis (2022: 222 ff.). According to that notion, constitutionalism is to be understood as a discourse and practice which projects in the constitution what Judith Shklar referred to as a "liberalism of fear" (1998: 3 ff.). Even though Kyritsis does not articulate that notion as tied with a conception of political representation by the constitutional jurisdiction, I believe the latter is a corollary of the former. In this vein, a constitutionalism of fear is precisely characterized by allowing the constitutional jurisdiction to *make present* that fear, thus permitting it to prevent a descension of political life into what is commonly feared.

Within a constitutionalism of fear – at least if the notion is understood as continuous with Shklar's "liberalism of fear" – constitutional adjudication is not a matter of institutionalized reason generating moral progress. I should stress that my point here is not necessarily to reject the fundamental beliefs of the Enlightenment in reason and progress. Even if these were to be accepted, even if a best moral light could be lit by reason or arguments could be weighted with no assistance of substantive assumptions, constitutional law should still not be construed in corresponding terms. In fact, even in that case, citizens still would not be conceivable in so demanding terms and therefore as commonly represented by an institution advancing them. Either the cause is their atavism or the fact that moral reason is necessarily conjugated in the plural, the fact remains that different moral lights persist, and arguments are weighted differently. A constitutional law – or corresponding constitutional jurisdiction – that ignored this would inevitably place itself "at the center of political conflict", losing in the process its overarching authority (Böckenförde 1992).

In sum, constitutional law and its jurisdiction are inviable as instruments of moral progress. The most one can expect is for them to persist as an antidote from known forms of moral regress. This means enforcing the corresponding institutions and procedures as means of depersonalization and dispersion of powers. This also means safeguarding individuals from known forms of cruelty, oppression, or intimidation. Regarding the latter, even though a "liberalism of fear" is not a "liberalism of rights" – and certainly does not depend on the assumption that there is a coherent and consistent public morality of rights (Yack 1996: 2–3) –, it is unthinkable without the guarantee of those "freedoms from" corresponding to basic rules of contemporary constitutions (prohibition of torture, prohibition of cruel and unusual punishments, criminal procedure rules, prohibition of discriminations based on degrading criteria, etc.).

As to principles, if there is a place for them in a constitutionalism of fear, it should be remembered at all times that their point must not be to offer "a *summum bonum* toward which all political agents should strive" but at preserving us from "a *summum malum*" (Shklar 1998: 10–11). Correspondingly, their construction must be cautious and restrained; above all it must not depend on naïve assumptions about outstanding capacities for moral rationality – least of all if the latter are to be embodied by a power of the state, that of its constitutional jurisdiction, which is after all to be feared like any other.

The practice of the German Federal Constitutional Court can be enlightening in this context. It is undoubtful that the construction of principles was a central part of it, namely the principles of "equality", "human dignity" or the "*Rechtstaat*". Moreover, the German Court developed a public record on the meaning of those principles, ascribing the *Willkür-Verbot* and the *Neue Formel* to equality, the *object formula* to human dignity, the *principles of proportionality* and *reliance* to the *Rechtstaat* principle. However, one cannot say that, when developing that record, the Court advanced a best moral version of those principles. On the contrary, at stake was only to assure citizens against known forms of arbitrariness or abuse, and that starting from the plausible assumption that citizens – regardless of their moral differences – commonly fear a descent into tyranny. In this sense, the framework in which the German Court developed constitutional legality was a framework of fear, at stake being a "constitutionalism of fear".

That is, when developing the said public record, the German Court was being cautious, not understanding constitutional reasoning as a medium of moral progress but as a stronghold of agreement (of common authority) in a context of disagreement. This interpretation of the German constitutional practice will be reinforced if one considers the purposes that were declared by those who originally developed the formulas used by the Court, namely Leibholz, Dürig or Forsthoff. I believe it's clarifying to consider Forsthoff's words (1964) when concluding that the Court should not go beyond the *Willkür-Verbot* when interpreting the *legal* meaning of "equality". In fact, he considered that restraint to be essential when we are living in "modern societies, spiritually non-homogeneous, which know few standards on the basis of which equality and inequality, justice and injustice can be convincingly determined in each case. In the vast domain in which one opinion is opposed to another, it cannot be the task of the Court to enforce its subjective opinion". This means, in other words, that the Court cannot lose sight of the extent in which it can represent a commonality of citizens.

4 Concluding Remarks

Many authors – including some of the contributors to this volume, namely Troper, Pasquino and Kyritsis – refuse the idea of political representation by the constitutional jurisdiction. Namely they claim that its legitimacy in contemporary constitutional democracies should be understood in light of other moral or political sources, unrelated to the representation of the citizenry. Before those other proposals, I could be accused of being too attached to a conceptual axiom, that axiom being that all organs of the constitutional state necessarily represent the people.

I believe however that the preservation of political representation as a constitutive concept of the constitutional state (outside which no constitutional legitimacy exists) is not arbitrary. As stated from the start, at issue is to preserve the unitary structure of the constitutional state in a way that reflects the democratic principle (national sovereignty or the sovereignty of "We the People") as its single source of legitimacy. In fact, the modern constitutional state was not constructed as a mixed regime in which different moral or political forces oppose one other, with different institutions reflecting different principles of legitimacy. That is, the modern constitutional state is not a facsimile of ancient Republics, namely of the Roman Republic with its moderating aristocratic Senate taming the passions of popular assemblies. Such an arrangement would be incompatible with the political self-definition of modern polities: something like the "Senate and People of Rome" can no longer exist in a political world in which "We the People" or "the sovereign nation" are the only political entities culturally susceptible of being *made present* by the powers of the state. In sum, political representation - i.e., representation of the people by all constitutional organs, majoritarian or counter-majoritarian - preserves and reflects the language of political legitimacy of the modern constitutional state.

As an axial element of the language of the constitutional state, political representation also means to ensure that considerations of legitimacy are necessarily tied to the definition of limits - which must be respected if constitutional organs are to remain to be adequately considered as representing the people (if a "relation between protection and obedience" is to remain, if one uses Hobbes's expression). I fear other moral or political forces, besides not preserving the theoretical or conceptual coherence of the modern constitutional state, may not have the same restricting effect on the constitutional jurisdiction they endow with legitimacy. Even though he was not addressing the specific problem of the constitutional jurisdiction, this is exactly the point that was made by Carré de Malberg when defending his theory of national sovereignty, i.e., of representation of the nation *by all organs* of the state. In his words, only by preserving the concept of political representation as a constitutive concept of the constitutional state, could one have "a firm basis to the modern system of limitation of powers" (1920: 28 ff; 1922: 30 ff.).

One other possible objection is methodological. By defending a constitutionalism of fear – and the possible representation of that fear by the constitutional jurisdiction – I may be accused of not mirroring that which is the actual practice of contemporary constitutional jurisdictions. Even if that is not the case in the practice of the German Federal Constitutional Court – as mentioned above – I admit that some constitutional practices have tended in these last decades to go far beyond the mere prevention of intolerable moral failures, envisioning themselves instead as agents of moral progress. However, an accurate account of constitutionalism cannot be exclusively aimed at fitting the practices which were implemented as "constitutional". Indeed, before emerging as a practice, constitutionalism is a purposeful language or discourse. It may therefore be the case that certain features of given practices deviate from it.

In this light, it is as a language or discourse that constitutionalism must be primarily reconstructed. My point in this chapter is that a corresponding exercise cannot abstract from a history which defined its purposes as political, i.e., as having essentially to do with the *political* legitimacy of *limited* powers (also that of the constitutional jurisdiction). Also, it cannot abstract from a notion of democratic citizenship, one which envisions citizens as participants in a common democracy - citizens who do not wish to renounce their partisanship while remaining well aware of the grave dangers they are exposed to in their collective enterprise. From my perspective, a concept of political representation that remains continuous with its classic formulations is an axial element of that language, organizing its features in a coherent scheme.

References:

Alexy R (2022) Balancing, constitutional review, and representation. The Ideal Dimension of Law. Oxford University Press, Oxford, pp 129–136

Böckenförde E-W (1992) Die Methoden der Verfassungsinterpretation – Bestandsaufnahme und Kritik. Staat, Verfassung, Demokratie, 2nd edn. Suhrkamp, Frankfurt am Main, pp 53–89

Carré de Malberg R (1920) Contribution à la Théorie Générale de l'État: spécialement d'après les données fournies par le Droit Constitutionnnel Français, I, Recueil Sirey, Paris

Carré de Malberg R (1922) Contribution à la Théorie Générale de l'État: spécialement d'après les données fournies par le Droit Constitutionnnel Français, II. Recueil Sirey, Paris

Coutinho LP (2020) The Masks of Sovereignty, Católica Law Review, IV/1, pp. 65–79

Dyzenhaus D (2022) The long arc of legality: hobbes, kelsen, hart. Cambridge University Press, Cambridge

Dworkin R (1978) Taking rights seriously. Harvard University Press, Cambridge Mass

Dworkin R (1986) Law's empire. Harvard University Press, Cambridge Mass

Dworkin R (1996) Freedom's law: the moral reading of the american constitution. Harvard University Press, Cambridge Mass

Dworkin R (2006) Justice in robes. Harvard University Press, Cambridge Mass

Ely JH (1980) Democracy and distrust: a theory of judicial review. Harvard University Press, Cambridge Mass, p 1980

Hobbes T (1998 [1651]) Leviathan: with selected variants from the latin edition of 1668 (ed. Edwin Curley). Hackett, Indianapolis/Cambridge
Kelsen H (1928) La Garantie Juridictionnelle de la Constitution (La Justice Constitutionnelle). Revue de Droit Public et Science Politique 35:197–258
Kyritsis D (2017) Where our protection lies: separation of powers and judicial review. Oxford University Press, Oxford
Kyritsis D (2022) Constitutional law as legitimacy-enhancer. In: Dyritsis D, Lakin S (eds) The Methodology of Constitutional Theory, pp 211–232. Hart, Oxford
Perry M (1978) The abortion funding cases: a comment on the supreme court's role in american government. Georgetown Law J. 66(5):1191–1245
Ratzinger J (2005) L'Europa di Benedetto nella Crisi delle Culture. Cantagalli, Sienna
Shklar J (1957) After utopia: the decline of political faith. Princeton University Press, Princeton
Shklar J (1998) The liberalism of fear. In: Hoffmann S (ed) Political Thought and Political Thinkers. Chicago University Press, Chicago and London
Sieyès (2003 [1789]) What is the third estate?. In: Sonenscher M (ed) Political Writings. Hackett, Indianapolis/Cambridge, pp 92–162
Vinx L (2007) Hans kelsen's pure theory of law. Oxford University Press, Oxford
Yack B (1996) Liberalism without illusions: an introduction to Judith Shklar's political thought. In: Yack B (ed) Liberalism without Illusions: Essays on Liberal Theory and the Political Vision of Judith N. Shklar. Chicago University Press, Chicago, pp 1–13

No Democracy Without Representation: Against a Certain Dualism in Constitutional Law

Miguel Nogueira de Brito(✉)

Faculty of Law, Lisbon Public Law Research Centre, Lisbon University, Lisbon, Portugal
miguelbrito@fd.ulisboa.pt

Abstract. This chapter is a plaidoyer against dualism in constitutional law. Dualism stands for the idea that constitutional law cannot be fully apprehended neither within the categories of ordinary law nor within the understanding of the constitution as a law. Moreover, according to dualism, "the political" can always irrupt in the normal legal order and conform it to its fundamental designs. Schmitt is the greatest herald of dualism in constitutional law, and Kelsen its foremost critic. Notwithstanding Kelsen's importance as a critic of dualism and the persistent relevance of his points of view on this issue, his pragmatic view of representation needs additional theoretical foundations regarding the concept of representation in a legal order. These additional foundations are provided by Hans Lindahl's legal work following the "Copernican turn of representation".

Keywords: Representation · responsiveness · dualism in constitutional law · Carl Schmitt · Hans Kelsen · Martin Loughlin · Hans Lindahl

1 Introduction

Constitutional law always begins with constituted powers and, in case it effectively presides over the political and legal life of a community, it evolves towards constituent power, never the other way around[1]. This is just another way of expressing the paradox of constituent power, but one, I hope, that points to an important insight: that constituent power is not antecedent to the constitution does not mean it can be dispensed with.

The paradox of constituent power is stated by Hans Lindahl in the following terms: "an act only succeeds – never fully, always provisionally – as the exercise of constituent power if, in hindsight, it appears to have been the act of a constituted power"[2]. For this

[1] In this sense, Henderson LM (2019), 1175, contends the "the imposition of a lawgiver as the representative of the people is not a one-off imposition at the beginning—it is an imposition each day anew and one that ultimately depends, day after day, on the people to recognize it as the legitimate lawgiver"; Corrias L (2011, 1571, also states that "the nation is dependent on the bearers of constituted power to the extent that the nation cannot act as constituent power without being represented by a constituted power". Both authors are influenced by the thought of Hans Lindahl, which this text claims to be the main demolisher of dualism in constitutional law.

[2] Cf. Lindahl H (2018) 402; see also, following Lindahl, de Brito MN (2023), 601–602, 608, 624, 646, 657.

L. Pereira Coutinho (Ed.): ICPRCR 2022, IUSGENT 124, pp. 38–57, 2025.
https://doi.org/10.1007/978-3-031-85983-0_4

author, neither the people nor the constitution are paramount – these two positions, as is well known, correspond to the views of Carl Schmitt and Hans Kelsen[3], respectively, on the problem of constituent power – but only "the constitution of a collective in the *verbal* sense of the word", as a narrative construction[4].

Lindahl's thought has the great merit of recovering representation as a central category of constitutional law in a political and cultural context in which disintermediation emerges as the watchword. In the following pages, I intend to explore how such a recovery allows not only to overcome the very visible danger of dissolution of constitutionalism, but also to ward off the danger – certainly less apparent, but no less real – residing in a certain fundamental dualism in constitutional theory. With this purpose in mind, I shall begin by addressing the dualist conception of constitutional law, whose greatest herald is Schmitt, whose foremost critic is Kelsen, and whose more consummate current exponent is Martin Loughlin. After that, I will explore the idea of representation as an irreducible category of constitutional law – democracy without representation being but an illusion –, its rescuing from dualism being therefore urgent. Precisely that is illustrated, albeit in different ways, in the works of Hauke Brunkhorst and Hans Lindahl.

2 Dualism in Constitutional Law and Its Critics

2.1 Carl Schmitt as the Master of Dualism in Constitutional Law

At its core, dualism in constitutional law simply means that this kind of law cannot be fully apprehended neither within the categories of ordinary law nor within an understanding of the constitution as a law. The most pregnant statement of dualism in this sense lies perhaps in Carl Schmitt's distinction between constitution and constitutional law. In his words, "the concept of the constitution is only possible when one distinguishes constitution and constitutional law"[5]. Having in mind the second term of this distinction, he further considered that "it is not acceptable to first dissolve the constitution into a multitude of individual constitutional laws and then to define constitutional law in reference to some external characteristic or even according to the method of its alteration"[6].

On the contrary, according to Schmitt "the act of establishing a constitution as such involves not separate sets of norms. Instead, it determines the entirety of the political unity regarding its peculiar form of existence through a single instance of decision. This act constitutes the form and type of the political unity, the existence of which is presupposed"[7].

In light of the aforementioned distinction, the constitution is prior to constitutional laws, in the sense that the political decision is prior to the norm: "constitutional laws are valid first on the basis of the constitution and presuppose a constitution. For its validity as a normative regulation, every statute, even constitutional law, ultimately needs a political

[3] Cf. Lindahl H (2007b), 9–14.

[4] Cf. Lindahl H (1998), 28 ss.; *idem* (2018), 402, 404; Ferrara A (2023), 141.

[5] Cf. Schmitt C (2008a), 75.

[6] Cf. Schmitt C (2008a), 75.

[7] Cf. Schmitt C (2008a), 75.

decision that is prior to it, a decision that is reached by a power or authority that exists politically"[8].

The distinction between constitution and constitutional law is a manifestation of a dualism that finds parallels in other distinctions especially present in Schmitt's thought: the distinction between constituent power and constituted power, the distinction between the exception and the norm, as well as the distinctions between representation and identity, representative democracy and direct democracy, state and society, or the political and the normative. At the same time, these distinctions – which are, ultimately, equivalent and express the primacy of politics in social life – make up the theoretical background against which a set of political-constitutional options are taken by Schmitt. Among these options it is worth mentioning the justification of emergency powers as a privileged mechanism to deal with government and economic crises[9]; the preference to entrust the defense of the constitution to the head of state, and not to a constitutional court[10]; the acceptance of a plebiscitary conception of democracy[11]; the affirmation of the separation between state and society and the essential role of the former in maintaining an economic order based on private property[12]; the unbounded conception of sovereignty in the context of a Eurocentric system of world order[13].

Therefore, the dualist basis of Schmitt's constitutional thought seems to be clear, as well as its closeness to the foundational distinction between friend and enemy which, according to him, is the core of the political[14]. The problem is that, by means of these dualistic schemes, solutions are proposed for questions of a political and economic nature. The apparently objective basis of the latter cannot disguise objectives which are purely political-ideological, or, at best, options of a metaphysical and theological nature, thus characteristic of "someone who still lives within a social imaginary shaped by the idea of a created world"[15].

Beyond this general assertion there is little agreement between Schmitt's commentators. Was Schmitt a modern Gnostic, as it appears to be the case in some passages of *Political Theory II*? Schmitt seems to be moving in that direction when, for example, he says that "the main structural problem with Gnostic dualism, that is, with the problem of the God of creation and the God of salvation, dominates not only every religion of salvation and redemption. It exists inescapably in every world in need of change and renewal, and it is both immanent and ineradicable. One cannot get rid of the enmity between human beings by prohibiting wars between states in the traditional sense, by advocating a world revolution and by transforming world politics into world policing"[16].

---

[8] Cf. Schmitt C (2008a), 76.
[9] Cf. Schmitt C (2014), 180 ss.
[10] Cf. Schmitt C (2015), 150 ss.
[11] Cf. Schmitt C (2008a), 131, 273, 278, 302–306; Schmitt C (2004), 59 ss.
[12] Cf. Schmitt C (1985), 192.
[13] Cf. Schmitt C (2006), 126 ss., 140 ss.
[14] Cf. Schmitt C (2007), 26.
[15] Cf. Kahn PW (2011), 115–116.
[16] Cf. Schmitt C (2008b) 125. On the possibility of this interpretation, see Herrero M (2015), 171 ss.; *idem* (2023), 16 ss. See, also, Paipais V (2016), 1615–1616; Groh R (1998), 163–164; *idem* (2014), 83 ss.; Griffioen S (2022), 103–106.

Differently, and even oppositely, it is also possible to sustain that Schmitt was in fact a critic of modern Gnostic dualism. This second interpretation points out that in *Roman Catholicism and Political Form*, first published in 1923, Schmitt, while acknowledging already that the current epoch is ruled by a radical dualism ultimately based on a modern conception of technicity and soul, claims that such a dualist conception is entirely alien to Catholicism. The latter "understands little of the dualisms of nature and spirit, nature and intellect, nature and art, nature and machine, and their varying pathos"[17].

However opposed the two interpretations may be, their outcome is not very promising: either Schmitt was a conservative revolutionary, or a sheer reactionary. Either he was an outright fascist, seeking a revolutionary reconfiguration of society in the context of a "bloody decisive battle" in the struggle between anarchistic atheism and the forces of faith and order[18]; or he was an authoritarian liberal, working for a "reactionary defence of bourgeois institutions, not least private property and state power, even if the endeavour was formulated in opposition to certain aspects of bourgeois ideology"[19]. In both cases, the dualistic schemes above mentioned – constitution and constitutional law, state and law, state and society, exception and norm – acquire a central importance, insofar as they allow, by their simple invocation, to present solutions that apparently break positive constitutional law on the basis that they are meant to express a more fundamental law, one that articulates the supposed primacy of the political.

If we choose dualism as a scheme for approaching constitutional law, it will be useful to oppose Schmitt's manifest embracing of it to its persistent criticism by Kelsen. It is also important to problematize the recovery of dualism by Martin Loughlin, who seems above all interested in exploring its critical potential in current conditions. One may say in this context that Kelsen represents the modernist critique of dualism in constitutional law, while Loughlin attempts a "postmodernist" recovery of it.

2.2 Hans Kelsen, Critic of Dualism (And of Carl Schmitt)

Kelsen arguably holds a "too dualistic distinction between normative and scientific propositions"[20], which could be attributed to his expressly acknowledged reception of Kant's theoretical reason (as to Kant's idea of a practical reason, it is rejected by Kelsen even if he adopts a cosmopolitan project that reveals striking similarities with Kant's[21]). One could claim that Kelsen's neo-Kantian sources and the empiricist and semanticist climate of Vienna at the turn of the 20th century are responsible for his sharp criticism of dualist categories in law.

Hauke Brunkhorst makes a much more ambitious claim when he says that "from the very beginning Kelsen's critique of dualism goes beyond the conceptual scope of neo-Kantianism and signifies a turn similar to and simultaneous with the pragmatic turn in philosophy that was performed by so different thinkers as John Dewey, the young

[17] Cf. Schmitt C (1996), 11. Leaning towards this second interpretation, see Falk H (2022), 13; Hiromura NT (2020), 37 ss.; Herrera HE (2020), 145, note 117.

[18] Cf. Schmitt C (2005), 59.

[19] Cf. Falk H (2022), 14.

[20] Cf. Brunkhorst H (2011), 496.

[21] Cf. de Brito MN (2020a, b), 311–315.

Martin Heidegger, the young Max Horkheimer, or the young Lukacs, and later Quine, Austin, Kuhn, Rorty, Gadamer, Davidson, Putnam, Brandom, Habermas, Bernstein and others. They all have a common starting point, and that is the critique of metaphysical dualism and its replacement by a continuum of differences"[22].

One way or the other, it seems unequivocal that there is a parallelism between the "anti-ideological tendence" of Kelsen's *Pure Theory of Law* and his criticism of dualist legal categories, such as *(i)* state and law; *(ii)* state and society; *(iii)* public and private law; *(iv)* law and decree; *(v)* international and national law[23]. In fact, "Kelsen considers as ideological the dualisms developed by nineteenth century positivistic legal doctrines. Notwithstanding, they are essentially still recognized by contemporary legal theory. These are the oppositions between public and private, subjective right and objective law, as well as the dichotomy of state and law, of law's application and law-making, which Kelsen viewed as ideological"[24].

Regarding, for example, the dualism of state and law, Kelsen considers that it "betokens not only a contradiction in the logically systematic sense; it is also more particularly the source of a politico-legal abuse. Under the guise of an argument in legal and political theory, it provides a way of enabling purely political postulates to break in upon positive law. The dualism of state and law becomes a dualism of two different and mutually contradictory norm-systems, of which one, under the names of 'state', reason or interest of state (also public welfare, public 'law'), is then repeatedly brought to bear whenever the other, namely 'positive' law, leads to a consequence unwelcome to the rulers, who are in truth identical with this 'state'"[25].

Once we let go of Kelsen's "residual dualistic elements" – still present in his own "neo-Kantian deductivism", such as the theory of the *Grundnorm*, the strict difference of analytical and empirical, of historical genesis and logical validity, of is and ought, etc.[26] –, we can fully appreciate that Kelsen's radical attacks on the above mentioned dualisms are directly aimed at "criticizing the construction of the realm of law and the state as a hierarchical and ontological order of categorically different spheres which are reciprocally impermeable and do not allow for interference". Instead, for Kelsen "there are only differences which can be reconstructed as a continuum of (quantitative or qualitative) differences, but there is no dualism of different spheres of being not allowing for reciprocal interference"[27].

According to Brunkhorst, the critique of dualism in Kelsen is closely related to his critique of representation, the latter being simply the other side of the former. He distances

[22] Cf. Brunkhorst H (2011), 506. In a somewhat different, but related, sense, Hans Lindahl also discusses Kelsen's criticism of natural law theory as an example of metaphysical dualism and a copy theory of knowledge: cf. Lindahl H (2000), 223–246. In spite of this criticism, according to Lindahl "the terms in which the Pure Theory construes the distinction between law application and law creation are entirely congenial to natural-law doctrines. Indeed, if the legal act produces a lower-level norm, does it not by the same token reproduce the higher-level norm?" [cf. Lindahl H (2000), 232].

[23] Cf. Brunkhorst H (2011), 498–501.

[24] Cf. Römer P (1971), 582 (my translation).

[25] Cf. Kelsen H (1973), 75–76.

[26] Cf. Brunkhorst H (2011), 502.

[27] Cf. Brunkhorst H (2011), 499.

himself from the view according to which "what is represented by our intellect, our statements, or our parliaments is the real world, the propositional content, or the people's real opinion (or their true interest etc.), hence, representation in the correspondence theory of truth as well as in the theory of parliamentary representation presupposes a dualism of the two realms"[28].

In opposition to this dualism, for Kelsen, "the 'People' is not, as is often naively imagined, a body or conglomeration of actual persons. Rather, it is merely a system of individual human acts regulated by the state legal order". Consequently "it is a fiction when the unity, which the state legal order fashions out of the multiplicity of human actions, poses as a 'popular body' by calling itself the 'People.' It creates the illusion that individuals belong to the People with their whole being, when in actuality they only belong to it through certain actions which are either commanded or prohibited by the political order"[29].

In this context, Kelsen has no illusions about the fictitious nature of representation, which "is meant to legitimate parliamentarism from the standpoint of popular sovereignty". And even though the fiction of representation "has been unable to fulfill its actual purpose of justifying parliament from the standpoint of popular sovereignty, it has served a function quite different from the one for which it was originally intended: It has managed to keep the nineteenth- and twentieth-century political movement standing under enormous pressure from the democratic ideal on a sensible and moderate path"[30]. Whether the fiction of representation is still able to discharge such a function in the contemporary digital condition – a condition characterized by "disintermediation" – is quite another question.

Furthermore, Kelsen believes that there is no access to the state as a collective body other than through the acts of its officials and, in this way, he avoids "ontologizing collective subjectivity", offering "an alternative to dualistic theories that postulate the state as an organic unity that first creates a legal order and subsequently subordinates itself to its creation"[31].

For Kelsen, in sum, there is no way out of representation in the political realm, even if (or because) representation is a fiction. There are no Peoples existing out there prior to their political representatives. This monistic view is directly opposed to Carl Schmitt's dualism of identity and representation as the "two opposing orientation points for the concrete formation of the political unity"[32]. In fact, it is even possible to claim that Kelsen develops "a conception of ideological criticism specifically orientated against the Schmittian position"[33].

Surely, Schmitt acknowledges that "even all active state citizens, taken as a whole, are not the political unity of the people. They merely represent the political unity, which transcends an assembly convened at a particular time and place"[34]. He also accepts that

[28] Cf. Brunkhorst H (2011), 506.
[29] Cf. Kelsen H (2013), 36.
[30] Cf. Kelsen H (2013), 50.
[31] Cf. Lindhal H (2007a), 487.
[32] Cf. Schmitt C (2008a), 240.
[33] Cf. Donhauser G (2019), 385.
[34] Cf. Schmitt C (2008a), 240.

"there is no state without representation because there is no state without state form, and the presentation of the political unity is an intrinsic part of the form". Furthermore, according to him, that "presentation, however, need not be production of the political unity. It is possible that the political unity is first brought about through the presentation itself"[35].

On the other hand, he posits that "there is no state without structural elements of the principle of identity. The principle of form of representation can never be instituted purely and absolutely by ignoring the people who are always somehow existing and present"[36].

The dualism of identity and representation is reproduced, so to speak, at the level of the very concept of representation, considered not as a "normative event", a "process" or a "procedure", but as "something existential".

Schmitt says that "[t]o represent means to make an invisible being visible and present through a publicly present one. The dialectic of the concept is that the invisible is presupposed as absent and nevertheless is simultaneously made present. This is not possible with just any type of being. Indeed, it presupposes a special type of being". In representation in constitutional law, as opposed to representation in private affairs, "a higher type of being comes into concrete appearance. The idea of representation rests on a people existing as a political unity, as having a type of being that is higher, further enhanced, and more intense in comparison to the natural existence of some human group living together"[37].

These dense formulations appear to confirm that there is no escape to representation in the political realm and even identity is produced by representation. Schmitt seems to assert, with his principle of identity, the "priority of presence over representation", but ends up acknowledging as inevitable that "there is no presence without representation", if we apply to his thought the categories developed by Lindahl regarding representation[38]. This does not lead him, however, to handle representation as a mere fiction, like Kelsen, but to reconfigure it, in a rather obscuring way, as an existential concept. In other words, identity is reintroduced in representation, as above mentioned.

Therefore, the opposition between identity and representation in Schmitt is untenable and can only be justified in political-ideological grounds. It is rather extraordinary how he manages to affirm, on the one hand, that "no state system can be fully formed according to the principle of identity without any representation", there being "a limit to the absolute implementation of the democratic principle of identity", and, on the other hand, that "[t]he theoretic consequence of the principle of identity will, indeed, validate itself again and again in a democracy and appear as something illuminating and self-evident", to the point of recognizing that "the people as an entity that is not officially organized become valid in individual moments and only by way of acclamation"[39]. The first assertion appears to be essentially correct – one is even tempted to say: it appears to conform to the "Copernican turn of representation" which, according to Hans Lindahl, "marks the

35 Cf. Schmitt C (2008a), 241.
36 Cf. Schmitt C (2008a), 241.
37 Cf. Schmitt C (2008a), 243.
38 Cf. Lindahl H (2000), 228, 235.
39 Cf. Schmitt C (2008a), 302.

demise of metaphysical dualism and a copy theory of knowledge"[40] – while the second, besides contradicting the first, looks like an irrational acceptance of the people as a real entity. Could it be that also for Schmitt "disintermediation turns out to be based on a hatred of mediation", as Roberto Calasso affirms, although in a different context? In any case, Calasso's verdict seems to apply: this is "fatal for thought"[41].

The question one is tempted to ask is, in fact, how it is possible that a thinker so conscious of the inescapability of representation in the political world ends up accepting the opposite principle of identity as bound to "the notion of embodiment in the (at first even physically present) people"[42]. Kelsen also poses a similar question to Schmitt regarding the related issue of the guardian of the constitution: "why [does] an author of such extraordinary intelligence as Carl Schmitt entangle[] himself in such manifest contradictions, only in order to defend the thesis that constitutional adjudication is legislation and notwithstanding the fact that his own insight implies that it can and must be both at the same time"[43]? Here we can ask, with at least equal pertinence, why does Schmitt entangle himself in such manifest contradictions to prove the thesis that democracy can be meaningfully defined as the real presence of the people, notwithstanding the fact that is own insight implies that democracy cannot exist without representation?

The answer to both questions is the same. The claim that constitutional adjudication is not a real form of adjudication "is taken to be crucially important, and it is defended even in the face of one's own conflicting theoretical insights, because it is considered to be indispensable for a legal-political demand"[44], that is, the assignment of the guardianship of the constitution not to a body of independent judges but rather to the head of the state[45]; in the same vein, one could also say that the reason standing behind the crucial claim that acclamation is the most perfect expression of democracy – which is defended even in the face of Schmitt's own conflicting theoretical insights – really is its indispensability for "a legal-political demand". The latter concerns the justification of the President of the *Reich* as a political leader against parliament in the troubled constitutional context of Weimar[46] or, from another perspective, it corresponds to a "fundamentally antipluralistic-authoritarian idea of the state" which is meant to break up the normative constitution[47].

In these processes we see the most dangerous feature of dualism in constitutional theory in action: a supposed theoretically grounded distinction between two concepts (identity and representation) really becomes a distinction based on none other than ideological-political grounds. The result is clear: while for Hans Kelsen – who clearly

---

[40] Cf. Lindahl H (2000), 236.

[41] Cf. Calasso R (2019), 72. This book can be read as an elegy to representation. On disintermediation and its perils for political life see also Guéhenno J-M (1999), 14, 72.

[42] This is how Habermas characterizes public autonomy in Rousseau (an author, by the way, that Schmitt systematically distorts with the purposes of enlisting him as a supporter of an identitarian concept of democracy): cf. Habermas J (1996), 300–301.

[43] Cf. Kelsen H (2015), 190.

[44] Cf. Kelsen H (2015), 190.

[45] Cf. Grimm D (2021a), 118–119.

[46] Cf. Schmitt C, (2008a), 370; see also, Schmitt C (2015), 172.

[47] Cf. Grimm D (2021b), 177.

rejects dualism – parliamentarianism lies at the center of the democratic process, Carl Schmitt – who affirms dualism – contrasts democracy and parliamentary representation, which he sees as an elitist and non-democratic element[48].

2.3 The Case of Constitutional Justice

A clear example of Schmitt's embracing of dualism in constitutional law and Kelsen's rejection of it is, as already hinted, the known controversy among the two authors regarding constitutional justice. This is not the place to develop the terms of this controversy[49], but it is important to point out that, in it, where Schmitt sees "categorial differences", Kelsen envisages only "gradual" ones[50]. For Kelsen, Schmitt's arguments against judicial review "rest on the erroneous assumption that there is an essential difference between the function of adjudication and 'political' functions, and in particular on the assumption that the decision on the constitutionality of a statute and the annulment of an unconstitutional statute are 'political' acts, from which it is inferred that such activities are no longer adjudicative". According to Kelsen, however, this conception "is mistaken because it presupposes that the process of the exercise of power ends with the legislative decision. This view overlooks or wants to overlook that the exercise of power necessarily continues in the courts, no less than it does in the other, administrative arm of the executive"[51].

Kelsen's criticism of Schmitt is really an indictment of dualism in constitutional law:

> "If one conceives of 'the political' as the authoritative resolution of conflicts of interest, i.e., if one conceives of it, to use C.S.'s terminology, as 'the decision', then one should admit that every court judgment contains, to a higher or lesser degree, an element of decision, an element of an exercise of power. The political character of adjudication is the stronger, the larger the sphere of free discretion that legislation, which is in its essence general, necessarily has to leave to adjudication. The view that only legislation is political, and that 'real' adjudication is not, is just as wrong as the belief that legislation alone is productive creation and adjudication nothing but reproductive application of the law. At bottom, these are only two variants of one and the same mistake. In authorizing the judge, within certain limits, to weigh conflicting interests against each other, and to decide conflicts in favor of one or the other interest, the legislator confers upon the judge a power to create law and hence a power that endows the judicial function with the same 'political' character that inheres, though to a higher degree, in legislation. There is only a quantitative but no qualitative difference between the political character of legislation and adjudication."[52]

48 Cf. Dreier H (1999), 74 ss.; *idem* (2019), 82–83.

49 See, generally, Grimm D (2021a), 105–122; Lepsius O (2007), 103–126; Jestaedt M (2007), 155–175; Schönberger C (2007), 175–195; Beaud O (2007), 197–208; de Brito MN (2015), 89–104.

50 Cf. Grimm D (2021a), 118.

51 Cf. Kelsen H (2015), 183–184.

52 Cf. Kelsen H (2015), 184.

By insisting on quantitative instead of qualitative differences Kelsen offers a way out of dualism without necessarily washing out traditional categories of constitutional law. We can still make sense of the political as a distinctive subject of constitutional law; what we cannot do anymore is to call for a mobilization of the political as the epitome of fundamental law, compared to which constitutional legalism would be just a fallen category.

2.4 Martin Loughlin's Recovery of Dualism

Martin Loughlin seems to recover dualism as the basis of his constitutional theory. His main contention apparently lies in the urgent need of saving constitutional democracy, both from the increasing administrative and technocratic overtones of contemporary constitutionalism, and the subordination of democracy to the affirmation of individual rights by courts.

Although Loughlin's constitutional theory is deeply indebted to Schmitt, dualism discharges a very different function in his thought[53]. In Loughlin's case, at issue is not to invoke the primacy of the political to justify solutions contrary to positive law, but to point out the dimensions of public law which he believes have been covered up or marginalized by the evolution of constitutions in a legalistic sense. Constitutionalism is defined by Loughlin as the result of this evolution, i.e., as "the primary medium through which an insulated elite, while paying lip service to the claims of democracy, is able to perpetuate its authority to rule"[54].

Whatever benefits constitutionalism might confer in terms of the protection of individual rights, "it is no longer the project of a people and no longer subject to popular control"[55]. For Loughlin, that is even more the case if constitutionalism is connected to the cosmopolitan dimension of modern constitutions, as explored by Alexander Somek[56], which results in the collective entity of the people being "disaggregated if not entirely dissolved", the distinction between citizens and foreigners being "permeated by the influence of antidiscrimination rights", and "the task of redistribution" being "replaced with that of 'inclusion'"[57]. Moreover, these developments take place in a context of growth of the administrative power, especially through police powers, of emergence of a "new ephorate"[58], and of rise of the "juristocracy"[59].

Loughlin's analysis poses the very urgent question of knowing whether an understanding of all constitutional issues primarily by the prism of rights has moved us all

53 Cf. de Brito MN (2020), 23 ss.

54 Cf. Loughlin M (2022), x. This idea is close to the core of Colin Crouch's concept of post-democracy, that is, the political condition in which corporate elites have learned to maintain and even enlarge their power while complying with "formal components of democracy", by reducing citizens to "the role of manipulated, passive, rare participants" [see Crouch C (2004), 21, 22].

55 Cf. Loughlin M (2022), 201.

56 Cf. Somek A (2014), 201 ss.

57 Cf. Loughlin M (2022), 190.

58 Cf. Loughlin M (2010), 448. The expression designates the growing number and importance of public bodies that "operate at some remove from electorally authorized sources of authority".

59 Cf. Loughlin M (2022), 124 ss.

along to one extreme of the continuum of differences that hold up the basic concepts of constitutional law. By moving towards the legalistic extreme of such continuum, we end up with the prospect of endangering the project of constitutional democracy and its key feature, which is the tension between collective self-rule and individual autonomy[60].

However, if we leave aside the critical dimension of Loughlin's theory (notwithstanding its crucial importance) and ask for its constructive dimension, the difficulties become manifest. As already mentioned, one of the features of "constitutionalism", in Loughlin's sense, is the rise of "juristocracy", a term coined by Ran Hirschl to express the transference of "an unprecedented amount of power from representative institutions to judiciaries", based on the "belief that judicially affirmed rights are a force of social change removed from the constraints of political power"[61]. The very presentation of the idea of juristocracy is based on dualistic assumptions, as it builds on a categorial opposition between courts and democratically accountable institutions. Before dwelling on that opposition, it is necessary to point out that Loughlin sees the path towards juristocracy as a way of advancing universal standards in the protection of rights, in the context of the cosmopolitan constitution[62], as well as a way of escaping the "classic scheme of the separation of powers" in terms that enable the courts to arrogate themselves "the critical role of overseeing the political process"[63].

In this case, dualism is no longer, as mentioned, a way of actively breaking "normal" law in the superior interests of the "political", but of deploring the loss of "political right" and the capability of citizens to effectively control the political process. However, Loughlin offers few solutions regarding the appropriate reaction at the level of constitutional law to the consequences of a so-called "second phase of modernity" and the processes of "individualization" it has given place to, if one uses the terms of German sociologist Ulrich Beck[64]. In this context, few differences remain between Loughlin's denunciation of the perils of constitutional review and the views of its most radical critics[65]. In both cases, the role of the courts is criticized in the name of a largely idealized view of democracy in contemporary societies. The problem is that in real world conditions the relationship between judicial review and democracy cannot be apprehended through a zero-sum mindset, according to which a less active role of the courts necessarily implies more deliberation by the people[66].

---

60 Cf. Loughlin M (2022), 196.

61 Cf. Hirschl R (2004), 1.

62 Cf. Loughlin M (2022), 190.

63 Cf. Loughlin M (2022), 134.

64 Cf. Loughlin M (2022), 193.

65 For those critics, see Grimm D (2021c), 357 ss.

66 As Dieter Grimm points out, after stressing the meagre possibilities people get to actually decide on concrete issues in real existing democracies, "those who can do more without judicial review than with judicial review are the people chosen in those state bodies that are based on popular elections, because judicial review is essentially about controlling norms, i.e., above all parliament" [cf. Grimm D (2021c), 371].

3 No Democracy Without Representation

3.1 Hans Lindahl and the "Copernican Turn of Representation"

According to Carl Schmitt, "the metaphysical image that a definite epoch forges of the world has the same structure as what the world immediately understands to be appropriate as a form of its political organization"[67]. Although it is questionable in what sense "an era's metaphysics sets the limits of political meanings"[68], there are certainly mutual influences between the philosophical views of a certain age and the political views adopted in it. But already at the time Schmitt wrote the above quoted sentence, the image of metaphysics forged by the corresponding epoch hardly suited his understanding of politics.

Indeed, it seems clear that the metaphysical dualism and the copy theory of knowledge rejected by Kelsen – and with which Schmitt maintained an ambiguous relationship, to say the least – does not correspond to the metaphysical image of our world, if there is one at all[69]. It is precisely in this context that Hans Lindahl, as already mentioned, speaks of a "Copernican turn of representation" that "marks the demise" of dualism, as well as its substitution by a monistic critical philosophy. The latter "postulates the priority of the relation between presence and representation"[70], not the priority of presence over representation.

The meaning of this Copernican turn is well captured in Lindahl's response to Thomas Fossen's criticism. According to Fossen, one must bear in mind that there are two modes of representation, which he exemplifies as follows: "(a) The lawyer represents her client before the court; (b) In her closing statement to the jury, the lawyer represents her client as an innocent bystander"[71]. In the first mode we have representation *of* (something), in the second we have representation *as* (this or that)[72].

The problem, for Fossen, is that in his book 2018 book *Authority and the Globalization of Inclusion and Exclusion*, Lindahl allegedly conflates these "two distinct senses of 'representation': acting-for-someone (or representative agency) and portraying-something-as-something (or representation-as), as he treats "this particular sense of the word (portraying-something-as-something) as the only sense there is"[73]. By overlooking representative agency and its specific demands Lindahl would be led to think "that all collective action, by definition, rests on dissimulated annexation".

For Fossen this means that, according to Lindahl,

---

[67] Cf. Schmitt C (2005), 46.

[68] Cf. Kahn P (2011), 115.

[69] In case that image is provided by quantum mechanics, Paul Kahn (2011: 115) accurately states that "there is no political theory" following from it. And even if there is such a theory, it is arguably not one in which politics occupies a central place in society. In any case, there surely is a post-metaphysical political theory as the work of Habermas eloquently testifies.

[70] Cf. Lindahl H (2000), 235, 236.

[71] Cf. Fossen T (2019b), 827.

[72] Cf. Lindahl H (2018), 109; see also, Lindahl H (2019a), 11. Lindahl alludes here to the work of Goodman N (1977), 27 ss.

[73] Cf. Fossen T (2019a), 384.

> "all collective action stems from a moment of illicit appropriation, a taking or seizure. Someone has to take the initiative to say 'we' in order to institute – to represent – 'us' as a collective. Insofar as the initiative succeeds, the addressees are swept up into a collective, and this ineluctably carries an element of violence. This moment of violence is then veiled because in order to succeed the initiatory act must present itself as legitimate. And in legitimating itself, Lindahl believes, it must appeal to the collective agent that it seeks to bring about. The initiator thus initiates while pretending that the initiative has already taken place."[74]

The conclusion is that, for Lindahl, at least according to Fossen's interpretation, we cannot escape violence at the origin of collective action, most notably in the exercise of the constituent power. Violence seems inherent in the fact that "collectives emerge by way of acts of representation that include and exclude without a prior authorization to do so by their addressees"[75]. And this fact is even explained by Lindahl using Schmitt's insight that an act of appropriation, a taking, is "the key to the genesis and structure of social orders"[76]. Consequently, the intimate connection between "representation-as" and violence is explicitly assumed by Lindahl, as for example when he states that "to call attention to the moment of seizure inherent to representation is to insist that violence, even if a productive (but never only productive) violence, is necessarily ensconced in all legal orders"[77].

But there is a second, and equally important, if not more, point in Fossen's criticism of Lindahl's views on representation. Fossen accuses Lindahl of sustaining that "all democracy is essentially representative democracy, joining a 'representative turn' among democratic theorists who contest the distinction between 'direct' and 'indirect' democracy, or between 'participation' and 'representation'". This understanding would obscure the sense of representation as acting-for-others, institutionalized by means of elections, that which corresponds to the ordinary meaning of "representative democracy"[78]. And only representation as acting-for-others can account for the priority of the represented, that is, "the idea that the actions of a representative purport to be justifiable in terms of the interests of the represented, and not the other way around"[79].

So, in Fossen's view, by reducing all representation to "representation as", Lindahl condones violence at the origin of every political community and obscures the responsiveness of representatives towards their electors. In this criticism of Lindahl, Fossen appears to conflate the establishment of categories in political representation with the development of ethical points of view regarding each of these categories. But this obscures the main point of Lindahl's views, which is to stress the two-dimensionality of all representational acts.

The acknowledgment that objectivity has a strictly representational structure is the crux of the Copernican turn in representation. Bearing that in mind, Lindahl defends

---

[74] Cf. Fossen T (2019a), 386.
[75] Cf. Lindahl H (2018), 232–233.
[76] Cf. Lindahl H (2018), 170.
[77] Cf. Lindahl H (2018), 181.
[78] Cf. Fossen T (2019a), 389.
[79] Cf. Fossen T (2019b), 835.

his theory from Fossen's criticism by pointing out that he is ethically induced to accept at least a residue of realism in order to save constructivism from the perils of violence and unresponsiveness. For Lindahl that is the purpose underlying the qualitative distinction between two categories of representation: "representational agency is a form of representation in which the represented individual or group already exists as this or that particular individual or group, prior to and independently of the representation itself. In turn, representation-as involves the *ab ovo* production of a collective, which only comes into existence with the acceptance of an invitation to participate in joint action"[80].

Fossen's purpose is to clarify how the represented can be both prior to representation and constituted by it, and in this he is influenced by Hanna Pitkin's dictum according to which "[a]s the 're' in 'representation' seems to suggest [...] the represented must be somehow logically prior; the representative must be responsive to him rather than the other way around"[81].

Lindahl gives a completely different meaning to the "re" in "representation". For him "everything turns on the particle 're' of representation, which refers to the fact that something is rendered present *as* this or *as* that. Hence collective unity is never given immediately or directly; there has to be a representational act absent which there can be no collective"[82].

Both Fossen and Lindahl accept that there are two modes of representation: "representation of" and "representation as". But if this is so, where do they really disagree regarding the way these two modes relate to each other? It seems that Fossen wants to save a minimum of "representation of" inherent in all political representation, whereas Lindahl wants to assert the irreducible moment of "representation as" in all representation, including political representation, as part of the *conditio humana.*

Fossen, as we have seen, wants to safeguard the priority of the represented in acting-for-others in a way that is compatible with constructivism. He is careful not to interpret the priority of the represented "as requiring a one-way causal influence, such that representatives' actions are supposed to be determined by the preferences of their constituents and not the other way around". The priority means "that the represented are entitled to a justification of the representative's actions in terms of their own interests, while they do

80 Cf. Lindahl H (2019b), 448.

81 Cf. Pitkin H (1967), 140; see also, Fossen T (2019b) 832.

82 Cf. Lindahl H (2018), 291. See also Lindahl H (2019a), 14: "The 're' of representation means that we (are deemed to) present ourselves anew as this or that unity, where 'anew' hovers somewhere between pure repetition and pure innovation, always introducing a difference, however minimal, into collective identity over time". The point is also made in Lindahl H (2000) 238–239: "The key to this question lies in the 're' of representation. If we reject the idea that this prefix means the duplication of an original, then to represent means literally to present again. On this reading, representation is a process, namely a context-bound iteration. Two cardinal implications flow from this insight. First, presenting 'again' means that each objectifying act links up to foregoing representations, not to an original. The series of acts whereby a 'form' is presented time and again does not take its point of departure in a pure presence. There is no 'original' of, for instance, a book; what we have is a sequence of human actions that treat things as books. Second, the same form is rendered present in different things: this book, that one, etc. Repetition introduces a difference, however minimal, with respect to earlier representations".

not owe the representative justifications in turn"[83]. Understood in this way, "the priority of the represented is not a metaphysical commitment to the existence of interests prior to the practices of political representation (in either sense), but a pragmatic commitment concerning the order of justification implicit in the idea of representative agency"[84]. Fossen appears to endorse a normative account of representative agency, or "representation of", but he also accepts that representation constitutes the represented, in a transformative and an initiatory sense, as happens with "representation as". However, he thinks this constructive dimension of representation "tells us little about representation in the sense of acting-for-others", and its ethical demands[85].

In view of the above it seems difficult not to conclude that Fossen's dualistic view on representation does not imply some form of realism, despite his claims to the contrary[86]. The true representative must always and above all defend the interests of the represented. He may start as enacting "representation as", but he is never true to his own mission if he does not aim to be a herald of "representation of". What is interesting in Fossen's view is that even if he seems to reject Cartesian assumptions regarding collective action, his dualistic view of representation still leads him to some form of realism. Here the judgment of Lindahl on Schmitt's views also applies: "dualism presupposes the priority of presence over representation"[87].

In the case of Lindahl the two modes of representation appear as two indissoluble dimensions of a phenomenological analysis of representational acts. According to Lindahl,

> "All representational acts have two dimensions which follow directly from the insight that to represent is to represent something as something. On the one hand, representation is the representation of (something); on the other, something is represented as (this or that). So also with the representation of collectives. Whoever claims to speak and act on behalf of a collective, for example by enacting a constitution, attributes the enactment of the constitution to the collective as a whole: representation of. On the other hand, the enactment does more than simply claim that the collective is a unity; the constitution must spell out, at least minimally, what "our" joint action is/ought to be about. It must articulate the point of joint action, what we* hold in common, enabling us to view our individual acts as part and parcel of joint action: representation as."[88]

[83] Cf. Fossen T (2019b), 834.

[84] Cf. Fossen T (2019b), 835.

[85] Cf. Fossen T (2019b), 834.

[86] As Lindahl H (2019b), 442, unequivocally claims: "Conceptualizing representational agency as a dyadic relation endorses a form of realism; Fossen's construal of representation-as champions constructivism. He cannot have it both ways".

[87] Cf. Lindahl H (1998), 29.

[88] Cf. Lindahl H (2019c), 265. "we*" stands for "we together" and is parsed by Lindahl "into three distinct we* positions: we* speaker, we* at stake, we* author. If the first of these positions concerns the spokesperson who speaks and acts on behalf of a collective, representing it as this or as that, the second is the referent of such representational acts, namely, the we* for the sake of which spokespersons speak and act. The third position concerns authorship, namely, when

As these two dimensions are intimately commingled, so are the moments of imposition and invitation in representational acts, as in the case of constituent power[89]. This means that Lindahl's articulation between the two modes of representation is essentially anti-dualistic. In his thought, it is not so much the case that even agents engaging in acts of "representation as" must observe the ethical dimension inherent in "representation of", but that "representation of" is to be recognized, first and foremost, also as a case of "representation as" whatever ethical demands may apply. As Lindahl says, the "interplay between representation of and representation as does all the work necessary to explain how representation in general, and political representation in particular, can be responsive"[90].

3.2 Representation and Responsiveness

The intimate connection between representation and responsiveness clearly distances Lindahl's views on representation from the ones defended by Ernesto Laclau. Granted, Lindahl would not have much trouble in accepting Laclau's finding according to which "the main difficulty with classical theories of political representation is that most of them conceived the will of the 'people' as something that was constituted *before* representation"[91]. But he would find, one reckons, Laclau's assertion that, once this finding is settled, "the only relevant question is how to *respect* the will of those represented, taking it for granted that such a will exists in the first place"[92] to be hopelessly confused. It appears that taking for granted that it does not exist is what gives Laclau a free ride in his populist reconstruction of democracy, based on the rise of a new political subject as the result of the "identification of the unity of the group with the name of the leader"[93]. On the contrary, Lindahl is interested in reconstructing "a political self without there being a subject which this self reflects"[94].

Both authors elaborate their views building on the thought of Claude Lefort and his famous definition of modern democracy as the regime in which politics has become an empty place[95]. But whereas Laclau wants to reoccupy such a place, Lindahl's project is premised on the persistence of its emptiness.

We now have to turn, once more, to Schmitt and Kelsen for, as Lindahl acknowledges, "the context of their discussion is the very problem which interests Lefort, namely, the continuities and discontinuities leading from medieval to modern politics", as well as "the

---

addressees of representational acts recognize themselves as authoring them, even though issued by spokespersons" [see Lindahl H (2019c), 275; Lindahl (2018), 98].

89 Cf. Lindahl H (2019b) 447.

90 Cf. Lindahl H (2019b), 443. Schmitt C (2008a), 241–243, also acknowledges the indissolubility of the two dimensions of representation when he points the specificity of political representation regarding representation in private law.

91 Cf. Laclau E (2005), 163–164.

92 Cf. Laclau E (2005), 164.

93 Cf. Laclau E (2005), 100.

94 If it is possible to use in this context the illuminating formulation of Van Roermund B (1997), 149.

95 Cf. Lefort C (1986), 291.

key notion of representation"[96]. It is now clearer, one hopes, how Schmitt's democratic theory is part of "a dualistic vision on the relation between state and law" in whose core "lies the age-old assumption that thinking represents being"[97]. And it is also clearer how for Kelsen modern democracy implies that "there is no substantial political unity preceding and conditioning an order of legal acts"[98].

To this rebuttal of dualism, Lindahl adds a substantive, so to speak, account of representation as something inherent in collective action. In Lindahl's words, "the representational dynamic of collective action suggests that two further features are part and parcel of social ontology: questionability and responsiveness. On the one hand, because an original unity can only be represented, without there being any direct access thereto, it is irreducibly questionable that a manifold of individuals is a collective, and what conjoins them as a collective. (…) On the other, and correlatively, collectives cannot but exist by responding, at every step of their career, to the practical question, 'What is/ought our joint action to be about?'"[99]. Beyond this correlativity, "responsiveness aims to render collective existence unquestionable"[100].

4 Conclusion

With Hans Lindahl's account of representation, Kelsen's indictment of dualism in public law is finally accomplished. Within the framework of his two-dimensional concept of representation, as well as the development of the correlativity of representation and responsiveness, one sees clearly how "participation is a form of representation"[101], how constituent power is the work of constituted powers[102], how courts are part of a "joint representational practice"[103], and how constituent power can occur beyond the states without excluding their "political primacy"[104]. The political is, however, not to be understood as something that precedes the juridical, but as a reality that constitutes itself in a representational practice that also already includes the juridical. The traditional pairs of concepts of public law – constituent and constituted powers, state and law, the "political" and the normative, norm and exception, state and society, etc. – cannot be deployed in such a manner that one concept in each pair expresses a privileged access to the real order of things. Instead, they all take part in the representational structure of collective action.

---

96 Cf. Lindahl H (1998), 28.
97 Cf. Lindahl H (1998), 29.
98 Cf. Lindahl H (1998), 32.
99 Cf. Lindahl H (2019), 487.
100 Cf. Lindahl H (2019), 491.
101 Cf. Lindahl H (2018), 109, 181.
102 Cf. Lindahl H (2018), 402.
103 Cf. Lindahl H (2018), 450.
104 See Lindahl H (2018), 415.

References

Beaud O (2007) Kelsen Contre Schmitt: Un Dialogue de Sourds?, In Beaud O, Pasquino P (eds) La Controverse sur «le gardien de la Constitution» et la justice constitutionnelle. Kelsen contre Schmitt. Paris, Éditions Panthéon-Assas, pp 197–208

de Brito MN (2015) Schmitt's spectre and kelsen's promise: the polemics on the guardian of the constitution. In: Coutinho LP, La Torre M, Smith SD (eds) Judicial Activism: An Interdisciplinary Approach to the American and European Experiences. Springer, Cham, pp 89–104

de Brito MN (2020a) Kelsen Redivivus, Kant Redimido: A Teoria Pura do Direito e a Relação entre o Direito Internacional e o Direito Interno. In: Lopes PM (ed), O Pensamento de Hans Kelsen: Influências, Contexto e Atualidade, Lisboa, AAFDL Editora, pp 293–332

de Brito MN (2020) Expanding legality and losing fundamental law: on martin loughlin's dualist conception of public law. In: de Brito MN, Coutinho LP (eds) The Political Dimension of Constitutional Law. Springer, Cham, pp 23–49

de Brito MN (2023) O Espectro de uma Nova Pangeia e a Perda do Poder Constituinte. In: Machete P, Ribeiro GA, Canotilho M (eds) Estudos em Homenagem ao Conselheiro Presidente Costa Andrade. Coimbra, Almedina, pp 681–738

Brunkhorst H (2011) Critique of Dualism: Hans Kelsen and the Twentieth Century Revolution in International Law. Constellations 18(4):496–512

Calasso R (2019) The Unamable Present, trans.: Farrar, Straus and Giroux, Richard Dixon, New York

Corrias L (2011) The legal theory of the juridical coup: constituent power now. German Law J 12(8):1553–1572

Crouch C (2004) Post-democracy. Polity Press, Cambridge

Donhauser G (2019) Nomos or Law? Hans Kelsen's criticism of carl schmitt's metaphysics of law and politics. In: Langford P, Bryan I, McGarry J (eds) Hans Kelsen and the Natural Law Tradition. Leiden/Boston, Brill, pp 372–398

Dreier D (1999) The essence of democracy – hans kelsen and carl schmitt juxtaposed. In: Diner D, Stolleis M (eds) Hans Kelsen and Carl Schmitt: a Juxtaposition. Gerlingen, Bleicher, pp 71–79

Dreier D (2019) Kelsens Demokratietheorie: Grundlegung, Strukturekemente, Probleme. In Jestaedt M, Paulson SL (eds) Kelsen im Kontext. Tübingen, Mohr Siebeck, pp 67–94

Falk H (2022) The modern epimetheus: Carl Schmitt's Katechontism as reactionary chronopolitics. Front Politic Sci 4:957094. https://doi.org/10.3389/fpos.2022.957094

Ferrara A (2023) Sovereignty across generations: constituent power and political liberalism. Oxford University Press, Oxford

Fossen T (2019a) Collective action, constituent power, and democracy: on representation in Lindahl's philosophy of law, Etica & Politica/Ethics & Politics, vol. XXI (3) pp 383–390

Fossen T (2019) Constructivism and the logic of political representation. Am Politic Sci Rev 113(3):824–837

Goodman N (1977) Languages of art: an approach to a theory of symbols, Indianapolis/Cambridge, Hackett

Griffioen S (2022) Contesting modernity in the German secularization debate. Leiden Boston, Brill

Grimm D (2021a) Recht oder Politik? Die Kelsen-Schmitt-Kontroverse zur Verfassungsgerichtsbarkeit und die heutige Lage. In: idem, Verfassungsgerichtsbarkeit. Berlin, Suhrkamp, pp 105–142

Grimm D (2021b) Zum Verhältnis von Interpretationslehre, Verfassungsgerichtsbarkeit und Demokratieprinzip bei Kelsen. In: idem, Verfassungsgerichtsbarkeit. Berlin, Suhrkamp, pp 172–181

Grimm D (2021c) Neue Radikalkritik an der Verfassungsgerichtsbarkeit. In: idem, Verfassungsgerichtsbarkeit. Berlin, Suhrkamp, pp 357–398

Groh R (1998) Arbeit an der Heillosigkeit der Welt. Zur politisch-theologischen Mythologie und Anthropologie Carl Schmitts, Frankfurt am Main, Suhrkamp

Groh R (2014) Carl Schmitts gnostischer Dualismus. Der boshafte Schöpfer dieser Welt hat es so eingerichtet (…). Berlin, Litt Verlag

Guéhenno, J-M (1999) L'Avenir de la Liberté. La Démocratie dans la Mondialisation. Paris, Flammarion

Habermas J (1996) Between facts and norms: contributions to a discourse theory of law and democracy (trans. Rehg W). The MIT Press, Cambridge, Massachusetts

Henderson LM (2019) Internalizing contestation in process-based judicial review. German Law J 20(8): 1167–1181

Herrera HE (2020) Carl schmitt between technological rationality and theology: the position and meaning of his legal thought. State University of New York Press, Albany

Herrero M (2015) The political discourse of carl schmitt: a mystic of order. Rowman & Littlefield International, London/New York

Herrero M (2023) Carl Schmitt's political theology of revolution. Open Theol 9. https://doi.org/10.1515/opth-2022-0223

Hiromura NT (2020) The concept of the human in the works of Carl Schmitt. https://bonndoc.ulb.uni-bonn.de/xmlui/handle/20.500.11811/8316. Accessed 8 July 2023

Hirschl R (2004) Towards juristocracy: the origins and consequences of the new constitutionalism. Harvard University Press, Cambridge, Mass/London, England

Jestaedt M (2007) Der 'Hüter der Verfassung' als Frage des Rechtsgewinnungsverständnisses – Ein etwas anderer Blick auf der Schriften von Carl Schmitt und Hans Kelsen. In : Beaud O, Pasquino P (eds) La Controverse sur «le gardien de la Constitution» et la justice constitutionnelle. Kelsen contre Schmitt, Paris, Éditions Panthéon-Assas, pp 155–175

Kahn PW (2011) Political theology: four new chapters on the concept of sovereignty. Columbia University Press, New York

Kelsen H (1973) God and state. Essays in Legal and Moral Philosophy (selected and introduced by Ota Weinberger, translated by Peter Heath). D. Reidel Publishing Company, Dordrecht, pp 61–82

Kelsen H (2013) The essence and value of democracy (ed. Urbinati N, Accetti CI, trans. Graf B) Lanham, Rowman & Littlefield Publishers, Inc.

Kelsen, H (2015) Who ought to be the guardian of the constitution?. In: The Guardian of the Constitution: Hans Kelsen and Carl Schmitt on the Limits of Constitutional *Law* (trans., introduction, and notes by Vinx L), Cambridge, Cambridge University Press, pp 174–221

Laclau E (2005) On populist reason. Verso, London / New York

Lefort C (1986) Permanence du Théologico-Politique? Idem, Essais sur le Politique, xixe-xxe Siècles. Éditions du Seuil, Paris, pp 275–329

Lepsius O (2007) Der Hüter der Verfassung – demokratietheoretisch betrachtet. In Beaud O, Pasquino P (eds) La Controverse sur «le gardien de la Constitution» et la justice constitutionnelle. Kelsen contre Schmitt, Paris, Éditions Panthéon-Assas, pp 103–126

Lindahl H (1998) Democracy and the symbolic constitution of society. Ratio Juris 11(1):12–37

Lindahl H (2000) Authority and representation. Law Philos 19:223–246

Lindahl H (2007) The paradox of constituent power. Ambig Self-Const Euro Union, Ratio Juris 20(4):485–505

Lindahl H (2007) Constituent power and reflexivity identity: towards an ontology of collective selfhood. In: Martin Loughlin M, Walker N (eds) The Paradox of Constitutionalism: Constituent Power and Constitutional Form. Oxford University Press, Oxford, pp 9–24

Lindahl H (2018) Authority and the globalization of inclusion and exclusion. Cambridge University Press, Cambridge

Lindahl H (2019) Inside and outside global law. Sidney Law Rev 41(1):1–34
Lindahl H (2019b) A-legality, representation, constituent power. Reply to critics. Etica Politica/Ethics Politics XXI (3): 417–501
Lindahl H (2019) Intentionality, representation, recognition: phenomenology and the politics of a-legality. In: Thomas Bedorf T, Herrmann S (eds) Political Phenomenology: Experience. Routledge, Ontology, Episteme, New York, pp 256–276
Loughlin M (2010) Foundations of public law. Oxford University Press, Oxford
Loughlin, 2022.Loughlin M (2022) Against constitutionalism. Harvard University Press, Cambridge, Mass/London
Paipais V (2016) Overcoming "Gnosticism"? Real Politic Theol Cambridge Rev Int Aff 29(4):1603–1623
Pitkin H (1967) The concept of representation. University of California Press, Berkeley
Römer P (1971) Die Reine Rechtslehre Hans Kelsens als Ideologie und Ideologiekritik: Hans Kelsen zu seinem 90. Geburtstag am 11. Oktober 1971 gewidmet, Politische Vierteljahresschrift 12(4): 579–598
Schmitt C (1985) Grundrechte und Grundpflichten (1932). Verfassungsrechtliche Aufsätze aus den Jahren 1924–1954. Duncker & Humblot, Materialien zu einer Verfassungslehre, Vierte Auflage, Berlin, pp 181–231
Schmitt C (1996) Roman Catholicism and Political Form (trans. Ulmen GL), Westport. Greenwood Press, Connecticut/London
Schmitt C (2004) Legality and Legitimacy (trans. Jeffrey Seitzer). Introduction by John P. McCormick. Duke University Press, Durham and London
Schmitt C (2005) Political Theology: Four Chapters on the Concept of Sovereignty (trans. George Schwab). Foreword by Tracy B. Strong, Chicago, The University of Chicago Press
Schmitt C (2006) The Nomos of the Earth in the International Law of the Jus Publicum Europaeum (translated and annotated by G. L. Ulmen). Telos Press Publishing, New York
Schmitt C (2007) The Concept of the Political (translation, introduction, and notes by George Schwab). Foreword by Tracy B. Strong. The University of Chicago Press, Chicago
Schmitt C (2008a) Constitutional Theory (trans. Seitzer J). Foreword Kennedy, E. Durham and London, Duke University Press
Schmitt, C (2008b) Political Theology II: The Myth of the Closure of any Political Theology (trans. Hoelzl M, Ward G), Polity Press, Cambridge
Schmitt C (2014) Dictatorship: From the origin of the modern concept of sovereignty to proletarian class struggle (trans. Michael Hoelzl and Graham Ward), Polity Press, Cambridge
Schmitt C (2015) The guardian of the constitution: Schmitt on pluralism and the president as the guardian of the constitution. In: The Guardian of the Constitution: Hans Kelsen and Carl Schmitt on the Limits of Constitutional Law (trans., introduction, and notes by Vinx L), Cambridge University Press, Cambridge, pp 125–173
Schönberger C (2007) Die Verfassungsgerichtsbarkeit bei Carl Schmitt und Hans Kelsen: Gemeinsamkeiten und Schwachstellen. In: Beaud O, Pasquino P (eds) La Controverse sur «le gardien de la Constitution» et la justice constitutionnelle. Kelsen contre Schmitt, Paris, Éditions Panthéon-Assas, pp 175–195
Somek A (2014) The cosmopolitan constitution. Oxford University Press, Oxford
Van Roermund B (1997) Law, narrative and reality. An essay in intercepting politics, Dordrecht, Kluwer

Representation Through Courts and Juries

Pierre Brunet(✉)

Sorbonne Law School, Université Paris 1, IRJS, Paris, France
pierre.brunet@univ-paris1.fr

Abstract. This chapter explores whether political representation by the constitutional courts can be taken as a form of democratic representation, even if non-electoral. To explore that possibility depends on exploring institutional alternatives to the present *status quo* which would make constitutional review more expressive of shared values in society and more dialogical in character. In this light, the systems of "constitutional juries" that were proposed by Horacio Spector, Eric Ghosh and Christopher Zurn are examined, regarding their potential to increase the legitimacy of constitutional review and their limits, which have to do with their strict individualistic logic, thus inattentive to the protection of increasingly relevant collective goods such as the environment.

1 Introduction

Today, constitutionalism is defined and characterized less by the existence of a written constitution than by the presence of constitutional courts as "guardians" of the constitution, which is required to contain a catalogue of fundamental rights. This model is now as widespread as it is accepted. Some dissenting opinions remain, although they are clearly in the minority. They point to the lack of democratic legitimacy of such control of the law by unelected judges and to the fact that there is ultimately no reason to believe that rights are better protected by the courts than by elected legislative assemblies.[1] The tendency is to show that the major problem is not so much the existence of these courts but their "supremacy": i.e. their exclusivity or interpretative monopoly (or even their power of having the last word). Accordingly, there are calls for a "dialogical constitutionalism" and a model of control based on "weak" constitutionality reviewing.[2] This seeks to establish a balance between a court (with the power to review laws and the capacity to alert Parliament over possible infringements of rights), and Parliament (the final judge of the merits of its own decisions to run the risk of restricting rights).

Yet here and there, in various forms, other opinions and dissent are being heard.

[1] In general, reference can be made to the work of Jeremy Waldron, in particular (2016: chap. 9).

[2] V. Stephen Gardbaum (2001: 707–747). The opposition between "strong- and weak-form judicial review" is due to Mark Tushnet (2003a: 813–838), who concludes: "With the demise of parliamentary supremacy as a system constitutionalists are willing to defend forcefully, weak-form judicial review provides constitution designers with a new choice within the universe of constrained parliamentarism"); see also Mark Tushnet (2003b: 353–379) and (2003c: 2781–2802).

L. Pereira Coutinho (Ed.): ICPRCR 2022, IUSGENT 124, pp. 58–73, 2025.
https://doi.org/10.1007/978-3-031-85983-0_5

For some, the criticism levelled at the courts on the grounds that they are undemocratic is inadmissible. On the one hand, it overlooks the fact that constitutional courts can be thought of as representatives in the context of a democracy that has ceased to be confined to the strict majority rule of procedure. On the other hand, it does not take into account the fact that the empirical and concrete functioning of the courts effectively leads them to allow themselves to be guided and influenced by majority social opinion.

For others, the "democratization of constitutional courts" has become the contemporary challenge facing contemporary societies. The very principle of constitutional courts is not called into question, but it is rather their mode of action, their 'political' line and their composition (as well as their claim to a monopoly in the interpretation of the constitution) that are called into question by envisaging the possibility of constitutional juries. It is undoubtedly too early to speak of a fundamental movement. But it is not too late to take an interest.

What all these innovations have in common is a challenge to the supremacy, exclusivity or monopoly of the courts in interpreting the constitution and protecting constitutional rights. This in no way prevents judges from claiming democratic legitimacy for themselves as "representatives of society".

My aim here is not to add a new proposal to an already full catalogue but, in a much more modest way, to present and, if not in an exhaustive manner, discuss a few of them.

2 Representation of Society by Courts

According to a thesis defended by Robert Alexy, constitutional courts participate in the process of institutionalizing practical reason that is characteristic of deliberative democracy and the discursive constitutionalism it promotes[3]. This thesis was very popular with some judges.

2.1 Alexy's Thesis: Constitutional Judges as Argumentative Representatives

This thesis is based on another well-known thesis, long defended by Robert Alexy, according to which constitutionality review as carried out by contemporary constitutional courts leads them to interpret the fundamental rights of individuals in the light of the principle of proportionality. This leads them to weigh up rights – or principles – that happen to conflict in a specific case. This balancing or weighting is not an irrational or arbitrary activity, as some (including Habermas) maintain, but is on the contrary based on a rational argument that the "formula of weights" makes it possible to reconstruct. There is no point in discussing Robert Alexy's first thesis here, so I will concentrate on the second: that constitutionality review is not only rational but also perfectly compatible with the requirements of democracy.

Alexy bases his argument on the concept of "argumentative representation". This form of representation is opposed to "decisional" or "volitional" representation, which is the relationship established by democracy when it is limited to the simple majority principle and the election of representatives of the people to parliament. This model of

[3] Robert Alexy (2005: 572–581).

democracy is inadequate: a democracy presupposes decisions but also arguments[4]. This is the condition for a deliberative democracy in which discourse is a means of producing public decisions. We therefore need to consider two forms of representation or representatives of the people: alongside parliaments, which act as "argumentative-decisional representatives", courts should be seen as "purely argumentative representatives" of the people. Alexy relies on the argument of the "claim to correctness" of representation[5]. For him, this is a structural argument: just as law is intimately and better conceptually linked to morality because it contains a claim to (moral) correctness[6] from which we can deduce that it has a dual dimension, both positive and ideal, so representation establishes a claim to (moral) correctness. It also has an ideal dimension in addition to having a normative and empirical dimension.

Alexy is aware that his presentation may appear to be an excessive idealization, and that some would be prepared to object that constitutional courts are free to declare all their arguments to be representative without ever having to verify or justify this assertion. But he believes in the objective rationality of legal argumentation in general and constitutional argumentation in particular. Indeed, we know how attached he is to the idea that legal reasoning is a form of practical rationality. Indeed, he regards his "formula of weight" as a form of argument in rational legal discourse[7]. He therefore considers that, in order to be deemed representative, constitutional courts cannot be satisfied with arguments that are plausible or coherent and correct from the point of view of practical rationality. This condition is necessary but not sufficient. There must also be "rational persons who are both able and willing to accept coherent and correct arguments for the good reason that they are coherent and correct. Such persons may be called constitutional persons"[8]. Alexy concludes that if these conditions are met, then it is not difficult to justify constitutionality review by a constitutional court: argumentative representation must prevail over electoral representation because it is a means of institutionalizing reason and moral correctness.

Alexy's thesis calls for a number of comments.

---

[4] Alexy (2005: 572–581, not. 578–579): "An adequate concept of democracy must, however, comprise not only decision but also argument. The inclusion of argument in the concept of democracy makes democracy deliberative. Deliberative democracy is an attempt to institutionalize discourse as far as possible as a means of public decision making. For this reason, the connection between the people and the parliament must not only be determined by decisions expressed in elections and votes but also by argument.".

[5] Alexy (2005: 579): "Representation necessarily lays claim to correctness. Therefore, a fully-fledged concept of representation must include an ideal dimension, which connects decision with discourse. Representation is thus defined by the connection of normative, factual, and ideal dimensions.".

[6] Alexy (1989a: 178): "The theory of claim states that individual legal norms and decisions as well as whole legal systems necessarily make a claim to correctness. Norm systems which do not explicitly or implicitly make this claim are not legal systems. So far the theory of claim is of defining character.".

[7] Alexy (1989b: 31).

[8] Alexy (2005: 580) continues: "Constitutional review can be successful only if the arguments presented by the constitutional court are sound and only if a sufficient number of members of the community are able and willing to exercise their rational capacities".

1) While Alexy succeeds in pre-empting the objection of the argument of authority that courts might derive from their status as argumentative representatives, he does not explain how the existence of what he calls "constitutional persons", i.e., "rational persons both able and willing to accept coherent and correct arguments for the good reason that they are coherent and correct", can be verified. Now, while Alexy acknowledges that parliamentary representation is determined by the election, he does not indicate precisely what would determine the link between the people and the constitutional court. Even if such "constitutional persons" did exist, it is still unclear how their degree of acceptance would be assessed or verified. Should we think of deliberative juries? Should we think of popular ratification of court decisions? Given that Alexy's thesis is very clearly aimed at securing and justifying the supremacy of courts over parliaments, any form of popular consultation seems out of the question. Given his ideal position, Alexy might be tempted to reply that such empirical questions do not concern him. It might then be objected that, although his argument refers to an ideal of democracy, the goal he is seeking to achieve and for which he charges constitutional review is indeed the institutionalization of reason; and that, in these conditions, he cannot do without a reflection on the practical and empirical modalities of this institutionalization. Moreover, he needs it since he bases his entire analysis on the actual practice of the courts, and in particular of the German court, whose art in practicing proportionality he likes to show, and whose jurisprudence has nourished his "formula of weight". In this case, however, there seems to be a double standard[9].
2) Following Mattias Kumm, it is doubtful whether an institution in a democracy can claim to represent the people by argument alone without even expressing a will[10]. Kumm therefore wonders to what extent a constitutional court does not represent the will of the people, even in a weak form. However, given that a court is generally appointed by elected representatives and that it must make decisions in accordance with the majority principle, it seems perfectly plausible to him to accept that a court also exercises decision-making representation, even if the judges are not elected. The argument overlooks a major difference, however: while election places a form of *accountability on* the shoulders of elected representatives, the same cannot be said of appointed judges, even if they were appointed by elected representatives – which is not always the case – and, moreover, the elected representatives who appoint judges are not themselves likely to control these judges, who enjoy the privilege of never being accountable for anything precisely because their decisions are not supposed to be political but legal, or even – according to Alexy himself – based on practical reason.
3) Alexy can be criticized for using the term "representative" with two very different meanings, referring to two different forms of representation which in reality have nothing to do with each other and thus can hardly coexist. Even if we acknowledge that both parliamentary representation and judicial representation are argumentative or discursive rather than merely decision-making, it is difficult to view the nature

9 See in particular Ricardo Guibourg (2010: 145–160).

10 Mattias Kumm (2012: 207): "there is no place in a democracy for an institution that can claim only argumentative representation".

of their arguments as being the same. The types of arguments mobilized in each context differ significantly. A parliament deliberates first and foremost to create new standards, whereas a constitutional court is supposed to deliberate first and foremost to decide whether or not a given new standard complies with an older standard. Moreover, while parliamentary representation is a matter of imputation and therefore of a constitutive justificatory fiction – a parliament expresses a will by taking the place of a collectivity whose existence is postulated by positive law, this justification being laid down by the constitution itself – the same cannot be said about a court that argues and decides, which is never designated as a representative. Therefore, to use representation to justify the function of the latter means to create a meta-legal concept of representation.

4) Alexy's assertion that representation – like constitutionality review and law in general[11] – "raises a claim to correctness" is inescapable. This claim is understood by Alexy not in an empirical sense but in a conceptual sense; it forms the basis of his thesis of the existence of a necessary – and not contingent – link between law and morality (*Verbindungsthese*). This thesis of the "claim to rightness" has been challenged from two points of view. From a logical one, because it leads to a pure tautology and explains nothing. Secondly, from a metaethical one, because it is based on an unverifiable cognitivist presupposition[12]. But it can also be misleading from a legal and constitutional point of view. It is tantamount to thinking about the objective nature of representation. On the one hand, all political systems that claim to be representative are careful not to define the very nature of representation that would make those they designate as such "authentic" representatives, whether at the ideal, normative, or empirical level. On the other hand, even if we believe we have uncovered the true nature of representation in a particular theory – whether devised by a philosopher, a jurist, or a member of a constituent assembly – we cannot consider it precise or morally just. At best, it can be said to adhere to legal "principles." However, this adherence does not inherently confer any moral value to those principles. Finally, the thesis is misleading in that it suggests that institutional representatives

[11] Robert Alexy (1992, 1994, 2002: 35–39; 1998: 205–221). On this subject, see George Pavlakos (2012: 15–30).

[12] Eugenio Bulygin (1993: 19–24) and (2000: 133–137), for whom this claim to moral correctness is by no means a characteristic and defining feature of legal systems, norms or decisions: it would be so only on condition that these unjust norms, decisions or systems cease to be considered as legal. But even Robert Alexy does not go so far as to admit that unjust legal norms are no longer legal. In his view, they are merely defective or erroneous. This amounts to saying that a legal norm that does not claim to be morally just is a morally defective legal norm. And as anyone can understand, this defect can only bother those who admit or dream of a conceptual connection between law and morality, but will not disturb those who do not believe in it. Moreover, even if the law were to claim moral rightness, there would be no way of proving this claim, and even if it were proved, there would be no guarantee that all the legal authorities likely to lay down norms would have an identical understanding of moral rightness or, more simply, justice, for who can say that the term "justice" is so univocal that it will be used in the same sense by everyone?

are justifiable when it is precisely representation itself that operates as justification in the constitutional system[13].

5) Alexy's construction leads him either to draw legislation to the side of practical reason or to draw constitutional jurisdiction to the side of political legislation. In the final analysis, it is not clear what legislation stands to gain from this, but it is fairly clear what constitutional judges stand to gain from the skillful justification Alexy has woven for them. Some judges were not mistaken.

2.2 Alexy Among the Judges

Two constitutional judges in particular (although others could be cited as well) have understood perfectly well what they could learn from Alexy: Aharon Barak[14] and Luís Roberto Barroso[15]. Based on certain decisions of the Brazilian Federal Supreme Court, the latter concludes that the Court was able to satisfy social demands that the Brazilian Congress did not meet (in terms of administrative morality, judicial reform or the sincerity and political loyalty of deputies to their party, and the financing of electoral campaigns)[16]. The Court is therefore clearly another – complementary, or even competing – interpreter of the "sentiments of the majority"[17]. Similarly, the Supreme Tribunal is one of the courts whose jurisprudence promotes social progress through the recognition of numerous new social rights.

However, it is interesting to note that this justification coexists with its opposite. For example, Luís Roberto Barroso acknowledges that, in very rare cases – cases that he declares to be "exceptional" – the Court sometimes takes counter-majoritarian positions (for example on civil unions for same-sex couples or on abortion in the case of fetuses with anencephaly). In so doing, the Court joins other constitutional courts that have

---

[13] Robert Alexy (1998: 208): "The core of the argument of correctness is the thesis claiming that such institutional acts are always connected to the non-institutional act of asserting that the legal act is substantially and procedurally correct. This assertion of correctness has consequences. Correctness implies justifiability.".

[14] V. not. Aharon Barak, *The Judge in a Democracy*, Princeton, Princeton University Press, 2008 or Aharon Barak, "Les juges comme gardiens de la Constitution sur l'acte de juger", *Cités*, n°69, 2017, p. 19–40.

[15] Luís Roberto Barroso, "Reason Without Vote: The Representative and Majoritarian Function of Constitutional Courts", in Thomas Bustamante and Bernardo Gonçalves Fernandes (eds) *Democratizing Constitutional Law: Perspectives on Legal Theory and the Legitimacy of Constitutionalism.* Dordrecht, Springer (2016), pp. 71–90.

[16] L. R. Barroso, *ibid*, p. 82: "The Court is performing, in slices, incompletely, and without the possibility of systematization, the political reform that society calls for".

[17] *Ibid*. p. 79: "For numerous reasons, the Legislature does not always express the sentiment of the majority.".

had to take courageous counter-majoritarian decisions[18]. But these decisions remain legitimate because they are justified by the protection of a fundamental right[19].

In other words, whether they take a majority position and respond to a social demand or adopt a counter-majority position to preserve the fundamental rights of individuals, constitutional courts in general, and the Brazilian Supreme Court in particular, are always democratic institutions. This illustrates the duality of both concepts "deliberative democracy" and "argumentative representation": while in Alexy's work it is argumentation that confers on the courts a quality of representation necessary to the law, in Barroso's work it seems that representation alone is a contingent argument in favor of the supremacy of the courts.

2.3 An American Concept of Representation by Judges

However, it would be wrong to think that only constitutional judges have an "interest" in adopting the idea that judges are "representatives". Without necessarily using this vocabulary, certain empirical academic works seek to show that a constitutional court can listen to public opinion and allow itself to be influenced by it. For example, as early as the late 1950s, Robert A. Dahl considered that the Supreme Court was unquestionably an institution that was an integral part of the political game, but whose role could not be "described or evaluated using simple concepts drawn from democratic or moral theory"[20]. In his view, the Supreme Court can pursue public policy at the national level, but on condition that it does so in a way that conforms to the majority and dominant public policies, at the risk of calling its legitimacy into question. For his part, Bickel sought to show that the Supreme Court maintains a form of "conversation"[21] with American society.

---

[18] Barroso cites the 1954 *Brown vs Board of America* decision of the US Supreme Court, which declared racial segregation in public schools unconstitutional; the *S v. Makwanyane and Another* decision of 1995, in which the South African Constitutional Court abolished the death penalty; and the Auschwitzlüge decision of the US Constitutional Court. *Makwanyane and Another* of 1995, in which the Constitutional Court of South Africa abolished the death penalty; the decision 90 BVerfGe 241 (1994) *Auschwitzlüge* of the Federal Constitutional Court of Germany, which definitively recognised that Holocaust denial could not claim freedom of expression; the decision *Public Committee Against Torture in Israel v. Israel* HCJ 5100/94 (1999), in which the Israeli Constitutional Court reaffirmed the absolute ban on torture, including in the context of interrogations of terrorism suspects.

[19] Barroso, *ibid*, p. 82: "These are emblematic examples of the enlightened role of the constitutional jurisdiction".

[20] Robert A. Dahl (1957: 293; 285): "the policy views dominant on the Court are never for long out of line with the policy views dominant among the lawmaking majorities of the United States. Consequently, it would be most unrealistic to suppose that the Court would, for more than a few years at most, stand against any major alternatives sought by a lawmaking majority".

[21] Alexander Bickel (1975: 111) speaks of the Supreme Court's "conversation" with society, the lower courts and the various political branches of government.

Later, other authors spoke of an "interpretive constitutional dialogue"[22] in order to capture the dynamic between the Supreme Court and public opinion in matters of constitutional interpretation, so that the Court ultimately appears to be far more majoritarian and democratic than that maintained by those who denounce the "counter-majoritarian difficulty". For Barry Friedman, all strata of society are involved, and the courts play a unique role in facilitating and shaping the national dialogue about the meaning of the constitution, particularly but not exclusively in relation to fundamental rights. This dialogue does not, therefore, pit an electorally (politically) accountable government, which alone would be legitimate, against politically unaccountable and illegitimate courts or judges. Jeffrey Rosen has a similar view, holding that the Supreme Court tends to reflect the constitutional conceptions of majorities[23].

However, this statement needs to be qualified or at least supplemented. As Corinna Barrett Lain has pointed out, the extra-legal factors envisaged by Barry Friedman - the process of recruiting judges, the method of majority decision (which gives significant weight to the most balanced opinion and to the pivotal judge), the desire of judges to be appreciated, the concern to make their decisions effective[24] – are not the only ones to explain the majority concern of the Supreme Court, which is expressed in many areas. This concern also has an argumentative dimension, which arises from the fact that constitutional provisions are largely indeterminate. Consequently, to justify their interpretative choices, which necessarily involve an axiological choice, the judges prefer to rely on the apparent objectivity of a count of state legislation to which they accord the status of a reflection of the majority will[25].

However, another model for democratizing constitutionalism is possible, based on a similar rationale.

---

22 Barry Friedman (1993: 577–682) and (2009: 382): "The magic of the dialogic system of determining constitutional meaning, however, is that it works whether the judges rule properly or not- precisely because everything important happens after they render their decision. What history shows is assuredly not that Supreme Court decisions always are in line with popular opinion, but rather that they come into line with one another over time".

23 Jeffrey Rosen (2006: XII): "Far from protecting minorities against the tyranny of the majority or thwarting the will of the people, courts for most of American history, have tended to reflect the constitutional views of majorities".

24 Barry Friedman (2009: 375): "The most telling reason why the justices might care about public opinion, though, is simply that they do not have much of a choice. At least, that is, if they care about preserving the Court's institutional power, about having their decisions enforced, about not being disciplined by politics. Americans have abolished courts, impeached one justice, regularly defied Court orders, packed the Court, and stripped its jurisdiction. If the preceding history shows anything, it is that when judicial decisions wander far from what the public will tolerate, bad things happen to the Court and the justices".

25 Corinna Barrett Lain (2010: 776): "In his focus on an extralegal account of Supreme Court decision making, Friedman misses the best evidence yet of the Court's majoritarian leanings: its widespread use of explicitly majoritarian doctrine". V. also Corinna Barrett Lain (2009: 391): "As Peter Westen recognized years ago, equality is an "empty idea" on its own, a precept that means nothing absent the value judgments used to fill it. In the end, those value judgments have to come from somewhere. Here, too, the majority position of the states is an obvious (and oft-used) choice." See also the earlier unorthodox but now "classical" views from Martin Shapiro (1964 and 1981).

3 Representation by Constitutional Juries

Indeed, those who want to see courts as representatives of society insist that courts are first and foremost morally representative, either because they express feelings that are morally shared in society, or because they express values that are necessary for society (and it doesn't matter that at the time they express them society may be opposed to them). In this way, what could justify or provide a basis for control of the courts would be the search for commonly shared values. But in this case, why not envisage associating members of society with judges in order to express these values? Hence the idea of constitutional juries.

Several convergent proposals envisage the constitution of constitutional juries associated with constitutional courts. However, they are not justified in the same way.

3.1 Horacio Spector's Proposal

Horacio Spector envisages a system of constitutional juries composed of 36 to 72 members, drawn by lot and to be convened at the request of the parties to a dispute when they wish to avoid the normal procedure of review by authorized courts[26]. Such juries, which would coexist with a system of constitutionality review by one or more courts, would not have general jurisdiction over compliance with the constitution by the public authorities, so they would not resolve conflicts of attribution in a federal system, for example. They would, however, have jurisdiction over disputes involving the violation of individual rights. Citizens would thus have an optional right to have a dispute decided by a jury rather than by a court, and these juries would therefore have the same power as a court to decide questions of constitutional interpretation and to annul a law deemed to be contrary to the constitution. This would be done on a case-by-case basis.

The great advantage that Horacio Spector attributes to the jury is that it makes it possible to resolve a problem inherent in classical constitutionality review, that of political equality. In his view, constitutionality review affects political equality in two ways: on the one hand, it contradicts majoritarian rule – as Rawls noted[27] – because, in order to overcome the contradiction between the law and the constitution, it will generally be necessary to have recourse to a qualified majority, which amounts to admitting that a minority can block or delay the adoption of a law (the law in question may itself be the law revising the constitution or a law that it is hoped to adopt once this revision has been completed). On the other hand, constitutionality review can be seen as a violation of the "one person, one vote" principle of political equality, with the court acting as if it had a veto that could block the majority. In other words: "The conclusion is that we can regard judicial review either as a form of restricting the power of majorities by giving minorities the power to impede a change, or as a grotesque violation of the one

[26] Horacio Spector (2009: 111–124). See also Horacio Spector (2014) chap. 7.

[27] "Whenever the constitution limits the scope and authority of majorities, either by requiring a greater plurality for certain types of measures, or by a bill of rights restricting the powers of the legislature, and the like, equal political liberty is less extensive", John Rawls (1957: 197), quoted by Spector.

person one vote principle. In either case, it is plain that judicial review is not a natural component of democratic regimes, and requires specific justification"[28].

We therefore need to rethink the justification for constitutionality review and envisage a specific way of applying it. Spector's justification is based on the idea that constitutional rights are procedural moral rights and that every citizen has a right to have his or her case heard, because a moral right has two sides: the power to express a claim and grievances, and the power to obtain an impartial and reasoned response when individuals believe that their right has been violated. Positive law must therefore provide this type of response. How can juries provide it? For Spector, constitutional juries achieve political equality because the drawing of lots is more egalitarian and democratic than choice by election can be. Moreover, Spector believes that constitutional juries are better able to deal with violations of rights than members of the judicial elite; it is therefore highly likely that the response from a jury will be more impartial than from a court because the constitutional jury system entrusts the function of interpreting the Constitution to the people themselves. Lastly, juries are perfectly capable of giving a justified and reasoned response and could escape the "discursive dilemma"[29] (or "doctrinal paradox" or the contradiction between individual opinions and collective judgments) if the members of the jury were to vote both on the reasons for the verdict and on the verdict itself at the same time. Although justified, these verdicts would not give rise to binding precedents; they would not be conceived as based on a *ratio decidendi*.

3.2 Eric Ghosh's Proposal

Ghosh points out that Spector does not justify the jury as an attempt to remedy elitism. What Spector wants is to remedy the lack of political equality in electoral democracy: it does not provide an equal opportunity for effective political influence.

The jury model proposed by Eric Ghosh is different. It is also rooted in Australia's constitutional reality, which does not have a Bill of Rights, and his proposal therefore presupposes a prior revision of the Constitution.

This would be a citizens' court comprising 200 people, chosen by lot, whose jurisdiction would be limited to the review of ordinary legislation and its annulment in the event of a violation of rights. The internal practice of this citizens' court would be based on the procedures already used for other consultations within the framework of the citizens' assemblies being experimented with in deliberative democracy. For example, documents would be provided prior to the deliberation, they would be asked to read them by means of a questionnaire, and decisions would be taken by a qualified majority of 60%, which would give great authority to the jury's decisions. Ghosh insists that this court should have significant power to select cases and not be limited to those presented

---

[28] H. Spector (2009: 112).

[29] In "social choice" theory, the discursive dilemma arises from the fact that the aggregation of opinions by a majority vote can lead to irrationality: "the problem is to know whether the views of the group respond completely to the individual views of its members, at the risk of collective incoherence, or whether the views of the group are collectively rational, even at the cost of compromising the group's response to individual choices", P. Engel (2005: 129–143). See also Roberto Vacca (1921: 52–59).

to it by the judges. That said, given the large number of cases the court could receive, advisory opinions could be offered by a panel of federal judges, themselves appointed by a parliamentary committee including minority parties, and the final choice would be made by lot. Hearings could be held over a few days to keep costs down, and here again the citizens would be assisted by three judges who could also preside over the hearings. Finally, Eric Ghosh's proposal makes room for constitutional dialogue because, on the one hand, the power to select cases would be conditional on parliament's ability to repeal the court's decisions by a qualified majority of 60% and, on the other hand, the same qualified majority would be required if parliament wished to pre-emptively prevent the constitutional review of a law. The basis for the decisions of this court of citizens would be a charter of rights which would include civil, political, and social rights, rights which would be understood very broadly in order to confer very explicitly a large discretionary power on the jury in its determination of "injustices"[30].

3.3 Discussion

As already pointed out, for both Spector and Ghosh, the defense of constitutional juries is first and foremost motivated by the idea that selection procedures based on the drawing of lots are the closest thing to political equality, even if they never fully achieve it.

The fact is that the drawing of lots is being used more and more frequently in contemporary theory of deliberative democracy. Indeed, it has been used successfully on a number of occasions. In Ireland, for example, a constitutional convention with a majority of members drawn by lot drafted the constitutional amendment that legalized same-sex marriage (after a referendum). As Horacio Spector and Eric Ghosh point out, along with many others (Fishkin, Manin, and Sintomer come to mind[31]), the merit of drawing lots is that it selects citizens who can fairly easily be expected to deliberate without regard to personal interests linked to their own careers or political commitments. And even so, the heterogeneity of the points of view will very probably negate any possibility of one personal interest prevailing over others. From then on, we can hope or imagine that a common good – if not the common good – will be taken into account.

So far, however, these proposals have not aroused great enthusiasm. There is no doubt that they are still too impractical, although their advocates are doing their utmost to show that they could be practical. Whatever criticisms may be levelled at them in detail (with regard to their possible costs, the complexity of their organization, or even the vagueness of certain procedural aspects), they seem to contradict all too explicitly the idea that has been conveyed since constitutional courts first existed, namely that constitutionality review is a matter for legal specialists, legal techniques, and therefore experts in law and not only in constitutional law. It is well known that, with a few exceptions, including France, most of the courts that review the constitutionality of legislative or executive

[30] Eric Ghosh (2010: 347): "an open-ended bill of rights would empower juries to determine what counts as an injustice. The bill of rights would include civil, political and social welfare rights, and also a catch-all phrase to capture cases of substantial injustice suffered due to action or inaction by any branch of government".

[31] V. James S. Fishkin (2011); Bernard Manin, (1995); Yves Sintomer (2011: 239–276) and the bibliography cited by himself in (2012).

acts are composed of legal experts who have demonstrated a perfect command of legal technique and argumentation.

Moreover, no one can deny that the effects of a constitutionality review – and first and foremost the annulment of a law – can have legal as well as social, economic, and political consequences, which need to be assessed and anticipated. Professional lawyers are undoubtedly useful here. Well, only lawyers? It is indisputable that constitutional review is increasingly linked with the assessment of the proportionality of laws. Proportionality review requires the courts to weigh up two equally important but conflicting objectives. This review therefore requires assessments that cannot be confined to the strictly legal sphere. Moreover, the proportionality review reveals the extent to which law is indebted to social sciences and the personal values of judges. We may therefore remain skeptical about the need to restrict the composition of courts to legal professionals alone.

Under these conditions, the question of whether a law violates a constitutional right or not – which technically amounts to asking whether a law that restricts the exercise of right X in pursuit of objective Y is justified or proportionate – could very well be left to a jury that is not identified with an elite. If, on the other hand, it is felt that specific epistemic skills and expertise in a wide range of subjects are required, then not only should all the courts have a large number of experts, but the judges who sit on them should also be sufficiently experienced to grasp the expert opinions they receive.

3.4 Christopher Zurn's Proposal

For his part, Christopher Zurn proposes another configuration which, on the one hand, entrusts to a specialized court the control of the constitutionality of ordinary laws but, on the other hand, provides that the revision of the constitution will call upon deliberative assemblies composed of ordinary citizens, drawn by lot, who will propose amendments which will then be submitted for ratification by referendum[32]. This system itself involves several stages. First, the amendments will have to be selected. In order to avoid making choices that could jeopardize the constitutional balance, while at the same time avoiding the risk of lapsing into systematic expertise, Zurn proposes involving a group of professional and independent jurists in the jury that will make the selection, and trusting the deliberative process to set aside the least relevant proposed amendments. Then comes the certification stage, which would be fairly complex, since it would involve three successive juries, each made up of different members drawn by lot and meeting at sufficiently long intervals. The complexity of this process is not sought for its own sake, but the aim is to make the most of the public consultations by seeking out the strongest and therefore best justifications for a particular amendment, without focusing on the author. The final stage would be a referendum on the proposed amendment – a "deliberation day" (as envisaged by Ackerman and Fishkin).

In other words, if the court decides to annul a law deemed unconstitutional and that annulment can therefore only be overcome by a revision of the Constitution, the people retain the possibility of voting in favor of that revision[33]. The idea behind this proposal is as follows: "the real normative worry about judicial review does not concern the mere

[32] Christopher Zurn (2007: 336).

[33] Zurn (2007: 274–300).

protection of constitutional provisions by a democratically unaccountable court, but rather the positive elaboration of constitutional content that reviewing courts inevitably engage in order to fulfil the demands of legal integrity"[34].

This whole process would give rise to numerous exchanges, justifications, questions and answers. In short, these arguments are likely to enlighten the public and constitute a moment of democratic deliberation. However, this procedure is by no means proposed as a panacea or a miracle solution[35].

Here again, quite apart from the organizational aspects, the approach emphasizes the importance of drawing lots. This system has already been practiced in Ireland. It runs the risk of encountering a limit. It is conceivable that the Court will attempt to preserve its supremacy in at least two ways: by increasing the number of interpretative reservations aimed at neutralizing the disputed law as much as possible, or by reviewing the constitutionality of the amendments themselves, a practice that is becoming increasingly common. In this regard, the rapid proliferation of techniques for reviewing revision laws is one of the most striking features of contemporary constitutionalism[36].

4 Concluding Remarks

A few years ago, Ran Hirschl noted how far "great" constitutional theory seemed to be from the reality of constitutional law. Entirely absorbed and obsessed by the "counter-majoritarian difficulty", it did not even seem to realize the rise in power of the courts, giving rise to a "juristocracy"[37]. However, this counter-majoritarian difficulty is primarily a political construct, not a legal one, arising from elected parliaments deferring the resolution of contentious issues to constitutional courts[38]. Consequently, those who delegate decisions to the courts retain the freedom to criticize the courts' actions. The discourse surrounding the "democratization" of constitutionalism[39] may indicate an increasing awareness within constitutional theory of this growing dynamic. Given certain pressing issues, such as environmental challenges, we must acknowledge the relative moderation or even overt passivity of elected representatives and political leaders. This situation suggests that increased intervention by "civil society" (referring to citizens engaged in

[34] Zurn (2011: 86).

[35] Ch. Zurn (2007: 341): "Let me be clear: I am not claiming that civic constitutional fora can solve all of the ills of contemporary political public spheres, nor more grandly yet, that it can solve all of the problems of constitutional self-government (…) I am claiming (…) that significant improvements can be made through relatively modest changes in current incentive structures for citizens, political actors, and the supporting political public spheres, and that these changes can be implemented through modest proposals to improve the procedures of democratic constitutional elaboration".

[36] On this subject, see Gonzalo Andres Ramirez-Cleves (2016: 213–229) and Yaniv Roznaï's acclaimed *Unconstitutional Constitutional Amendments. The Limits of Amendment Powers* (2017).

[37] Ran Hirschl (2004: 6).

[38] V. Mark A. Graber (1997: 35–73) and Carlo Guarnieri and Patrizia Pederzoli (1996, not. Chap. 3).

[39] Thomas Bustamante and Bernardo Gonçalves Fernandes (2016).

politics without it being their profession) could potentially enhance the protection of certain rights.

However, the jury systems proposed by Spector, Ghosh, and Zurn are limited by their focus on individual rights, which may undermine their effectiveness in addressing these broader concerns. Regarding environmental issues, the focus would shift to defending collective rights – such as the rights to health, access to water, a healthy environment, a minimum level of food security, and reliable information about consumable products. This approach would empower society to hold companies, whose primary concern is not these rights, accountable for compliance with the law. This is also the fragility of theses that make judges representatives of "society", since the latter ultimately appears to be very little integrated into the economic circuit. Ultimately, when considering the protection of future individual rights, which inherently have a collective dimension and require profound changes in the economic and social system, it is doubtful that judges will be effective in advocating on behalf of "society." In this context, the beneficial role of cross-intervention by elected representatives becomes clear. However, the pursuit of the common good would have to prevail over economic interests. We could then envisage linking constitutional juries and the "constitutional dialogue" that some people are calling for[40] and thus pave the way for the defense not only of individual rights but also of collective rights.

References

Alexy R (1978, 1989b) A theory of legal argumentation. The theory of rational discourse as theory of legal justification. Oxford UP, Oxford

Alexy R (1989a) On necessary relations between law and morality. Ratio Juris 2:167–183

Alexy R (1992, 1994) Begriff und Geltung des Rechts, Freiburg, Herder. English translation (2022) The argument from injustice. A reply to legal positivism. Oxford, Clarendon Press

Alexy R (1998) Law and correctness. Curr Leg Probl 51(1):205–221

Alexy R (2005) Balancing, constitutional review, and representation. Int J Const Law 3(4):572–581

Manin B (1995) Principes Du Gouvernement Représentatif. Calmann-Lévy, Paris

Bickel A (1975) Morality of consent. New Haven, Yale UP

Bulygin E (1993) Alexy und das Richtigkeitsargument. In: Rechtsnorm und Rechtswirklichkeit (ed) Duncker & Humblot, Berlin

Bulygin E (2000) Alexy's thesis of the necessary connection between law and morality. Ratio Juris 13:133–137

Bustamante T, Gonçalves Fernandes B (eds) (2016) Democratizing constitutional law: perspectives on legal theory and the legitimacy of constitutionalism. Springer, Dordrecht

Zurn C (2007) Deliberative democracy and the institutions of judicial review. Cambridge UP, Cambridge

Zurn C (2011) Judicial review, constitutional juries and civic constitutional fora: rights. Democr Law. Theoria 58(127):63–94

Dahl RA (1957) Decision-making in a democracy: the supreme court as a national policymaker. J Public Law 6:279–295

Engel P (2005) Croyances collectives et intentions partagées. In: Leroux A, Livet P (eds) Leçons de philosophie économique, tome 1, Economica, Paris, pp 129–143

40 Stephen Gardbaum's work springs to mind (see 2013 not. Chap. 3); see also Roberto Gargarella (ed.) (2014).

Fishkin JS (2011) When the people speak. Deliberative democracy and public consultation. Oxford UP, Oxford
Friedman B (1993) Dialogue and judicial review. Mich Law Rev 91:577–682
Friedman B (2009) The will of the people. how public opinion has influenced the supreme court and shaped the meaning of the constitution. Farrar, Straus and Giroux, New York
Gardbaum S (2001) The new commonwealth model of constitutionalism. Am J Comp Law 49:707–747
Gardbaum S (2013) The new commonwealth model of constitutionalism: theory and practice. Cambridge University Press, Cambridge
Gargarella R (ed) (2014) Por una justicia dialógica, Buenos Aires, Siglo Veintiuno
Ghosh E (2010) Deliberative democracy and the countermajoritarian difficulty: considering constitutional juries. Oxf J Leg Stud 30(2):327–359
Graber MA (1997) The non-majoritarian difficulty: legislative deference to the judiciary. Stud Am Polit Dev 7(2):35–73
Guarnieri C, Pederzoli P (1996) La puissance de juger: pouvoir judiciaire et démocratie. Michalon, Paris
Guibourg R (2010) On Alexy's weighing formula. Archiv für Recht und Sozial Philosophie. Beiheft 124
Kumm M (2012) Alexy's theory of constitutional rights and the problem of judicial review. In: Klatt M (ed) Institutionalized reason. The jurisprudence of Robert Alexy. Oxford UP, Oxford, pp 201–217
Lain CB (2009) The unexceptionalism of evolving standards. UCLA Law Rev 57(2):365–420
Lain CB (2010) The doctrinal side of majority will. Mich State Law Rev 775–793
Pavlakos G (2012) Correctness and cognitivism. Remarks on Robert Alexy's argument from the claim to correctness. Ratio Juris 25(1):15–30
Ramirez-Cleves GA (2016) The unconstitutionality of constitutional amendments in Colombia: the tension between majoritarian democracy and constitutional democracy. In: Bustamante T, Gonçalves Fernandes B (eds) Democratizing constitutional law. Law and philosophy library, vol 113. Springer, Cham, pp 213–229. https://doi.org/10.1007/978-3-319-28371-5_10
Hirschl R (2004) "Juristocracy" - political, not juridical. Good Soc 13(3):6–11
Rawls J (1957) I. Justice as Fairness. J Philos 54(22):653–662. https://doi.org/10.2307/2021929
Rosen J (2006) The most democratic branch: how the courts serve America. Oxford University Press, New York
Roznaï Y (2017) Unconstitutional constitutional amendments. The limits of amendment powers. Oxford University Press, London
Shapiro M (1964) Law and politics in the supreme court, new approaches to political jurisprudence. Free Press of Glencoe, New York
Shapiro M (1981) Courts: a comparative and political analysis. University of Chicago Press, Chicago
Sintomer Y (2011) Délibération et participation: affinité élective ou concepts en tension? Participations 1(1):239–276
Sintomer Y (2012) Tirage au sort et démocratie délibérative. Une piste pour renouveler la politique au XXIe siècle? La Vie des idées, 5 June 2012. ISSN: 2105-3030. http://www.laviedesidees.fr/Tirage-au-sort-et-democratie-deliberative.html. Reproduced in Le Pillouer A (ed) À quoi servent les élections, Paris, PUF, pp 73–89
Spector H (2009) The right to a constitutional jury. Legisprudence 3(1):111–124
Spector H (2014). Un sistema democrático de control constitucional. In: Gargarella R (ed) Por una justicia dialógica. Buenos Aires, Siglo Veintiuno
Tushnet M (2003a) New forms of judicial review and the persistence of rights - and democracy - based worries. Wake For Law Rev 38(2):813–838

Tushnet M (2003b) Forms of judicial review as expressions of constitutional patriotism. Law Philos 22(3/4):353–379

Tushnet M (2003c) Alternative forms of judicial review. Mich Law Rev 101(8):2781–2802

Vacca R (1921) Opinioni individuali e deliberazioni collettive. Rivista Internazionale di Filosofia del Diritto 1(52):52–59

Waldron J (2016) The core of the case against judicial review. Yale Law J 115:1346–1406. Reprinted in (2016) Political Political Theory. Harvard University Press, Cambridge

Constitutional Courts as Trustees: Protecting the Representative Balance

Pedro Lomba(✉)

Faculty of Law, University of Lisbon, Lisbon, Portugal
pedrolomba@fd.ulisboa.pt

Abstract. How does the *idea* of representative constitutional courts relate to the dominant traditions of political representation? To begin with, both traditions impose limits on the understanding of the representative nature of constitutional courts. First, once introduced into the dual representational scheme of divided power, constitutional courts run the risk of becoming another instance of competitive political division, producing its partisans and detractors. Second, understood as a power that must be responsive to the democratic community and its multiple and conflicting claims to representation, constitutional courts may end up being too dependent on the "advocacy" of political representation, thus becoming the "masters" of the representative process.

The way to contain these limitations is not to exclude courts from the representative device, but to identify a representative function that may be appropriate for a constitutional court. While constitutional courts, as a form of state authority, ultimately derive their power from the people, their representative function is to maintain the people's trust in the constitutional value of representative balance. In other words, constitutional courts do not represent the people; rather, they represent the people's trust in the representative balance enshrined in a constitutional democracy.

1 Setting the Scene: Courts as Representative Institutions

It has been repeatedly suggested that constitutional courts are representative institutions. This assertion, which has accompanied the expansion of judicial power around the world, takes various forms. For some, once we accept the legitimacy of judicial review in a constitutional democracy, especially the exercise of judicial review of the scope, content and limits of fundamental rights, we are forced to consider constitutional courts as representative bodies, although the degree of this representative role may be anchored in several institutional variables[1]. For others, most notably Robert Alexy (2005: 572–581), constitutional review can be conceived of as representation of the people, not because of its connection to electoral politics, but because courts perform an "argumentative function", which is a distinctive form of representation based on rational arguments and discourse. As Alexy put it, the argumentative representation put forth by constitutional courts "can succeed only if the arguments put forth by the constitutional court are sound and only

[1] See Mattias Kumm (2019: 281–291).

L. Pereira Coutinho (Ed.): ICPRCR 2022, IUSGENT 124, pp. 74–84, 2025.
https://doi.org/10.1007/978-3-031-85983-0_6

if a sufficient number of members of the community are able and willing to exercise their rational capacities" (for Alexy, such members are referred to as "constitutional persons[2]").

Another line of thought emphasizes the role of constitutional adjudication in compensating for democratic deficits, since courts - because they are not elected and do not engage in competitive politics - can take advantage of their own insulation from the political branches to achieve better outcomes.[3]. Brazilian Federal Supreme Court Judge Roberto Barroso goes even further, arguing that "in certain contexts, paradoxical as it may seem, courts are more representative of social aspirations and demands than traditional political bodies."[4] Barroso describes the courts as playing an "enlightened" role in this respect.

On the relationship between representation and judicial review courts, John Hart Ely famously sought to justify a particular approach to judicial review in which courts - as "political outsiders" - are well placed to provide "representation-enhancing" review "concerned with procedural fairness in the resolution of individual disputes and with ensuring broad participation in the processes and distribution of government," so that courts will effectively "police the process of representation."[5]. And more recently, Rosalind Dixon has argued for a more robust and expansive role for representation through the idea of responsive judicial review, capable of overcoming various situations of democratic deadlock or dysfunction, as well as promoting forms of "constructive choice."[6].

My aim in this article is not to extend the concept of political representation to the courts. I will argue that constitutional courts should not be treated as representative bodies, nor should they purport to act in a representative role. Constitutional courts do not derive their authority directly from the people, but from the constitution. But because constitutional courts rule on how democratically representative bodies exercise their powers, it is an illusion to think that constitutional courts can be indifferent to the representative mechanism. As I will argue, one way of framing the issue, rather than demanding that constitutional courts actively engage with forms of political representation, is to be fully aware of the paradox of political representation and its constitutional implications. The paradox of representation requires the protection of what I define as the representative balance. As such, one way to approach the paradox is a matrix of judicial action that is faithful to the idea that constitutional courts are expected to maintain the citizens' trust in the representative balance. This is the conception of constitutional courts as representative trustees.

[2] Robert Alexy (2005: 572, 581).
[3] Dieter Grimm (2016: 220–221).
[4] Luis Roberto Barroso and Alise Osorio (2019: 175).
[5] John Hart Ely (1980: 102–103).
[6] Rosalind Dixon (2023: 93–98).

2 Representative Power: Two Dominant Traditions

I will begin by identifying the meanings of political representation that are relevant to this paper. These two meanings have shaped the development of representative institutions in our political traditions. In many ways, they have become the dominant conceptions of political representation. However, we must not forget that there are other relevant concepts of representation: in his seminal work, Hannah Pitkin has notably distinguished between formalist, symbolic or virtual concepts of representation.[7]. The point is not that they are unimportant, but that while some are essentially historical conceptualizations of representation in non-democratic and non-liberal societies, others, for various reasons, have not prevailed in our traditional constitutional democracy because they are incapable of explaining the characteristic features of the modern system of power.

2.1 Divided Representation

The first idea that shaped our system of power is "divided representation". In the aftermath of political representation, political power was conceived as divided in two correlated senses: between the representatives and the people and between two different representative powers: the legislative and the executive, both of which are endowed with representative functions. The two representative powers have produced their partisans[8] who, having delegated power to their representatives, expect them to *stand* for them under certain conditions, so that the will of the state emerges from an interplay of mutually limited representative wills.

The two representative powers, with their own bodies and institutions - but also, as mentioned, with their own partisans - stand in relation to each other. There is an element of confrontation in this relationship: in Montesquieu's terms, the positive and negative forces are the "*faculté de statuer*" and the "*faculté de empecher*".

One power dictates and prescribes, the other prevents and denounces. However, as Montesquieu also explains, this competition operates according to an articulated mechanism. It is not static, but dynamic. Montesquieu speaks of a "*necessary movement of things*", which stems from the idea that both powers - because they require *movement*- are forced to act together[9]. Because one representative power cannot control the other, citizens understand that the power that represents them, the power that they have chosen to represent them, is a limited power, or a power "held in respect by another power". In fact, a will is limited by the presence of another will: a system of mutually representative wills.[10].

---

[7] Hannah Pitkin (1967: 38–92).

[8] Pierre Manent (2004: 31).

[9] Montesquieu (2011: 177): "Ces trois puissances devraient former un repos ou une inaction. Mais, comme par le mouvement nécessaire des choses elles sont contraintes d'aller, elles seront forcées d'aller de concert.»

[10] Pierre Manent (2004: 31).

2.2 The *Political* Political Representation

The second dominant idea is an allegedly democratically committed concept of political representation. On the one hand, it is partly a reaction to a criticized feature of modern representation, namely alienation. Alienation arises from two different phenomena. The tradition of shared power is based on what Pierre Manent has called the "double game" of political representation: "As soon as a power, any power, is supposed to represent the citizen, the latter's desire for identification is inseparable from a feeling of alienation." This stems from "a kind of general powerlessness: the general powerlessness of the citizens to act much together, the powerlessness of the divided power to oppress the citizens".[11]

It is now understood that political power cannot be completely divided and that citizens cannot be powerless. The political conception of representation is a response to the alienation and powerlessness that results from divided representation. This is what Urbinati writes in her powerful book on representation when she speaks of a "political conception of representation": "In a government that derives its legitimacy from free and regular elections, the activation of a communicative current between civil and political society is essential and constitutive, not only for the government to be elected, but also for the people to be represented.[12]." Urbinati thus describes representative politics not as a form of divided power. Representation should be located not in the scheme of divided and competitive power, but as an unceasing political process of creating and recreating consent in society.

Second, *political* political representation can also be interpreted as a conception that abhors the crystallization of the common will. Let us recall that Sieyès wrote that political society developed from the transformation of separate wills into a unifying representative "common will": "The community needs a common will; without this '*silence* of will' it could not succeed in being a willing and acting body."[13]. In the tradition of Sieyès, the *representative* common will that resides in the body of representatives is neither complete nor unlimited; it is a mere portion of the great, common, national will.

Since the will of the representatives is not complete, the purpose of representation must be to ensure the completeness of the great common will. One way to do this is not to dissolve representation into a competitive mechanism of multiplying wills, but to reconstruct political representation in a unifying process of participation and will formation.

Against Sieyès' grand common will, authors such as Urbinati propose a "political vision of representation". "In sum," Urbinati writes, "political representation is far more than a system of division of labor and a state institution; it involves a complex political process that activates the "sovereign people" far beyond the formal act of electoral authorization. Representative politics has the power to unify and connect (through friction or agreement) the "fluctuating" "atomic units" of civil society by projecting citizens into a future-oriented perspective. It has the power to keep the sovereign in perpetual motion"[14].

[11] Pierre Manent (2004: 32).

[12] Nadia Urbinati (2006: 20).

[13] Emmanuel Sieyès (2002: 52).

[14] Nadia Urbinati (2006: 5).

This is a perspective that presents democratization and representation as having the same origin and the same destination.

2.3 Constitutional Courts and Representative Politics: Visible and Invisible Powers

Let us now contrast the two prevailing conceptions of political representation with the actual role of constitutional courts. Montesquieu alluded to the famous distinction between visible and invisible powers. The representative powers are visible; the judicial powers are invisible. Since the visible representative power is divided, the citizens have the possibility to choose between different powers to represent them. When citizens entrust a power, they do not lose their independence. Citizens are indeed possessed of a "double concern": "that the power which they have elected should represent them and stands for them, but is also a power that can betray them, that can be too different from them."[15] When and if that happens, they can turn to the opposite power.

Constitutional courts are judicial bodies. In Montesquieu's terms, they belong to the invisible powers. However, when constitutional courts conduct the judicial review of laws and declare laws null and void, they make their presence and power extraordinarily visible. The question is: can constitutional courts be as "visible" as the other two branches of representation?

On the one hand, as discussed above, political representation is a dual system of powers, a mechanism of political competition and rotation between the various powers and, through them, between society and the state. By joining the same mechanism of political concurrence, constitutional courts run the risk of becoming another source of competitive political division, having their partisans and their detractors.

On the other hand, if seen through the lens of participation and advocacy, courts may also end up being seen as superior forms of political representation -as in the position of Brazilian Judge Barroso- and therefore ultimately rejected by their constituencies. As Urbinati also writes, "voters choose their representatives on the basis of who will be the best advocates for the issues that matter most to them."[16]. The danger, then, is that the constitutional courts will become too reactive and dependent, and, in the prescient words of Böckenförde, moving "from safeguarding the constitution into domination over the constitution – and over representation – and thus departing from the democratic ground[17]". This is a serious risk, that of courts engaging in a *political* political representation.

2.4 John Hart Ely and His Discontents

The risks we have alluded to are remarkably present in the reactions to John Hart Ely's proposals as developed in his famous and seminal book, Democracy and Distrust. Note that Ely's approach was that questions of trust and distrust are not about mere disagreements over policy outcomes, or the disadvantages produced by representative politics, or

[15] Pierre Manent (2004: 32).
[16] N. Urbinati (2006: 53).
[17] Ernst-Wolfgang Böckenförde (2017: 190).

even the inevitable creation of winners and losers by the representative process. Courts are not expected to correct these situations. But Ely saw other situations of "dysfunction" in which the representative system no longer deserves confidence, with courts then "clearing the channels of political change" and "facilitating minority representation". As Ely said:

> "Dysfunction occurs when the *process* is unworthy of trust, when (1) the ins clog the channels of political change to ensure that the ins stay in and the outs stay out, or (2) when no one is actually denied a voice or a vote. Representatives beholden to an effective majority systematically disadvantage a minority out of simple hostility or a prejudiced refusal to recognize common interests, thereby denying that minority the protection afforded other groups by a representative trust.[18]".

Ely argued that it was not incompatible with American democracy for courts to engage in representational enhancement. He sought a middle ground between the two opposites, in which courts were either not authorized to make value-enhancing commitments or, alternatively, to substitute their own salvific commitments for the choices of democratic politics. Yet Ely's approach has been heavily criticized by those who claim that Ely blatantly failed to conjecture that "the comparative superiority of judges in policing the democratic process has proved untrue. From this perspective, Ely "ignored ideological affiliation (focusing exclusively on personal self-interest)", assuming instead "that judges, with their independence and tenure, are less likely to act in self-dealing ways than politicians.[19].

Ely has also been criticized within his own camp of neo-Elysian studies by other prominent voices who argue that it is impossible to distinguish between substantive and procedural issues, and that Ely's theory is "arguably under-inclusive even from the perspective of substantive commitments to equality."[20].

3 Constitutional Adjudication and the Protection of the Representative Balance

The brief argument I have sketched so far is that the two traditions of political representation confront the paradox between identification and alienation in different ways - from the articulated mechanism of the system of powers to the reunification of political will through forms of democratic participation - and that constitutional courts are ill-suited to occupy the position of either a countervailing representative power in the divided mechanism of representation or an advocate of substantive claims that have not been channeled through the representative process. We have also noted how John Hart Ely's proposal of a "third way" to the debate has been seen as inadequate and has generated his dissatisfaction.

In this part of my paper, I will argue for a representative function of constitutional courts in a narrow sense: if it is limited to preserving and protecting the value of representative balance.

[18] John Hart Ely (1980: 103).

[19] Ryan D. Doerfler and Samuel Moyn, (2023: 769).

[20] See, recently, Rosalind Dixon (2023: 97).

3.1 The Paradox of Political Representation

We can begin by focusing on the relationship between modern democracy and political representation. The collective will of the state is not the result of a majority of individual autonomous wills in competition with each other. Modern democracy develops within a political framework based on the separation of the representatives and the represented. Representatives are chosen and organized to embody the collective will of the state and to represent the diversity of society. In this sense, representation is a necessary condition both for the exercise of individual freedom and for the formation of the collective will of the state.

In this system, modern freedom consists of the freedom of the represented to decide who their representatives are, but also to identify the needs, desires, or interests that they wish to see represented and supported in the political sphere. Although exercised to elevate and distinguish a category of citizens in the social order[21] political freedom does not lose its purpose of self-determination. Representation is an ongoing activity - not just a device for allocating power - through which representatives act institutionally to make present the needs, desires, or interests of those they represent.

As argued elsewhere[22], democracy is thus a form of organizing political freedom through the expansion and socialization of representation. The main consequence of this expansion was that citizens - the people - could freely bring their interests, claims, or aspirations into the space of political representation and thus seek their recognition by the representative state. The process by which these aspirations and interests are incorporated into the representative space is an essentially contextual process, prone to multiple and conflicting political strategies that may or may not translate into normative commitments.

The project of modern representative democracy thus operates according to several discernible currents:

(i) The movement of *inclusion*, leading to the extension of citizenship rights to the people as a whole, without discrimination: the "unity" of the people is organized through representation.
(ii) The movement of *politicization*, which breaks the rigid separation between political and social issues; it has thus politicized social issues seeking political recognition or satisfaction.
(iii) The movement of *freedom*, which recognizes the rights of individuals to equal agency and autonomy, granting them forms of political participation and representation of their interests and claims.

These different movements socializing political representation cannot be described, however, as an innocuous activity. This is because the more democracy socializes representation, the more the State is increasingly pressured by the 'desire for satisfaction' of the represented; and, on the other hand, the more the State aims to satisfy the represented, the more the individual's own sphere of agential freedom may end up being dependent on the domain of the State.

[21] Bernard Manin (1997: 150–153).

[22] Pedro Lomba (2015: 30–46).

As a result, the activity of representation – which presupposes the separation between the represented and the representatives - can be distorted in light of the various participatory capacities from particular social demands, interests or groups. Such different degrees of participatory capacity can foster a situation in which political representation ceases to be a movement of inclusion, politicization, and freedom. This is a phenomenon that the political philosopher Pierre Manent has aptly described as the "paradoxical game of representation". Manent writes:

> "The vitality of the representative process presupposes that the people to be represented, in the diversity of its components, *exists and desires to exist independently of representation* and thus of the representative state. To be represented, one must first be. To really be is necessary to exist, according to a *'condition' independent of representation.* The desire to be represented presupposes, contains, if I may say so, the refusal to be represented, or the disgust or the aversion to be represented.[23]".

The implications of this paradox are twofold. First, the project of representative democracy is that citizens, though represented, must be treated as "independent" agents within the representative scheme. Why should there be representation if citizens do not exist or seek to exist beyond representation? As such, and as Manent astutely describes, citizens simultaneously desire and reject representation. They admit that they need to be represented, but they also show a "reluctance" to be represented. The "reluctance" to be represented also stems from the desire to live an independent existence that must never disappear. It is certainly a paradox, but it is within this paradox that "the vitality of the representative process" must ultimately be guaranteed.

3.2 Inclusion and Exclusion

The paradox of political representation requires the protection of what we will call the *representative balance.* The logic of representation is that the independent condition of citizens must coexist with the dependency inherent in the representative framework. The independent "active people" are also the represented "passive people. Representative democracy needs both.

When the independent status of citizens ceases to manifest itself in the broader representative apparatus, when citizens are transformed into mere administrative objects, or when the "passive" condition of people prevails over their independent status, the movements we described above as part of the representative system are reversed. In this respect, the prevailing movement may no longer be one of inclusion, but of exclusion: exclusion of those who are unable to have their say in the representative process; exclusion of unorganized social groups or claims; exclusion of members who are unable to articulate their interests (e.g., future generations) or are even prevented from doing so; in a word, exclusion of members who either refuse or are prevented from being represented.

Consider, for example, how contemporary democracies have witnessed the rise of parties representing disaffected citizens, be they "taxpayers, pensioners, the unemployed, migrants, families, and other political groups who no longer believe or *trust* the promises

---

[23] Pierre Manent (2008: 46). See, also, Luís Pereira Coutinho (2019-187–191).

of representation. While representation is inherently a socializing feature of the modern state, the crisis of representation fosters an entirely different dynamic of de-socialization. When citizens no longer see themselves as represented by the "whole," they turn their energies to the margins.

This is not the promotion of the separation between the representatives and the represented, which, as has been pointed out, pervades modern representative democracy. The phenomenon we are now discussing is that of separation *within* the represented; in other words, it is now the citizens who are separating from each other. As a result, they become hostile to representation, which is plagued by the emerging "discontentment" and distrust of an increasing number of those represented. These citizens thus refuse to conduct their political existence within the sphere of representative equilibrium. On the contrary, they seem to want to regain the direct representation of themselves, while affirming their own political and social differences.

Under these transformations, we come to a point where the state and the law may become defectively representative. We may then be in the presence of a form of state that no longer has political representation as one of its main pillars.

3.3 The Role of Courts as Representative Trustees: Institutional Sensitivity and Representative Balance

In another work, I have alluded to the circumstance of constitutional law intervening in a society scattered by political *overrepresentation* and *underrepresentation.*[24]. The coexistence of over- and under-represented citizens is not an illogical reality. Rather, it is a scenario resulting from a representative process undermined by forms of imbalance and persistent mistrust.

Matters of trust and distrust in political representation are not simply disagreements about policy outcomes, nor about the harms caused by policy decisions, nor even about the fact that representative politics inevitably produces its winners and losers. Courts are not expected to correct the normal outcomes of political competition.

On the other hand, maintaining confidence in the law and the constitution requires that courts possess and observe certain institutional characteristics, such as a culture of professionalism, judicial independence, and fidelity to the law. As noted by Böckenförde, "the expectation that a decision will be independent and made solely on the basis of legal reasoning rather than hidden political considerations is traditionally greatest with a court."[25]. Our focus is not on how courts are expected to enforce the general trust in law by respecting such institutional features. The focus is on how constitutional courts can act as trustees of the representative system, that is, as guardians of our trust in the constitutional value of representative balance, thus avoiding the dynamics of desocialization, exclusion, and distrust in the vitality of the representative mechanism. The task of constitutional theory is precisely to identify instances and contexts where and how such a role can be legitimately exercised. For this role, one of the most indispensable conditions is what we will call institutional sensitivity.[26].

[24] Pedro Lomba (2015: 45)

[25] See Böckenförde (2017: 191)

[26] Alan D. P. Brady (2012: 76–82).

The logic of institutional sensitivity implies that while John Hart Ely's critics seem to want the state to correct broader democratic dysfunctions, and thus impose positive duties or obligations on the state, the role of the courts in strengthening trust may work in the opposite direction, i.e., toward the fulfillment of negative duties by the state. The paradox of representation makes it clear that, in certain cases, the correction of the representative process may require deliberately self-limiting judicial decisions in order to ensure the protection of "independent existence" within the sphere of citizens. We can consider some examples of this approach, each of which may be subject to further development:

(i) *Freedom of communication, disinformation and the regulation of online speech.* Freedom of expression is the first right by which citizens demonstrate their allegiance to political representation. Courts may consider that the affirmation of the positive role of the state in creating an enabling environment for freedom of expression and equality should not be used to suppress disturbing, undesirable or minority opinions. This applies to the invocation of supposed new fundamental rights (e.g. the right to disinformation[27]), which can also be used to enforce viewpoint discrimination.

(ii) *Social reform.* It has been said that "the citizen, the taxpayer and the beneficiary of social rights are three faces of the same person.[28]". While this overlapping of social roles is a reality, it can be said that the balance between them is also inherently unstable. When reviewing laws that require an assessment of the distributive aspects of the social and fiscal activities of the administrative state, the courts must be particularly attentive to the principle of representative balance, preventing the state from adopting increasingly aggressive forms of action (for example, a sharp coercive apparatus to collect taxes), even if they serve the purposes of social provision. The definition of the limits of the fiscal state expresses an institutional sensitivity necessary to avoid ruptures in the social consensus.

(iii) *Social Differentiation and Group Rights.* The protection of minority groups and interests was a classic example of the procedural positioning of John Hart Ely's representative-reinforcing perspective. While it is true that courts, in applying the principles of equality and nondiscrimination, may be obliged to protect minority social groups in order to defend and reintroduce their interests into the representative process, it is also true that this protection may itself lead to the same phenomena of overrepresentation of interests, especially when other minorities and social groups are kept hidden by this enhanced representation. Protecting the balance of representation thus requires courts to pay institutional attention to the effects of minority representation in order to correct cases in which the legislature may have created imbalances of protection and silenced other unorganized, invisible, or merely politically less powerful groups.

[27] Paolo Cavaliere (2024: 1–10); also, Domingos Farinho (2021: 1–20).

[28] Michael Stolleis (2014: 248).

References

Alexy R (October 2005) Balancing, constitutional review, and representation. Int J Const Law 3(4)

Barroso LR, Osorio A (2019) Democracy, political crisis, and constitutional jurisdiction – the leading role of the Brazilian supreme court, in Christine Landfried. In: Judicial power – how constitutional courts affect political transformations. Cambridge University Press

Böckenförde E-W (2017) Constitutional jurisdiction: structure, organization, and legitimation. In: Constitutional and political theory: selected writings. Oxford University Press

Brady, ADP (2012) Proportionality and deference under the UK human rights act - an institutionally sensitive approach. Cambridge University Press

Cavaliere P (2024) Freedom of expression after disinformation: towards a new paradigm for the right to receive information. J Media Law. https://doi.org/10.1080/17577632.2024.2362482

Coutinho LP (2019) O Estado como Representação – do Momento Hobbesiano aos Problemas Contemporâneos. Associação Académica da Faculdade de Direito da Universidade de Lisboa

Dixon R (2023) Responsive judicial review – democracy and dysfunction in the modern age. Oxford University Press

Doerfler RD, Moyn, S (2022) The ghost of John Hart Ely. Vanderbilt Law Rev 770

Ely JH (1980) Democracy and distrust

Farinho D (2021) The new "right to protection against disinformation" in Portugal. E-Publica 8(3)

Grimm D (2016) Constitutionalism – past, present and future. Oxford University Press

Kumm M (2019) On the representativeness of constitutional courts: how to strengthen the legitimacy of rights adjudicating courts without undermining their independence. In: Landfried C (ed) Judicial power: how constitutional courts affect political transformations. Cambridge University Press

Lomba P (2015) Democracia, representação política e Constituição social. Democracy, political representation and social Constitution. e-publica

Manent P (2004) Cours familier de Philosophie Politique. Gallimard

Manent P (2008) A Razão das Nações. Edições 70

Manin B (1997) The Principles of representative government. Cambridge University Press, Cambridge

Montesquieu (2011) L'esprit des lois, Paris, Classiques Garnier

Pitkin H (1967) The concept of representation

Stolleis M (2014) History of social law in Germany. Springer, Heidelberg. https://doi.org/10.1007/978-3-642-38454-7

Sieyès EJ (2002) Qu'est-ce que le Tiers état ? Éditions du Boucher, Paris

Urbinati N (2006) Representative democracy - principles and genealogy. The Chicago University Press

A Misguided Quest?

Representation, Constitutional Courts, and Divided Power

Pasquale Pasquino(✉)

Politics Department, New York University, New York, NY, USA
pasquinopasquale@gmail.com

> First Chinese speaker: "The Standing Committee does usually have two roles. The first one is that it is a sort of institution for power sharing. So, this is a value as which, in all the interests you know, factions, clicks, groups within the party right, get *representation* and get the recognized and acknowledged right by having a seat". (Columbia University, 31st October 2022, seminar on the 20th Congress of CCP).

Abstract. Starting from the classical definition of representation as the term designating the authority authorized and accountable via popular elections, the chapter claims that the institutions exercising constitutional adjudication cannot be considered representative – at least not in the same sense. Given that electoral representation is the mark assigning legitimacy to law-making state organs of modern democracy, the chapter explores a better path to justify the rationale for the existence of constitutional courts in stable liberal democracies, going back to the Western doctrines of good government as *divided power*.

Keywords: Representation · constitutional adjudication · non-democratic legitimacy · divided power

The term representative/representation was introduced in Western modern political language by Samuel Sorbière in his French translation of Hobbes' *De Cive*[1] and later systematically employed in English by the author of *Leviathan* in his major work.

This exergue shows the need to give a clear definition of the term/concept of representation. This is not a natural object like silver or wood. There is no true concept of representation, only stipulative ones. In Chinese *political* language (the only one I'm considering) it has no connection with the standard Western idea of popular election of the governing authorities, the one from which I start in my contribution.

[1] The term *representation* first appeared in political language in the French translation by Samuel Sorbière of De Cive's Latin version (chap. 6.1, Remark: *Multitudo*): "D'où l'on peut voir la différence que je mets entre cette multitude que je nomme le peuple, qui se gouverne régulièrement par l'autorité du magistrat, qui compose une personne civile, qui nous *représente* tout le corps du public, la ville, ou l'État, et à qui je ne donne qu'une volonté; et cette autre multitude qui ne garde point d'ordre, qui est comme une hydre à cent têtes, et qui doit ne prétendre dans la

L. Pereira Coutinho (Ed.): ICPRCR 2022, IUSGENT 124, pp. 87–92, 2025.
https://doi.org/10.1007/978-3-031-85983-0_7

Representative in the modern Hobbesian language, which has in general been accepted, refers to the subject(s) or institution (for instance an assembly) *authorized* by the citizens to exercise public authority in a commonwealth[2]. For the modern Western political culture, there is no public authority without authorization, authorization by the citizens not by God or nature – like the authority of a King or nobility. Representatives is the name of those who can give citizens orders/laws because they have been authorized by them.

At the end of XVIII century (notably starting with US's constitution and the French Revolution) the idea of authorization took the distinct legal form of repeated, free, and competitive elections, and the political regime based on the elections the name of *republic* (characterized at its outset by the limited franchise – in French: *suffrage censitaire*). This political order based on the authority of elected and electorally accountable officials, during the 19th century, also because of the extension of the franchise and not only because of Tocqueville, got the misleading name of (representative) democracy – where the crucial term is the adjective – so that it would be better to speak of representative government *tout court*. I say *misleading* because what we call representative democracy is not a popular government, but a regime where the public authority is authorized but non exercised by the citizens[3] – as it was exceptionally and in radically different historical circumstances in the Athenian *demokratia*.

So said, if we identify our representative regime with elections and electoral accountability of political authority, as contemporary descriptive political science does, thus accepting the claim that there is no representation without election – which can be attributed to Sieyes (Pasquino 2008) –, then constitutional adjudication by a court of justice is not a representative (in the usual parlance) a democratic institution. Given that it is an institution controlling or better moderating representative democracy, as I shall try to explain.

Before arguing this claim, I need to specify the meaning of some words/concepts I will use in my remarks.

The language of representative government (*vulgo* democracy, as Norberto Bobbio used to say) is a rhetoric based on a double synecdoche, that is a figure of speech in which a term for a part of something is used to refer to the whole.

(1. First) The will of the representatives (which is an artifact produced by the algorithm we call electoral law) is identified with the will of the people, where in fact what is called popular will is just the will of the representatives.

---

république qu'à la gloire de l'obéissance." Available at http://classiques.uqac.ca/classiques/hobbes_thomas/le_citoyen/le_citoyen.html, p. 81: Remarque. This text seems in fact to be missing in the Latin version of the same work; published in Amsterdam in 1647. The French translation of 1649 was prepared by Sorbière jointly with Hobbes who was living in Paris.

[2] The specific form of authorization according to Hobbes is a question not relevant in the context of this chapter. But it is connected to his theory of equal rights of the members of a political community, which destroys any forms of natural hierarchy and natural authority among them, as famously in Sir Robert Filmer's *Patriarcha or The Natural Power of Kings*, published after his death in 1680.

[3] As Schumpeter argued clearly in his book on *Capitalism, Socialism, and Democracy* (1942). His theory, being deskriptive, was disqualified as elitist!

(2. Second) The will of the majority of the Parliament as such it is attributed is predicated on the will of the institution as such.

We need moreover to consider that most political systems we know nowadays in the West are a combination between representative government and *Rechtstaat* (in English *rule of law*). We designate this combination as a *liberal democracy* – an expression systematically used notably in the text of German *Grundgesetz* – the constitution of 1949[4].

Given that constitutional courts are not made up by elected and electorally accountable public officials we can agree that they are not representative institutions, at least in the standard meaning of the term that I just presented.

For sure it is possible to play with the semantics of the term[5] – representation is not a natural object, and its meaning does depend on the definition we stipulate. Rather than exploring other possible meanings of the term, allowing through a redefinition, to show that Constitutional Courts are representative, my choice is to explore an alternative historical and not simply normative foundation and genealogy of constitutional adjudication.

Recent political developments in our societies gave birth to regimes designated by their leaders as "illiberal democracies", such as they exist nowadays in Hungry and Poland, which are a clear instantiation of political systems that refuse any form of control upon the double synecdoche of the parliamentary majority. Relevant in this perspective the texts by Béla Pokol[6].

In the following short remarks, I will present briefly what I believe is the non-democratic/non-representative legitimacy of constitutional adjudication showing that it is an essential element of the contemporary structure of divided power (in the American traditional language "checks and balances") - a point hinted but made not sufficiently clear by Hans Kelsen in his criticism of Carl Schmitt's theory, who in his *Hüter der Verfassung* [1931] against Kelsen wanted to assign the function of guardian of a rigid constitution to an *elected* accountable and hence democratic – as he said – president. I shall consider moreover the *conditions of the success* of constitutional adjudication, which presuppose at the same time specific rules for the appointment of the members of the Court, as well as a firm culture of liberalism inside the citizens of a given society.

I need to give a clear definition of the terms I use. By *divided power*, I mean the idea, typical of Western political thought, which opposes any form of monocratic power. From Aristotle through Montesquieu the classical doctrine of divided power was based on an anatomy of society, which presupposed the existence of distinct parts of the city (*mere tes poleos*, in the Aristotelian doctrine). They could check each other to avoid the structure of monocratic authority, a topic revived in Modern Europe in the fight against absolutism. The existence of such anatomy of the society based on the existence of

---

4 "*Freiheitliche demokratische Grundordnung*" (art.11, 18, 21, 87a, 91).

5 Think of the following American usage of the term; you call Citibank, and you get an automatic answer saying: "Stay on the line, you will speak with the next available *representative*"!

6 A member of the Hungarian Constitutional Court, appointed by Viktor Orban: *A Sociology of Constitutional Adjudication*, Passau, 2015 and "The Juristocratic Form of Government and its Structural Issues", Pázmány Law Working Papers, 2016/9.

ranks, estates, or *Stände* as the foundation of the anti-absolutist model of government is exposed in Montesquieu's chapter 6 of the Book xi of his *Spirit of Laws* where we read:

> *"Il y a toujours, dans un état, des gens distingués par la naissance, les richesses ou les honneurs: mais, s'ils étoient confondus parmi le peuple, & s'ils n'y avoient qu'une voix comme les autres, la liberté commune seroit leur esclavage, & ils n'auroient aucun intérêt à la défendre ; parce que la plupart des résolutions seroient contre eux. La part qu'ils ont à la législation, doit donc être proportionnée aux autres avantages qu'ils ont dans l'état ; ce qui arrivera, s'ils forment un corps qui ait droit d'arrêter les entreprises du peuple, comme le peuple a droit d'arrêter les leurs. Ainsi, la puissance législative sera confiée & au corps des nobles, & au corps qui sera choisi pour représenter le peuple, qui auront chacun leurs assemblées & leurs délibérations à part, & des vues & des intérêts séparés."*[7]

The cultural revolution introduced by the American Constitution and theorized notably by James Madison (see *Federalist Papers* # 47–51) aimed to reproduce the mechanism of anti-monocratic power introducing the divided power in the *republican* model of a *society without qualities*, a society of equal citizens that rejected inside the structure of the new divided power both the King and the nobility (Montesquieu's *gens distingués par la naissance, les richesses ou les honneurs*). The solution as we know was the distribution of the *sovereign legislative power* among the three elected and electorally accountable branches designated by the constitution to exercise that supreme authority: the House of Representatives, the Senate, and the President (thanks to his legislative veto power).

As Rick Pildes and Daryl Levinson showed in a seminal article some years ago[8], the advent of political parties able to control the three branches may defeat the system of counterpowers imagined by Madison. This problem is even more evident in parliamentary systems where the relation between executive and legislative cannot be characterized most of the time as a structure of checks and balances. (Even though the Parliament can dismiss the government and in some constitutional systems the executive disbands the Parliament). I do not need to enter here into the details of these crucial questions. My point is to draw attention to the weakness of the counterpowers structure in the contemporary representative governments, which are indeed *Parteienstaaten* (Kelsen). Therefore, the need of looking outside the representative electoral regime to restore in some way the project of a moderate, anti-monocratic regime, in a society where the citizens are not divided in ranks or estates with unequal rights.

---

[7] The old translation of that text in English by Thomas Nugent (1752) says: "In such a state there are always persons distinguished by their birth, riches, or honours: but were they to be confounded with the common people, and to have only the weight of a single vote like the rest, the common liberty would be their slavery, and they would have no interest in supporting it, as most of the popular resolutions would be against them. The share they have, therefore, in the legislature ought to be proportioned to their other advantages in the state; which happens only when they form a body that has a right to check the licentiousness of the people, as the people have a right to oppose any encroachment of theirs."

[8] "Separation of Parties, Not Powers", *Harvard Law Review,* 2006.

Carl Schmitt hostile to the judicial review of the legislation, recognizing the need for a guardian of the constitution (unlike other more radical theorists of the so-called *juris-tocracy* – Schmitt was not a critic of constitutional guardianship), suggested to assigning this function to the *elected* – democratic, he said – president of the Republic, chosen by the citizens and accountable to them, as the regular representatives.[9] Unfortunately, in his attempt to utilize Constant's theory of the *pouvoir neutre*, Schmitt disregarded the inevitable partisan character of any elected and accountable official, who may be the expression of the same segment of the political forces controlling the Parliamentary majority. This is the reason why only non-elected officials, under the conditions I will specify, may try to guarantee a structure of divided power.

Hans Kelsen in his polemical answer to Schmitt, *Wer soll der Hüter der Verfassung sein?* (1931) in a long footnote (n.10) quotes his text *Wesen und Entwicklung der Staats-gerichtsbarkeit* (1929) where we read the following interesting remarks concerning the objection that the constitutional adjudication violates the separation of powers:

"In the annulment of a law by a court one could thus see as much an 'interference' in legislative power as the entrusting of legislative power to two organs [...] So it happens, for example, when, in the constitution of constitutional monarchy, legislation, that is, the production of general legal norms, is as a rule entrusted to parliament together with the monarch [...] And the concept of the distribution of power among various organs and not so much for the purpose of their mutual isolation as for the purpose of their mutual control." (my translation).[10]

The conditions of which I spoke are 1. First - independence of the judiciary, 2. Second - appointment of the judges by the super-majority of the representative assemblies, 3. Third - political culture of the citizen supporting the Rule of law (*Rechtstaat*).

I want to finish quoting the French Constitution 1791, section 7, art. 8 reads:

"The National Constituent Assembly entrusts the safekeeping thereof [the guardian-ship of the constitution] to the fidelity of the legislative body, of the King, and of the judges, to the vigilance of fathers of families, to wives and to mothers, to the affection of young citizens, to the courage of all Frenchmen"[11] (We know that the King, Louis the 16th was not respectful of the constitution and not to his benefit).

---

[9] See his *Der Hüter der Verfassung*, Berlin 1931.

[10] " *Man könnte somit in der Aufhebung eines Gesetzes durch ein Gericht ebenso wie einen „Eingriff" in die gesetzgebende Gewalt die Übertragung der gesetzgebenden Gewalt auf zwei Organe verstehen...So, wenn z.B. in der Verfassung konstitutioneller Monarchien die Geset-zgebung, d.i. die Erzeugung genereller Rechtsnormen, zwar in der Regel dem Parlament in Verbindung mit dem Monarchen übertragen wird ... Es ist der Gedanke der Aufteilung der Macht auf verschiedene Organe, nicht so sehr zum Zweck ihrer gegenseitigen Isolierung, als vielmehr zu dem ihrer gegenseitigen Kontrolle"*. (German edition, Mohr Siebeck, Tübingen, 2019, p.79–80).

[11] " L'Assemblée nationale constituante en remet le dépôt [de la constitution] à la fidélité du Corps législatif, <du roi> et des juges, à la vigilance des pères de famille, aux épouses et aux mères, à l'affection des jeunes citoyens, au courage de tous les Français".

References

Filmer R (1680, 2012) Patriarcha or the natural power of kings; contemporary edition: Patriarcha and other writings. Cambridge University Press, Cambridge

Hobbes Th (1649) De Cive, French translation by Samuel Sorbière. http://classiques.uqac.ca/classiques/hobbes_thomas/le_citoyen/le_citoyen.html

Kelsen H (1929) Wesen und Entwicklung der Staatsgerichtsbarkeit. In: Wesen und Entwicklung der Staatsgerichtsbarkeit. Verhandlungen der Tagung der Deutschen Staatsrechtslehrer zu Wien am 23. und 24. April 1928, new edition. Mohr Siebeck, Tübingen pp 30–84

Kelsen H (1931, 2019) Wer soll der Hüter der Verfassung sein? Berlin-Grunewald: W. Rothschild, new edition. Mohr Siebeck, Tübingen

Madison J, Hamilton A, Jay J (1788, 2012) The Federalist papers; contemporary edition: Cambridge University Press, Cambridge (2012)

Montesquieu (1748, 1989) L'esprit des lois, contemporary English translation, the spirit of laws. Cambridge University Press, Cambridge

Pasquino P (2008) Constitution et pouvoir constituant: le double corps du peuple. In: Figures de Sieyes. Publications de la Sorbonne. de la Sorbonne, Paris, pp 13–23

Pildes R, Levinson D (2006) Separation of parties, not powers. Harv Law Rev 119(8):2312–2385

Pokol B (2015) A sociology of constitutional adjudication. Schenk Verlag, Passau

Pokol B (2016) The juristocratic form of government and its structural issues. Pázmány law working papers 9

Schmitt C (1931) Hüter der Verfassung. Dunker & Humblot, Berlin

Schumpeter JA (1942) Capitalism, socialism, and democracy. Harper & Brothers, New York City

Sieyès EJ (1875) Reprise de la discussion sur l'organisation du pouvoir législatif et la sanction royale, lors de la séance du 7 septembre 1789. Archives Parlementaires de 1787 à 1860 - Première série (1787–1799), Tome VIII - Du 5 mai 1789 au 15 septembre 1789. Librairie Administrative P. Dupont, Paris, pp 592–601

The Representation of the Representation or Is This a Pipe?

Michel Troper(✉)

University of Paris X, Nanterre, France
Michel.troper@gmail.com

Abstract. This chapter discusses various attempts to reconcile judicial review with the democratic principle, in particular the claim that constitutional courts do not go against the general will expressed by elected representatives, because these elected representatives represent the general will only in accordance with the Constitution, or because one ought to consider the courts themselves as representatives. These attempts fail, so that the contemporary constitutional systems cannot be described as democratic, but only as mixed governments comprising a democratic element, the elected representatives, and an aristocratic element, the constitutional judges.

Keywords: constitutional courts · representative democracy · representation of representation · mixed government

1 Judicial Review: Strategies of Legitimation

This chapter addresses a relatively simple question: can the existence and action of constitutional courts be reconciled with the idea of representative democracy? This question, referred to as the "the counter-majoritarian difficulty" on the other side of the Atlantic, results above all from the fact that the constitutional courts, composed of judges generally unelected and chosen in any case not for their opinions but for their technical competence, are able to invalidate laws adopted by elected representatives of the sovereign people (Bickel 1986; Troper 2003).

A first group of arguments simply denies that there is a contradiction. Two opposed strategies can be involved in that denial. A first strategy contends that the court does not enjoy any discretion and therefore cannot oppose the will of the majority. A second strategy, while admitting that the court does have some margin of discretion, contends that the will expressed by Parliament which can be invalidated by the court is not really the will of the people.

The first strategy depends of course on the argument that the court merely applies the constitution, which is set out in a clear text or at least endowed with a meaning that competent jurists can discover by means of certain appropriate methods, without their personal preferences affecting their interpretation. There is thus no contradiction between constitutional review and democracy.

L. Pereira Coutinho (Ed.): ICPRCR 2022, IUSGENT 124, pp. 93–103, 2025.
https://doi.org/10.1007/978-3-031-85983-0_8

A variant of this thesis, devised by Kelsen and widespread in France under the name "switchman's theory", consists in maintaining that the constitutional court does not rule on the substance of the law, but only on the procedure: if it invalidates an act of Parliament, it is only because Parliament has acted outside of the limits prescribed by the constitution, i.e., the rule it wanted to prescribe could not have been adopted according to the legislative procedure but only in the form reserved for constitutional amendments (Vedel 1988 [1991]: 209–219). Therefore, the Constitutional Council, like a switchman, redirects the rule to its proper track which is the constituent power.

In its two variants, the first strategy of denial faces a major difficulty: the text of the constitution is written in ordinary language, which is necessarily vague and ambiguous, and must therefore be interpreted. Interpretation is a function not of knowledge but of the will, its result being a decision, which as such cannot be true or false but only valid or invalid (valid when it emanates from an authority empowered for that purpose; invalid in other cases). However, interpretations given by a constitutional court are not subject to appeal. They are therefore valid by definition, whatever their content – they are considered authentic – and, as long as they have not been overturned by a new interpretation, the constitutional text has no other meaning than the one given to it by the court. This idea also applies to the "switchman", who, before determining which procedure should have been chosen, must have interpreted the constitutional text in order to find what are the limits of Parliament's power.

If it is true that the decision is not a matter of legal technique, but of will – being therefore valid whatever its content – it follows that the judge does have a discretionary power, being able to assert his preferences – whether moral, religious, political, or economic.

The second strategy of denial that there is a contradiction is to change the concept of democracy, which will then no longer be defined as the power of the people or their majority. Thus avoiding the "counter-majoritarian difficulty", some authors will argue that democracy essentially consists not in some specific procedural rules, but in the guarantee of certain objective values, in particular the protection of fundamental rights.

It is important to note that those who thus change the concept of democracy do not always admit that the court exercises discretion. The so-called "new-constitutionalists" also deny that the court exercises discretion but they do so on slightly different terms than those who argue that the court merely follows classic legal methods. The assumption that appropriate methods allow the competent jurist to determine an objective legal meaning is no longer at stake, but rather the defense of the idea that the court has the means to discover objective values, its decisions reflecting them in a neutral and impartial manner (Comanducci 2002: 72; Pozzolo 2020).

A third strategy of defense of judicial review does not aim at denying that there is a contradiction between judicial review and democracy. Rather, it focuses on the need for limits to democracy, considering it a threat to liberty when it is conceived as absolute. Proponents of this thesis refer to Montesquieu, who stressed that "it is necessary that, by the arrangement of things, power shall stop power". From this perspective, the court is therefore considered as a necessary counter-power. Some authors go so far as to admit that a political system with a constitutional court is not a democracy but a mixed regime (a mix of democracy and aristocracy) or a divided government (Pasquino 2013).

However, this strategy is problematic: it may be tricky to acknowledge that the court is not a democratic institution when the constitution claims to be democratic in its text, and the court itself claims to apply it. Thus, in order to reconcile the exercise of significant power by non-elected judges with the principle of democratic government, it becomes necessary to imagine the courts not as anti-democratic but a as democratic institutions.

Those who go in that direction stress that the courts are not cut off from the people nor do they make general and abstract decisions, but that, although not elected, they are profoundly influenced by public opinion (Friedman 2009). Such theories have not gained much attention in France: they would be implausible in a context, such as the French, in which public opinion has been for a very long time completely indifferent to the Constitutional Council. Moreover, the sociological nature of the argument could hardly be accepted in a constitutional law culture whose concepts, going back to the Revolution, have been channeled through the German school of public law, having consequently been framed within a legal dogmatics tinted with metaphysics.

It becomes therefore necessary to reason in terms of sovereignty and representation. Hence the temptation of some leading French philosophers and legal scholars to construct a theory by which the Constitutional Council is a democratic institution, not because it is elected but because it is nonetheless a representative of the sovereign people. It is this temptation that I wish to analyze in this chapter. I will first examine the origins of the temptation to make the constitutional judge a representative, then describe some attempts in this direction and finally show the formidable difficulties that make it impracticable.

2 The Temptation

For French constitutionalists, the temptation has its origin in the revolutionary conception of representation as it was expounded by Barnave on August 10, 1791. Let me briefly summarize this conception.

According to Article 6 of the Declaration of the Rights of Man and the Citizen of 1789, "[t]he law is the expression of the general will. All citizens have the right to participate personally or through their representatives in its formation". It is therefore necessary that, in the absence of personal participation, which is mentioned only regarding natural law, the law must be made exclusively by representatives. But who are or should these representatives be?

After 1789 it took two years to answer this question. In fact, the Constituent Assembly only faced it at the time of the "revision" of the constitution; "revision" meaning in this context the process of giving the text a final reading in order to make it more coherent before its final adoption. The text submitted to this process by the constitution committee of the Assembly included a provision stating that "the French constitution is representative and the representatives are the legislative body and the king". This proposal was strongly criticized by the left, notably by Roederer and Robespierre, for whom the King, for lack of being elected, could not be called a representative. Their secret purpose was, should they succeed in removing the King's qualification as a "representative", to deprive him of the legislative power that had previously been granted to him. Indeed, since the law is defined as the expression of the general will, only a representative of the people should be entitled take part in that expression.

Against Robespierre and Roederer, Barnave turned the reasoning upside down and stressed that the King does not participate in the exercise of the legislative power because he is a representative. Rather, he is a representative because he participates in the legislative power. That he does was a question already answered in the affirmative as early as the autumn of 1789, when the constituent assembly had decided that the King could either grant or withhold his assent to the laws approved by the legislative body. Since that had already been settled, at this moment Mit was only pertinent to discuss the best justification for the solution, i.e., to reconstruct the logic of the Declaration of the Rights of Man. Barnave points out that the Declaration does not state that the law *should* be the expression of the general will, but that, as a consequence of natural law, there is a presumption that every legitimate law necessarily expresses the general will. Hence, all those who participate in the adoption of the law participate in the expression of the general will and cannot be called anything but representatives of the sovereign, i.e. of the nation.

Therefore, in this logic, representation has nothing to do with a method of appointment, being instead a justification for a constitutionally granted participation in the legislative branch. Besides, if the status of representative were to depend on an election, local authorities and judges, appointed by popular election, would have to be called "representatives", which would obviously be absurd. The logic thus imputed by Barnave to the Declaration is crucial for understanding the temptation. Within it, representation is no longer a predicate depending on election by the people but on the legislative power one has received or that one claims.

Carré de Malberg has rightly pointed out that this conception of representation is a monistic one: unlike representation in private law, which is a relationship between two persons (by which a representative entrusts a mandate to a representative to will and act on his behalf), in constitutional representation there is only one entity: the sovereign, people or nation. Because the sovereign is only a collective and abstract entity, it is unable to form and express a will that it could transmit to the representative. Therefore, the will formed and expressed by the representatives *is* the general will (Carré de Malberg 2004).

Hence the temptation to mimic this reasoning in order to justify constitutional justice: if the judge, by exercising discretion when reviewing the constitutionality of laws, is actually a part of the legislative power – if, therefore, like the king in 1791, he is a co-legislator –, then he participates in the expression of the general will and he too must therefore be considered a representative of the sovereign.

Yet, it would be very difficult to use Barnave's model to justify constitutional review in a modern political system, particularly in the Fifth Republic. Saying that the constitutional judge is a representative depends on identifying the entity he is representing and also what will he is supposed to express. In a monist model that entity – and that will – can be none other than the general will. But how could one plausibly claim that the court represents the general will, i.e. the sovereign people, against its own elected representatives? The only possibility is to claim that the latter do not really express the "true" general will, i.e., that the judge is able to compare the will expressed by the sovereign with the "true" general will. However, such a claim is absurd in a monist model, since it does not allow for any conceptual difference, and thus for any comparison, between the general will as expressed and a "true" general will.

Because of this impossibility, Georges Vedel, a famous law Professor who was also a member of the Constitutional Council, forged a formula, which the Council repeated many times when justifying some important decisions. According to this formula, "the law expresses the general will only in accordance with the constitution". Thus, judicial review of legislation does not consist in a comparison between the will expressed by the representatives and the "real" will of the sovereign people. Rather, it is a simple verification that the Parliament qualifies as a representative, compliance with the constitution being therefore a mere identification tool. Unfortunately, this theory only works well if the identification is made by confrontation with procedural rules (e.g. rules regulating elections and deliberations).

The mechanism of Vedel's theory works like the mechanism of any legal presumption (*v.g.* the presumption of paternity according to which the husband of a married woman is the father of her child). In both cases, the mechanism only works when it is easy to verify whether the condition is satisfied. But the situation is entirely different when the so-called "verification" depends on a value judgment and thus on a decision. For example, if the Constitution directs the legislature to treat all subjects equally, it cannot be ascertained whether or not the law has subjected this or that category to equal treatment without first interpreting the word "equally". As we know, this is a decision even if based on a legal text.

In sum, whether Parliament is a representative depends, not on a verification, but on a decision by the Constitutional Council. Contrary to Vedel's claim, the proposition "*Parliament is a representative*" (or "the law expresses the general will") is not a consequence of the proposition "*the law is in accordance with the constitution*". In fact, the two sentences are synonymous and express one and the same decision. Vedel's theory is thus only a variant of the flawed idea that the judge does not decide, but merely ascertains the meaning of the law.

Therefore, those authors who wish to maintain that Parliament is a representative not because of a presumption or a fiction, but because it really expresses the will of the people must switch from a monist to a dualist conception, within which the people and their representatives are seen as two real beings, both capable of forming and expressing a will. The supposed existence of two wills allows for a comparison. Moreover, if one departs from a democratic ideology, a dualist conception apparently has great advantages, since in it "the people" is finally given its own voice. One way or the other, the Constitutional Council unmistakably is a beneficiary of this conception: its authority is now conceived as that which makes the "true" will of the people prevail over that of its elected representatives.

However, this pattern leads to another formidable difficulty: if the will of the people is no longer the one expressed by its elected representatives, how can it be expressed and how can it be known? The proponents of this version of the dualist conception have a ready answer: the people are represented by the constitutional judge. This answer is question-begging, since the real problem is to know how a non-elected judge can be justified in expressing the will of the people in its place – assuming that the people is a real, non fictitious entity who could after all express its own will.

This is the reason why this theory has been abandoned by most authors, giving way to another, more sophisticated, but just as fragile, theory: that the Council is the medium that allows for the functioning of a representative democracy.

3 A Tentative Theory: The Representation of Representation

Because they dare not go as far as to write that the Constitutional Council is a representative of the people, a few prominent authors resort to a rather strange construction, which they illustrate with the help of a few formulas that vary slightly and which moreover are sometimes combined with the simpler and more traditional ones. I will briefly analyze two of these authors, Dominique Rousseau, professor of constitutional law and Marcel Gauchet, a philosopher, although Pierre Rosanvallon, a sociologist and historian uses very similar argument. It is remarkable that all of them are scholars and that neither the Constitutional Council as a body nor any of its members feel the need to use the justification they propose. What is common to the constructions designed by these authors is the idea that what the Constitutional Council represents is not some abstract entity like the people or the sovereign, that must necessarily be represented because it is essentially incapable of expressing or even forming a will. What the Constitutional Council represents is representation itself.

Dominique Rousseau begins by admitting that the constitutional judge has discretionary power, that he participates in the formation of the law and that we live in a "competitive regime of enunciation of the general will" in which take part the executive, which has the initiative and prepares bills, the parliament which votes them, and the constitutional judge which verifies whether they comply with the constitution. The judge is therefore recognized as a co-legislator. However, Rousseau is reluctant to follow Barnave's logic and thus to consider the Council a representative of the people.

No doubt this hesitation is due to the fact that Barnave's logic is based on a monistic conception of representation, which is difficult to reconcile with the democratic nature of control. As seen above, in the monistic conception, the sovereign only exists and wills through its representatives. However, democratic control, according to Dominique Rousseau, should consist in comparing what representatives do with the real will of the represented. Still, Rousseau accepts the idea that the Council actually makes decisions – being a co-legislator – and he cannot be satisfied with a mere transposition of Vedel's argument, which was still part of a monistic vision and thus radically incompatible with the idea that the constitutional judge compares the will expressed by the Parliament with a real will.

Rousseau therefore clearly calls for a dualistic vision: *"By "evidencing" that the two spaces – the will expressed by the elected representatives and the people's will – may not coincide and that, in the event of a conflict, the will of the citizens prevails over that of the representatives, the constitutional judge prohibits the representatives from claiming that they are the sovereign*" (2015: 230).

According to Rousseau, the very existence of the constitutional judge, and its power to invalidate unconstitutional laws, give evidence that laws voted by Parliament do not always express the general will – although they sometimes do. Therefore, the will of the representatives should not be confused with that of the sovereign, a gap separating the representatives from the represented. The Constitutional Council thus highlights the nature and limits of political representation while "putting representation in representation"[1]. This dualistic vision of representation purports to be more democratic and to provide for a democracy understood as the rule of citizens of flesh and blood. It theoretically achieves that result since citizens are understood to express their will in a continuous manner and not only in periodical elections. In sum, the Constitutional Council is understood here as the main instrument of a "continuous democracy".

The same observation can be made about Marcel Gauchet's thesis, which proposes an original and nuanced version of the Kelsenian or Vedelian theory while continuing Dominique Rousseau's reflection on continuous democracy, to which he refers expressly (Gauchet 1995: 44 note 1)[2]. It is also the thesis that gives representation the most important role.

Like Rousseau, Gauchet seeks a way to ensure continuous control of the rulers outside election moments. For him, it is the constitutional judge who makes it possible without being himself a representative. Gauchet is clear regarding this point, affirming that the constitutional judge "in no way affects the functions of the representatives; it does not introduce a competition of representations". Rather, he "represents the fact that [the sovereignty of the people] must have the last word".

Gauchet warns us not to confuse the sovereign people, who must have the last word, with Parliament, or even with the voters, who are themselves the representatives of the true sovereign. "The people who choose and vote are themselves only momentary representatives of the power of the perpetual people, the one who endures identical to itself through the succession of generations and who constitutes the true holder of sovereignty." Therefore, the present people cannot derogate the corresponding constitutional principles, the constitutional review of legislation being a "perpetual appeal to the people against the present people".

4 Objections to the Theory

4.1 The Difficulties that Make the Theory Impracticable

The theory that the Constitutional Council, without being a representative of the sovereign people, *represents representation itself* faces several difficulties: we may distinguish ideological difficulties (Sect. 4.2), institutional difficulties (Sect. 4.3) and intellectual difficulties (Sect. 4.4).

4.2 Ideological Difficulties

In a democratic culture, the people that claims representation supposedly is the real, concrete people. This claim can hardly be matched with a justification for the existence of a Constitutional Council that qualifies it as a representative. The theories under scrutiny presuppose the monistic conception that the people, either is the constituent people

[1] Rousseau borrows this formula from Gauchet, whose theory will be analyzed shortly.

[2] Gauchet writes that "the constitutional judge is not in charge of representing the sovereignty of the people… He is in charge of putting in representation the fact that she must have the last word." (1995: 42).

(whose will is embodied in the text of the constitution adopted many decades or even centuries ago) or a totally fictitious perpetual people, the latter being the case in Gauchet. In both cases, the will expressed by elected representatives is subject to a superior will, which cannot really be considered as democratic. As Pierre Joxe, a former socialist MP, once said of the Constitutional Council (before becoming himself a member): "we represent the people, they represent politicians, majorities of yesteryear"[3]. Joxe was indeed merely paraphrasing Jefferson in a letter to Madison "I set out on this ground, which I suppose to be self evident, 'that the earth belongs in usufruct to the living' that the dead have neither powers nor rights over it [and] no society can make a perpetual constitution, or even a perpetual law" (Jefferson 1958: 392–8).

4.3 Institutional Difficulties

The Constitutional Council must necessarily claim that it is applying the constitution. However, the constitution is based on a theory of representation that makes every organ participating in the exercise of the legislative power a representative. Therefore, the Constitutional Council could not claim to be a representative without acknowledging at least a participation in the legislative power. Since that is not acceptable from a democratic point of view, the Council consistently and expressly denies exercising such a power, explaining that "it does not have the same discretion as Parliament". Above all, the constitutional judge has no need to claim to be a representative in order to give himself legitimacy, since it is sufficient for him to repeat that he is limited to applying the constitution and that this constitution is democratic, provided that democracy means a set of fundamental values.

4.4 Intellectual Difficulties

It must first be emphasized that in the expressions "representation of representation" or "to put representation in representation", the word "representation" in taken in two different senses: in a first sense, it means that one evidences, shows or highlights something, as it happens with a pictorial or theatrical representation; in a second sense, a legal or political sense, it means the capacity to speak or to act in the name of some other person or of an abstract entity. The French or the English language use the same word for these two different concepts while the Italian language has two different words: *rappresentazione* for illustration and *rappresentenza* for political representation (Albertone, Troper 2021).

Certainly, this distinction between the two meanings of the word "representation" does not disqualify the theory that the Constitutional Council represents representation. We might even think that it clarifies it. The theory can be restated as meaning that the Council's very existence shows that we live in a representative democracy. The existence of the Constitutional Council and its jurisprudence allow us to understand that members of Parliament are representatives, not because they have been elected, but because the Constitution establishes them as such. Representation is thus an institutional fiction

---

[3] Quoted by Alain Delcamp, «Le Conseil constitutionnel et le Parlement» [archive], www.cairn.info, janvier 2004.

whose legitimating function only works within limits: representatives are only those who respect the Constitution.

Basically, we would be in a situation opposite to that of Magritte's famous painting "This is not a pipe", which is the image of a pipe with the inscription "this is not a pipe" underneath. Indeed, it is not a real pipe, but only the representation of a pipe. Magritte surely did not want to stress the obvious for who would mistake the painting of a pipe with a real pipe that one can smoke? Rather, by writing that phrase on the painting itself, his intention seems to have been to criticize a certain conception of painting, i.e., to denounce a certain conception of art, according to which it gives access to the essence or truth of things. Magritte, in that sense was denouncing idolatry, by stressing that what art does no more than represent appearances.

The theory of representation of representation does the opposite. Indeed, at stake here is no longer to denounce, but to rehabilitate idolatry. Instead of telling us that representation is not the real thing, the theory tells us: representation is a good thing, representing the perpetual people is a good thing and the Constitutional Council that represents representation is the instrument to construct this idol. Thanks to the Council, we understand that you live under a representative government. "This is indeed a pipe" is what is meant.

The theory is thus coherent in the sense that it does justify the existence of the Constitutional Council and its relation to representation. However, being coherent is not sufficient for such a theory. Indeed, the theory must also fulfill its purpose, which is to justify both the existence of the Constitutional Council and its necessary character in the context of "democratic representation". This means that the theory must demonstrate that the system is a democracy while not using arguments that could compromise the claimed legitimacy of the Constitutional Council in such a system. Unfortunately, the theory does not satisfy those two conditions.

It does not show that the system is democratic, because it cannot demonstrate in dualistic fashion that a comparison is made by the Constitutional Council between the will of the real people and the will of its representatives. On the contrary, what is being really compared is the will of the elected representatives with the will of the Constitutional Council as it transpires in its decisions when interpreting the Constitution. In truth, the conception of representation that is being proposed by the theory is not really dualistic but monistic. That is, the theory depends on the argument that representation is a necessary fiction (or that we live with that fiction) without ever showing that behind the fiction the people in whose name laws are made is real and able to form a will with which the will of representatives could be compared.

On the other hand, far from showing the necessity or even the usefulness of the theory for the Council, these authors fail to mention the fact that the Council carefully avoids it, never claiming that it is a representative or a co-representative. It is worth remembering that while every act of Parliament, every single judicial decision in France starts with the words "in the name of the French people", the Constitutional Council merely decides in its own name.

In fact, using the theory of representing representation would be counterproductive, even more so if it involves claiming that the supreme authority is a perpetual people and not the real people. Indeed, a claim that transfers sovereignty to a purely abstract entity – in truth nothing but the dummy of a ventriloquist Council – is very much vulnerable to the accusation that it is antidemocratic.

The Constitutional Council reveals itself to be more astute than the said theorists in what concerns its own legitimating tools. As long as the Constitutional Council maintains the myth that it merely applies the constitution in a neutral and impartial manner, thus claiming not to exercise any discretion, it has no need to present itself as a representative of the people, and even less to resort to sophisticated theories that conceive it as a representative of representation. In order to claim that it does not oppose the elected representatives of the people and that it does not constitute a limit to democracy, it is enough for it to repeat the magic formula "the law expresses the general will only in accordance with the constitution".

5 Conclusion

Finally, it is only the myth that the judge is neutral and impartial, being merely the "mouthpiece of the constitution" that is used to pretend that the Council is, if not a democratic institution, at least not an undemocratic one.

However, recognizing that it is a myth should not lead us to think we live in a pure and simple government by the judiciary or a juristocracy. It is more accurate to think that ours is a mixed government, in which political power is exercised *jointly*, as one used to say in 18th century England. Indeed, power is exercised both by a democratic element, at least as it is traditionally called (an elected Parliament) and another element, not usually called aristocratic, but that in fact can be predicated in that way since its competence is justified by the supposed skill and wisdom of its members. In this mixed government, each of the elements exercises political power in a particular way because of the specific constraints to which it is subject. In the case of parliament these constraints result from the electoral process, party politics, the influence from the executive or the practical necessities related to the matters to be regulated. Those on a constitutional court result from the need to conceal its discretionary power, referral procedures, deliberative rules, the need to maintain as consistent a case-law as possible, and the strategic relations it maintains with the authorities, with which it shares political power (Troper 2006; Paour 2023).

References

Albertone M, Troper M (2021) La représentation politique. Anthologie; Classiques Garnier, Paris

Bickel AM (1986) The least dangerous branch: the supreme court at the bar of politics, 2nd edn. Yale University Press, New Haven

Carré de Malberg R (2004) Contribution à la Théorie générale de l'État. Dalloz, Paris

Comanducci P (2002) Forms of (neo)constitutionalism: a metatheoretical recognition. In: Giappichelli (ed) Neoconstitutionalism and (supra) national protection of fundamental rights, Turin

Friedman B (2009) The will of the people: how public opinion has influenced the supreme court and shaped the meaning of the constitution. Farrar, Straus and Giroux, New York

Gauchet M (1995) La Révolution des pouvoirs. La souveraineté, le peuple et la représentation, Gallimard, Paris, pp 1789–1799
Jefferson T (1958) Thomas Jefferson to James Madison. In: The Papers of Thomas Jefferson, vol 15, 27 March 1789–30 November 1789. Princeton University Press, pp 392–8
Paour R (2023) Le pouvoir des cours constitutionnelles. Société de législation comparé, Paris
Pasquino P (2013) A political theory of constitutional democracy. On the legitimacy of constitutional courts in stable liberal democracies. The Joseph and Gwendolyn Straus Institute for the Advanced Study of Law & Justice. https://www.law.nyu.edu/sites/default/files/siwp/WP4Pasquino.pdf
Pozzolo S (2020) Neoconstitutionalism. In: Sellers M, Kirste S (eds) Encyclopedia of the philosophy of law and social philosophy. Springer, Dordrecht, pp 1–4. https://doi.org/10.1007/978-94-007-6730-0_87-2
Rousseau D (2015) Radicaliser la démocratie: propositions pour une refondation. Seuil, Paris
Troper M (2006) Le gouvernement des juges, mode d'emploi. Presses de l'Université Laval, Sainte-Foy, Québec
Troper M (2003) The logic of justification of judicial review. Int J Const Law 1
Vedel G (1988) Le Conseil constitutionnel, gardien du droit positif ou défenseur de la transcendance des droits de l'homme. Pouvoirs 45:49–59

Legitimacy and the Misguided Quest for a Representative Constitutional Court

Dimitrios Kyritsis(✉)

Essex Law School, Colchester, UK
d.kyritsis@essex.ac.uk

Abstract. This chapter casts doubt on the view, put forward in recent years by Robert Alexy among others, that the legitimacy of constitutional review rests (at least in part) on the fact that constitutional courts are representative institutions. It mounts a three-pronged challenge against Alexy's account. First, it proposes the following litmus test for accounts, such as Alexy's, which portray courts as representatives: they must offer a convincing explanation of the distinctive contribution that the courts' putative representative character makes to political legitimacy such that it justifies that they be given the power of constitutional review. Second, it criticizes Alexy's claim that courts are argumentative representatives in the sense that they represent (many) citizens *qua* rational agents through the way they reason their decisions. However, if the standard of reasoning that judicial decisions must meet is demanding, akin to correctness, then it is not representation that does the moral heavy lifting. And if it is understood as mere plausibility, then it is unclear why we would be bound by a decision solely because it satisfies it. Second, the chapter seeks to undercut the motivation for Alexy's account by arguing against the proposition -which he seems to presuppose- that the legitimacy of a democratic regime depends on its being willed (in the appropriate sense) by the people. In its place the chapter offers a different understanding of legitimacy, informed by the ideal of separation of powers, that provides that government ought to be shaped by different moral forces -not all of which refer back to the people's will. On this understanding, it is morally appropriate, all else being equal, for power to be assigned to a multiplicity of institutions, some representative, some not representative. The upshot of this understanding is that proponents of constitutional review do not have to defend it by fitting it into the representation straitjacket.

1 Introduction

Your country's highest court (or its constitutional court, if it has one) has just decided that the national constitution does not guarantee a right to abortion that would conflict with (and override) any primary legislation excessively hindering or even banning this

I presented earlier versions of this chapter at a conference on political representation and constitutional adjudication at the University of Lisbon and at a workshop on judicial representation organized by Pompeu Fabra University. I thank all participants for their helpful comments. I am especially grateful to Joel Colon-Rios, Luis Pedro Dias Pereira Coutinho, and Pablo Magaña for detailed written feedback.

L. Pereira Coutinho (Ed.): ICPRCR 2022, IUSGENT 124, pp. 104–115, 2025.
https://doi.org/10.1007/978-3-031-85983-0_9

procedure.[1] You disagree vehemently with that decision. Are you nonetheless morally bound by it and on what grounds? For some theorists a big (though by no means the only) part of the answer to this question makes reference to the constitutional court's putative representative credentials. Arguably, to the extent that it is a representative institution, its decisions are in a morally relevant sense *ours* and hence *pro tanto* binding. This view -let's call it the representative-constitutional-court view (RCC)- contrasts sharply to what is probably the dominant justification of constitutional review, according to which constitutional courts are supposed to act as guardians of constitutional norms against an encroaching representative legislature.

In this chapter I want to take issue with RCC. I shall use as my foil the well-known version of it put forward by Robert Alexy, but my interest goes beyond Alexy. I want to offer a general strategy for thinking through the use of political representation in matters of constitutional design, which has at its heart the concept of political legitimacy. My assessment of RCC employs this strategy. Accordingly, I shall make three closely interconnected claims, one methodological and two substantive, all of which develop the theme of political legitimacy. On the methodological front, I shall suggest that the litmus test for evaluating RCC is whether the representative character it attributes to courts makes a distinctive contribution to the political legitimacy of the respective regime. Applying this method, I shall then advance my first substantive challenge against Alexy. I shall argue that Alexy fails to show that the putative representativeness that he attributes to courts makes judicial decisions *our* decisions. It is a stretch to contend, as he does, that such an identification comes about as a result of a constitutional court representing citizens as rational agents.

I recognize, however, that this part of the argument is not without its difficulties. The main one arises from the fact that the concept of representation is very broad and at times ambiguous and seems to leave room for a broad range of different conceptions, including, arguably, those that are congenial to RCC. With this caveat, the second prong of my challenge comes into play. I claim that RCC is insufficiently motivated. Legitimacy is key to this part of the challenge, too. I argue that the extension of the concept of representation it proposes is driven by the wrong understanding of political legitimacy, which says, roughly, that all power must be willed, directly or indirectly, by the people. I canvass a different understanding, whereby legitimacy requires that government ought to be shaped by different moral forces -not all of which have their source in the people's will. On this understanding, it is morally appropriate, all else being equal, for power to be assigned to a multiplicity of institutions, some representative, some not representative. The upshot of this understanding is that proponents of constitutional review do not have to defend it by fitting it into the representation straitjacket.

2 Legitimacy, the Yardstick of Constitutional Theory

Before I proceed with the substantive claims of the paper, in this section I wish to explain the methodology I shall employ. So how ought we to evaluate RCC (and indeed any account of political representation)? One option would be to try to show that the

[1] *Dobbs v. Jackson Women's Health Organization,* No. 19–1392, 597 U.S. ___ (2022).

conception of representation underpinning RCC is not faithful to the understanding of the concept that has been handed down to us from the history of theorizing and practicing representation. Call it what you want, says this critique, but don't call it representation, because we mean something different by 'representation' around here.[2]

This is not only a matter of the correct use of language. The critique has a moral edge as well. Modern political discourse assigns the relationship between the representative and the people a key role for political legitimacy. Hence, if the critique is sound, then a defence of constitutional adjudication cannot rely on any positive moral connotations of seeing judges as representatives of the people; constitutional adjudication will have to stand on different moral ground. But note the order of explanation. It is a historical fact (which understanding of the concept is being or has been practiced around here), not a moral fact, that picks out the correct meaning of political representation. It just so happens that the historical fact has important moral implications. So, morality comes in at a logically subsequent stage.

Although I have some sympathy for this line of argument, I am not going to pursue it in this chapter. Clearing the ambiguities of the concept of representation and tidying up its nuances, tensions, and wrinkles is a risky undertaking. To begin with, the history of the concept is itself untidy and complex. Both the abstract ideal and the historical manifestations of representation have been the focal point of -politically charged- contests and struggles among competing understandings of what it means and requires. Relatedly, it is not clear what theoretical standard governs this exegetical undertaking. On the one hand, we are not seeking historical accuracy, otherwise we would have to rest content to report all the inconsistencies and conflicts in the discourse and practice of representation, but, on the other, we lack the vantage point from which we can dismiss some of the inconsistent and conflicting uses of the concept as mistakes.

That vantage point, I propose, is political morality. Our aim should be to work out a conception of representation that is appealing in light of some broader moral principle such as political equality, democracy and the like. In previous work I have claimed that the particular prism through which we must assess theories about the proper constitutional allocation of power is political legitimacy (Kyritsis 2022; see also Hickey 2022): We must make a case for a certain allocation on the basis that it enhances the legitimacy of the relevant political order. That case will typically proceed from the characteristics of a political institution (e.g. its composition, decision-making process) and then seek to establish what I have elsewhere called a 'purposive interrelation' (Kyritsis 2017, 42–4) between those characteristics and the government task in question. In other words, it will show that, in light of the institution's characteristics, legitimacy recommends that it be assigned the task. Legitimacy is understood here as a moral, not sociological, concept. It is a moral warrant by virtue of which the decisions of a political regime are binding on those who live under it.[3] Needless to say, it is also a controversial concept, so there

[2] Notable examples of this approach are Manin 1997 and Urbinati 2008.

[3] In the philosophical literature on legitimacy a distinction is commonly drawn between the legitimacy of a regime, its ability to bind those subject to it, and its authority, its moral title to govern in a certain territory, whether or not those subject to it have an obligation to obey it. There are important continuities between the two concepts, but representativeness, which is our topic here, pertains more to legitimacy.

is little beyond this abstract formulation that everybody is likely to agree on. Even so, it gives our inquiry a certain shape. We are not engaged in ideal theory, looking for the most just institutional arrangement. Rather, taking into account the challenges and imperfections of actual political regimes we seek to determine how they can nonetheless earn such a moral warrant (if they can).

This is the methodology that I suggest we apply in assessing RCC. To be successful, it must do a good job of articulating the link between representation and legitimacy. It must offer a convincing account of the distinctive contribution that the courts' putative representative character makes to political legitimacy such that it justifies that they be given the power of constitutional review. Put simply, it must show that this power is legitimate (at least in part) *by virtue of the courts' representative character*. This is a test that, as we shall see, RCC fails.

Note the difference with the aforementioned hermeneutic methodology. On my preferred approach, political morality enters stage from the get-go. It explicates how representation should be construed, at least in broad terms, and why and how it matters. Accordingly, past and present practices of representation become the targets of our legitimacy-inflected moral evaluation rather than fixed points that candidate conceptions must respect. Actual practices of representation are also instructive targets of moral evaluation, as they show, in their complexity and historical unfolding, how abstract moral principles can be realized and combined in institutional forms.[4] Furthermore, based on the moral evaluations that this approach recommends, we can make the sort of relative judgment that I argued above the hermeneutic approach would be hard pressed to make. We can side with one understanding of a constitutional concept as against others because it offers a better moral account of the way representation contributes to legitimacy.

It could be objected against the approach adopted here that, despite its emphasis on legitimacy rather than ideal justice, it still does not capture the correct relationship between moral principles and constitutional practice. In fact, so the objection goes, we are not trying to identify a conception of representation that matches an external moral standard, whether that be legitimacy or justice, but simply one that can make *some* moral sense of existing constitutional practice. On this understanding, a successful conception aims at vindicating the practice in the sense that it identifies an even sub-optimal value that can truly be served by the practice, as we find it. Alexy (2005, 428) can be said to have such a limited ambition.[5] His starting point is the following provision of article 20 (1) (1) Basic Law of the Federal Republic of Germany: "all state authority proceeds from the

[4] Institutional and political practice also plays a separate and much more critical role in my account. It helps us identify the institution of which we will ask what powers it should possess. Accordingly, it supplies the main parameters for our exercise in purposive interrelation. Thus, when I speak of courts, I have in mind the institution that is typically organized so as to give impartial judgment on specific disputes in accordance with pre-existing law. I readily acknowledge that some institutions that we call courts have characteristics that make them depart from that simple picture. To the extent that they do, my claim may apply less to them. Likewise, my claim leaves open that we may want to reform this kind of institution so as to beef up its representative character. Such a reform may be in tension with other roles that courts are typically assigned, but I shall not pursue this line of reasoning further.

[5] Möller (2012) calls this method 'moral reconstruction'. It should be noted, however, that for both Alexy and Möller the value we ascribe to the practice must be genuine, not doctored.

people,'[6] Arguably, an account of representation that shows courts to be representative institutions has a better fit with practice insofar as it upholds the requirement of art. 20 (1) (1), as it applies to judicial authority. It is thus pro tanto superior (at least as an account of judicial authority under the German constitution and others similar to it) over accounts that are further removed from practice, even if the latter have an advantage at the level of moral theory.

As a general matter, this style of argument is plausible. However, we should be wary of relying too heavily on the typically very abstract and succinct constitutional text. You can interpret the provision of the German Basic Law mentioned above in a number of possible ways. Even interpretations that refrain from postulating that courts are representative institutions can fit it. For example, it may be suggested that all art. 20 (1) (1) requires is that state authority be exercised *in the name of the people* conceived of as a community of free and equal persons rather than in the name of, say, an absolute monarch. If judicial authority satisfies this criterion, it need not additionally be construed as representative in a thicker sense. Regardless of the merits of my suggestion, the provision under consideration cannot be taken in isolation. It must be seen in relation to other salient elements of the practice. If, as I will argue below, the picture of representation Alexy paints is defective, this may give us reason to go back to the practice and find alternative ways of combining and accounting for its elements.

3 Representation, Only not Responsive

At its most basic, the representation relationship involves someone acting or speaking on behalf of someone else with warrant. Typically, the relationship is structured such that the representative will reliably reflect the interests and opinions of the person being represented. In turn, this is commonly understood to require an effective causal mechanism between the representative and the represented such as, for example, periodic elections ensuring that the representative *heeds* the interests and opinions of the represented. However, arguably there is more than this *responsive* type of representation. Recently Philip Pettit (2010, 428) has proposed a different type of representation which he calls *indicative*. Whereas responsive representation works by constraining the role of the representative so that she gives effect to or heeds in a suitable sense the interests and opinions (including opinions about their own interests) of those being represented, indicative representation works by assigning a representative function to a person or body whose views systematically mirror the views of those being represented. He writes that on the responsive model 'the preferences, attitudes, opinions, etc., of representees 'are the causal source of the attitudes displayed by the representer' (ibid). By contrast, on the indicative model, 'the attitudes displayed by the representer are non-causal signs of the attitudes held by the representee' (ibid).

Pettit mentions courts as one institution that could represent in this indicative manner but does not elaborate how they ought to be organized so as to achieve that. He discusses at length citizen's assemblies, which he thinks are meant to provide a cross-section of societal views by virtue of the fact that participants are chosen randomly from the

[6] There are similar provisions in many other constitutions.

general population. The thought is that, if they are organized properly, then the fact that the citizens' assembly makes a decision is indicative of the decision that would have been taken by the citizenry at large without the need for participants in the assembly having to heed the views of anyone else.

Can something similar be said about constitutional courts? Obviously, constitutional judges are not expected, at least officially, to take into account citizens' interests and opinions.[7] Consequently, the responsive model seems ill-suited to motivate RCC. On the other hand, random selection does not determine who will be a constitutional judge, so there is no straightforward analogy with citizens' assemblies; we need a different explanation of how courts can act as indicative representatives. Such an explanation has indeed been offered by other authors.[8] Thus, Chris Eisgruber (2007) writes that the fact that US Supreme Court Justices are nominated by the President and confirmed by the Senate means that their decisions are not radically at odds with views widely held in US society. I am not going to evaluate this proposal because most constitutional systems do not follow this highly politicised mode of appointment, and also because this is not the only or the most significant consideration that Eisgruber marshals to justify constitutional review. Instead, I am going to focus on the account put forward by Robert Alexy. Alexy concedes that courts are not responsive representatives. However, he argues they can still be said to represent the people, albeit in a distinctive, *argumentative*, way. When their decisions are based on 'correct or sound' reasons, they appeal to the rational capacities of citizens. And if we assume that in a well-ordered constitutional system 'a sufficient number of members of the community are able and willing to exercise their rational capacities' (Alexy 2005, 580), that is, 'accept an argument on the ground that it is correct or sound' (ibid), then we can say that judges are indeed representatives. They are argumentative representatives. In fact, says Alexy, it is appropriate that the argumentative representation provided by courts should take precedence over the representation afforded by democratically elected institutions. Starting from the premise that '[d]iscursive constitutionalism, as a whole, is an enterprise of institutionalizing reason and correctness' (ibid, 581), it would follow quite naturally that its goals are best advanced by a system that puts sound arguments ahead of responsiveness to the electorate.

Notice the difference between this account and Eisgruber's. Eisgruber claims that the US Supreme Court is representative, because by design the Justices have moral views that many people in American society hold. So, if I am conservative, I can be confident that there is someone fighting my corner on the bench. And likewise if I am liberal. Of course, it so happens that nowadays the conservatives are in the majority, so the decisions of the institution as a whole will more likely reflect conservative views. But arguably that is no different from a democratically elected legislature. I can still think that the legislature is a representative institution, even though the legislators that share my views are in the minority. By contrast, for Alexy what matters is the quality of the argumentation as opposed to the moral views of this or that judge or a majority of judges.

[7] See contra Dixon 2023.

[8] The authors I examine below do not refer to the distinction between responsive and indicative representation -indeed their defence of RCC predates Pettit's article. I use the distinction because it helpfully frames what is taken by these authors to be distinctive of judicial representation.

What would Alexy make of the example with which we started? Recall that we are looking for an explanation of our constitutional court's abortion decision which will show that its moral bindingness depends on whether judges have acted as argumentative representatives of the people. Recall also that for Alexy argumentative representatives speak for rational persons, those willing and able to exercise their rational capacities. What is the standard that courts' reasoning must meet in order for them to count as genuine representatives? At times Alexy seems to adopt a particularly strong understanding. As already mentioned, he writes that rational persons are those that accept an argument on the grounds that it is correct or sound. Presumably, they also do not accept an argument that is incorrect or unsound. Let's assume that the arguments advanced by the court are not correct or sound. On the strong understanding, it would seem to follow that the abortion decision is not even an instance of genuine argumentative representation. The problem with this move is that it yields an overly strict criterion of representativeness. For one thing, many people would treat that decision as binding because they happen to believe that the court has got it right. Are we then to say that actually the decision does not even represent *them* because it is not correct? More generally, people who are otherwise willing and able to exercise their rational capacities will sometimes make mistakes in their reasoning. Does the court only represent them when they (and the court) have got it right, whereas it does not represent them when it has got it right but they have erred?

Alexy himself seems to back away from this move. Elsewhere he writes that it is sufficient that representative judicial decisions are 'backed by arguments that are recognized as good *or, at least, plausible*, by all those who accept the constitution' (Alexy 2005, 580, emphasis added). This qualification appears to invoke a weaker understanding of the standard to which argumentative representatives are to be held. It thus arguably avoids the problems already mentioned. It also chimes with the commonsensical thought that an argument can be rational though not fully correct. However, it would be beset with difficulties of its own. To examine these, it is necessary to get clearer on the meaning of 'at least plausible' arguments. How can an argument retain that status while still falling short of correctness?

One might be tempted to say that all it takes is that the argument conform with rules of formal rationality. When assessing the merit of government measures interfering with human rights, these rules are furnished, according to Alexy, by the laws of balancing. Alexy (2017, 20–22) distinguishes this formal dimension of rationality from the substantive dimension which comprises true moral principles. So, perhaps an argument is plausible provided it has applied the laws of balancing, even if it has assigned, say, free speech an incorrect moral weight relative to personal reputation.

This suggestion must be rejected. A purely formal notion of rationality which would remain completely agnostic about true moral principles would be, in Alexy's words, 'empty' (Alexy 2017, 21).[9] Instead, our account of 'at least plausible' arguments must 'intrinsically [connect] the formal and the substantive dimension' (ibid) of rationality, such that even erroneous arguments must make a genuine attempt to get the substantive

[9] I have argued against a similarly weak notion of reasonableness in public law based on the notion of 'rational requirements' (Broome 1999) in Kyritsis 2017, 169.

principles right in order to count as plausible. It is not clear how this can be done. Regardless, it is doubtful that plausibility furnishes an adequate criterion for representativeness. Let's suppose that the constitutional court's abortion decision passes the threshold of plausibility. It does not go without saying that you should regard it as yours, as representing you, just because it is plausible, despite being in your eyes horribly wrong. Furthermore, what if you simply refuse to be bound by the decision precisely because you do not think that it is correct or sound? Surely, it is a mistake to say that you are thereby not even a rational person.[10]

What has gone wrong? We have seen that, if the standard to which we hold the reasoning of courts is understood very weakly, as plausibility, then argumentative representation produces an anaemic constitutional result. We are not particularly moved by a decision, just because it is plausible. Conversely, if we beef up the standard and equate it with moral correctness, then, although this has obvious and significant constitutional purchase, what is doing the work is moral correctness, not representativeness. And that is not what we are after. We are not simply debating whether it matters morally that constitutional decisions are backed by correct or sound arguments. Of course it does. Alexy, though, is trying to show something more specific, namely that such arguments promote -are a vehicle of- representativeness. It is this proposition that is problematic. If my argument until now is sound, political representation cannot be understood simply to vindicate our rationality. In fact, my argument suggests a stronger conclusion, namely that political representation is meant to encompass much more of us as persons, our interests, our opinions, and our desires. However, these are all aspects of our personhood that argumentative representation brushes aside.

But maybe the stronger conclusion is premature. It could be objected that one cannot infer from argumentative representation's demise that representation should always strive to 'make present' citizens with their interests, opinions, and desires in the way just suggested. There may be value, so the argument goes, in having a more austere type of representation as well, which seeks to capture what citizens have in common rather than what pulls them apart.[11] If so, then the institutional forum that instantiates this type of representation should be one that gives expression to those moral demands, say, of freedom and equality that can be thought of as constitutional essentials of a legitimate political society. And it would not be implausible to think of the constitutional court doing just that when it interprets and enforces the constitution. On this view, Alexy is onto something that is morally significant. Where he goes astray is in thinking that what

[10] Note that I do not mean to suggest that plausibility or something like it has no role to play in constitutional law. Neither am I claiming that it would be morally permissible for you to take yourself as not bound by a suitably plausible decision whenever it is incorrect or unsound. I am making the narrower claim that it is unconvincing to portray a plausible decision as *for that reason* representative.

[11] See Pereira Coutinho (2025). This conception of representation should not be confused with the view, put forward by, among others, Wil Waluchow, whereby a constitutional court that enforces the demands of equality and freedom represents citizens by virtue of the fact that it gives effect to their authentic wishes, even against their expressed ones. For Waluchow this is because the court adheres to the abiding moral commitments of a political community, as these are enshrined in that community's constitution. See Waluchow 2007, 89ff. I have argued against this view in Kyritsis 2017, 132–5.

the constitutional court represents is the commonality of rational persons. What it does represent is citizens as free and equal.

Here I cannot fully evaluate the proposal sketched in the preceding paragraph. Suffice it to point out that it misdescribes the moral import of the constitutional demands of equality and freedom. Compliance with these demands contributes directly to political legitimacy, because a legitimate polity is one that treats its citizens as free and equal, not indirectly, because these demands reflect *our* values and thus a body that gives effect to them speaks for *us*. So, again, on this view, representativeness seems not to be making any distinctive contribution to legitimacy. At best, it collapses into moral correctness.

4 My Way or the Highway?

But let's suppose that I am wrong, and that argumentative representation is indeed a bona fide type of political representation. Do we really need to go to such lengths to establish the representative character of constitutional courts in the first place? Well, Alexy thinks we do. He writes: 'The only way to reconcile constitutional review with democracy is to conceive of it … as representative of the people' (Alexy 2005, 578). So, the overall project is the reconciliation of constitutional review with democracy. This is a project I share. What I resist is the my-way-or-the-highway quality of Alexy's claim.

I shall begin by offering the following proposition, which I shall call the democratic thesis: Political equality demands that elected bodies like, primarily, the national legislature should have a consequential role in government.[12] It also demands that other state institutions respect that role. I presume that a proponent of RCC will not object to the democratic thesis. However, I submit that the democratic thesis does not entail a further one, namely that all law must be 'people's law', to use Richard Bellamy's (2014, 1027) apt expression. Let's call this the unitary legitimation thesis. What is meant by it is that at least all the general assignments of legal rights and duties (with the exception, perhaps, of the development of the common law in the shadow of statutory law) be traceable to a decision-making process with (direct or indirect) popular credentials. If you are persuaded by the unitary legitimation thesis and want to defend systems of constitutional review that give constitutional courts the power to cancel or neutralize some general assignment of legal right or duty endorsed by a democratic legislature, then it makes

[12] Needless to say, political equality is not the only basis for the democratic thesis. I focus on it because it brings into sharp relief the counter-majoritarian difficulty with constitutional review and thus does a good job of motivating RCC. If the original problem with constitutional review is that it violates political equality because it gives the views of a few unelected judges superior voting weight over the views of ordinary citizens, then presumably we have reason to try to ameliorate the tension between constitutional review and political equality by construing courts as representative institutions. In addition, political equality furnishes a deontological basis for the democratic thesis which is immune to the kind of context-sensitive calculation that instrumentalist justifications of democracy notoriously necessitate. It thus allows us to test whether my claim holds up when the case for RCC is particularly strong. Finally, political equality is crucial for legitimacy (as well as justice), so appeal to it is in line with the methodology I adopt in this chapter.

sense for you to try to bolster the courts' representative credentials.[13] Doing so may not provide the whole of the answer to the counter-majoritarian difficulty (for one thing, you would still need to explain why constitutional courts should win in their contest with another representative body), but it goes a long way.[14]

How can we stop short of the unitary legitimation thesis, if we accept the democratic thesis? Quite apart from its philosophical merits, the insistence that all law be 'people's law' is hard to square with some salient features of the legal orders that we are most familiar with.[15] There, we notice that political equality is only one of the many moral forces that shape institutional design. Institutional design is also shaped by considerations such as the rule of law, checks and balances, efficiency, stability. This pluralism of institutional considerations is part of the reason that governing is assigned to a multiplicity of institutions. Because we care about political equality, we design the joint project of governing so that it includes a strong input from institutions that embody it. Because we care about other moral principles, we admit into the joint project of governing contributions from institutions that are set up to foster those. Thus, we build hierarchical control into institutions from which we expect efficiency and expedience. Or we bestow independence on institutions that are supposed to instantiate impartiality. That is why in earlier work I suggested that the legal orders with which we are familiar are polyphonic (Kyritsis 2017, ch 2). They are polyphonic since an individual institution can only be expected to realize a more or less narrow set of political virtues. To a great extent the moral appeal of polyphonic legal orders lies precisely in that they seek to combine the distinctive political virtues of different institutions.

Of course, even with the best intentions we cannot avoid that one value must on occasion give way to another. This is not a merely pragmatic observation, though. The openness to countenance trade-offs between different values, including democracy, exhibits a certain attitude towards the problem of political legitimacy, a wariness, due to the awesome power of the state, to put all of one's eggs into one basket. We have a political ideal that, properly understood, captures this attitude in all its complexity: separation of powers. Very aptly, Waldron distinguishes three things that we want separation of powers

[13] It might be suggested that the unitary legitimation thesis is easily satisfied whenever constitutional review is authorized by a constitution that has been drafted and/or ratified by the people or a popularly elected body. It falls outside the purview of this chapter to assess this suggestion. But it is important to contrast it to RCC, which is my sole focus here. RCC offers a different reconciliation of the unitary legitimation thesis and constitutional review, whereby it is judicial decision-making itself that has the requisite democratic credentials because it instantiates representativeness. RCC and the suggestion sketched above are not mutually exclusive. One could argue that the legitimacy of constitutional review turns *both* on the representativeness of constitutional adjudication *and* its proper constitutional authorization. I am grateful to Joel Colon-Rios who urged me to make this clarification.

[14] Conversely, it is at least arguable that the democratic objection to constitutional adjudication diminishes, the more we beef up its democratic pedigree. Bellamy (2014) has pursued this path in his work on the ECHR.

[15] Notice that my argument is not that the unitary legitimation thesis is unsound *because* it does not fit the legal orders with which we are familiar. Rather, it is that there is an attractive moral story that can be said about these legal orders, which vindicates their rejection of the 'people's law' view of legitimacy.

to achieve, 'a qualitative separation of the different functions of government' (Waldron 2013, 434), so that they may be assigned to bodies that are well suited to perform them, the avoidance of 'excessive concentrations of political power in the hands of any one person, group, or agency' (ibid, 433), and the checking and balancing of one power-holder by others. By bringing the ideal of separation of powers to bear on the controversy over the representative character of constitutional adjudication, we can better appreciate the difference between the democratic and the unitary legitimation thesis. The former is compatible with the idea that, in the name of checks and balances or in order to stave off excessive concentration of power, the institution that realizes political equality must sometimes yield to the institution that embodies independence from party politics. This is an idea that the latter thesis largely rejects. However, a legal order that subscribes to a 'people's law' criterion of legitimacy across the board is poorly equipped to address the manifold threats that separation of powers warns against. It thus risks being oppressively monophonic. Legitimacy abhors such a result.

For the same reason it will not do to say, as a proponent of the unitary legitimation thesis might be tempted to, that this thesis states a *pro tanto*, not an all things considered requirement.[16] On this construal, laws with popular credentials are always preferable, all else being equal. But because all else is sometimes not equal, it may be permissible to override such laws on occasion due to the presence of a weighty competing consideration. This construal of the unitary legitimation thesis misunderstands the lesson of the previous paragraph. Because of the grave risks associated with excessive concentrations of power, it is never enough simply to check that a law has democratic credentials. We must always keep an eye on the rest of the political order within which this law was enacted to make sure that this order as a whole adequately takes into account all the other considerations that pertain to legitimacy. Consequently, even in a system of parliamentary sovereignty it is not the case that the unitary legitimation thesis holds sway. Rather, the legitimacy of the system (assuming that it is indeed legitimate) depends on a judgment that the system as a whole sufficiently accommodates the other sources of legitimacy even absent a system of constitutional review.

5 Conclusion

Well-designed representative institutions enhance the legitimacy of a political regime. This is the animating thought behind RCC, the view that constitutional courts, too, are meant to represent the people. But, as I have argued in this paper, RCC puts us on a wild goose chase. Legitimacy shows why. In fact, it delivers a double blow against RCC. On the one hand, I have suggested that it is unconvincing to cash out whatever legitimacy gains do accrue from constitutional adjudication in terms of representation. On the other, I have stressed that legitimacy demands much more from a political order than that it be representative of the people; well-designed representative institutions are not the only thing that can enhance legitimacy. Hence, there is no compelling reason to establish a connection between constitutional adjudication and representation. Quite the opposite, there may be good reason not to refer all state institutions to the same source of legitimacy.

[16] I am indebted to Pablo Magaña for suggesting this objection.

Of course, here I have focused on only one, albeit prominent, version of RCC. There are others. But, if my claims are sound, then we have a yardstick for how to evaluate those, too. The concept of representation can perhaps accommodate lots of different types of representation. However, they are of no use to RCC, unless they provide a framework for understanding how the putative representative character of constitutional courts contributes to political legitimacy. That is a tall order.

References

Alexy R (2005) Balancing, constitutional review, and representation. Int. J. Const. Law 3(4):572–581

Alexy, R.: Proportionality and rationality. In: Jackson, V., Tushnet, M., (eds.) Proportionality: New Frontiers, New Challenges. University Press, Cambridge (2017)

Bellamy, R.: The democratic legitimacy of international human rights conventions: political constitutionalism and the European convention of human rights. Euro. J. Int. Law **25**, 1019 (2014)

Broome, J.: Normative requirements. Ratio **398** (1999)

Dixon, R.: Responsive Judicial Review: Democracy and Dysfunction in the Modern Age. Oxford University Press (2023)

Eisgruber C (2007) Constitutional Self-Government. Harvard University Press

Hickey T (2022) Legitimacy - not justice - and the case for judicial review. Oxf J Leg Stud 42(3):893–917

Kyritsis, D.: Where Our Protection Lies: Separation of Powers and Constitutional Review. Oxford University Press (2017)

Constitutional law as legitimacy-enhancer. In: Kyritsis, D., Lakin, S. (eds.) The Methodology of Constitutional Theory, pp. 211–231. Hart Publishing (2022)

Manin B (1997) The Principles of Representative Government. Cambridge University Press

Möller K (2012) The Global Model of Constitutional Rights. Oxford University Press

Pettit P (2010) Representation, responsive and indicative. Constellations 17(3):426–434

Pereira Coutinho, L.: In search of what is common: political representation by the constitutional jurisdiction. In: Pereira Coutinho, L. (ed.) Political Representation and Constitutional Adjudication, Part I, vol. 124, pp. xx–yy. Springer, Heidelberg (2025). https://doi.org/10.1007/978-3-031-85983-0_9

Urbinati, N.: Representative Government: Principles and Genealogy. Chicago University Press (2008)

Waldron J (2013) Separation of powers in thought and practice. Boston Coll Law Rev 54:433

Waluchow W (2007) A Common Law Theory of Judicial Review. Cambridge University Press

Can Political Representation Legitimately Determine Constitutional Adjudication? Judicialization, Politicization, and Judicial Candor

Bojan Spaić(✉)

Faculty of Law, University of Belgrade, Belgrade, Serbia
bojan.spaic@ius.bg.ac.rs

Abstract. Constitutional courts decide on many political issues in contemporary democracies. In doing so, they formulate conceptions of constitutional concepts. In many cases, the formulated conceptions coincide with those of political representatives. This gives the impression that constitutional courts are influenced by political representations and the appearance of illegitimate influence of political representation on constitutional adjudication. The chapter discusses the politicization of the constitutional judiciary and the judicialization of political issues to determine (1) whether political representation determines constitutional adjudication and (2) whether there are cases in which the influence of political representation on constitutional adjudication is justified. The initial discussions lead us to argue for (3) a piecemeal approach to the legitimacy of constitutional adjudication and (4) in favor of the strategy of dialogization that relies on the virtue of judicial candor to increase the likelihood of popular legitimacy of constitutional adjudication.

1 Introduction

Philosophy of law often paints a too-broad or a too-narrow picture.[1] At times, it deals with the justification of the very practice of constitutional review under some normative, conceptual, and empirical assumptions.[2] Other times, it focuses on a specific principle or concept in constitutional adjudication, hoping that the problems surrounding it can be solved by terminological or conceptual analysis.[3] In most cases, it intentionally or unintentionally omits the real-life workings of institutional arrangements on constitutional adjudication in different contexts and jurisdictions.

[1] This chapter results from research conducted within The Horizon Twinning project "Advancing Cooperation on The Foundations of Law – ALF" (project no. 101079177). ALF is coordinated by the Faculty of Law University of Belgrade (coordinators Miodrag Jovanović and Bojan Spaić) in partnership with University of Genova (coordinator Andrej Kristan), University of Lisbon (coordinator David Duarte), University of Surrey (coordinator Hrafn Asgeirson). The project is financed by the European Union.

[2] See: (Jovanović, 2015).

[3] Methodological positions in constitutional theory have recently been the object of study in: (Kyritsis and Lakin, 2022).

L. Pereira Coutinho (Ed.): ICPRCR 2022, IUSGENT 124, pp. 116–138, 2025.
https://doi.org/10.1007/978-3-031-85983-0_10

One of the stable characteristics of adjudication is that it involves the interpretation of underdetermined legal texts under various influences that often determine the normative content of sources of law within a jurisdiction. An important source of influence that has been discussed in political science and political theory but has at the same time been neglected in the philosophy of law is the formal and informal relations between the courts and other institutions in contemporary democracies. The interpretative theory has, in recent decades, shifted towards considering judicial reasoning from an institutional perspective in the work of Shapiro, Waldron, Vermeule, Sunstein, Victoria-Nourse (Spaić, 2019). The same interpretative theory has shied away from discussing informal institutional influences on constitutional adjudication, especially from those considered illegitimate influences. One illegitimate influence in contemporary democracies is the influence that representative bodies and political representatives have on constitutional adjudication.[4]

At the same time, constitutional and political theory have long been arguing that contemporary politics have been judicialized and that the adjudication of constitutional courts has been politicized (Nogueira, 2020; Vallinder, 1994). Constitutional courts have increasingly become important political actors, with their decisions often publicly challenged by political actors. For the most part, justices keep out of political debates, but the judicial opinions often reflect one of the current political positions when reversing or upholding previous judicial decisions. This has mostly been understood as a problem in some jurisdictions like the US, where constitutional courts' practices have been scrutinized for decades. In other jurisdictions, the debates on the role and legitimacy of constitutional adjudication seem to be completely absent (Rosenfeld, 2004).[5]

In this chapter, I adopt a piecemeal approach to the influences of politics on constitutional adjudication. The main issue I discuss is whether political influences or, more precisely, the influences of political representation on constitutional adjudication can be justified. To do this, I'll try to (1) explain the judicialization of politics and the politicization of the constitutional judiciary, (2) argue that political representatives and representative bodies, as a matter of fact, influence constitutional adjudication, and (3) inquire into whether these influences can be justified, in order to finally (4) argue for a dialogical approach to constitutional adjudication that overly includes the views of political representatives in judicial opinions.

2 Front-Door Judicialization, Back-Door Politicization

Contemporary democratic politics increasingly relies on constitutional courts and judicial process as a "means for addressing core moral predicaments, public policy questions, and political controversies." We call this process "judicialisation of politics" (Hirschl, 2008, 2011). Judicialization is marked by the fact that political issues across the globe

[4] Dieter Grimm writes "application of the law is a matter for the legal system, and in this process political motives are illegitimate" (Grimm, 2016, p. 204).

[5] The fact that judicial review is scrutinized in the US with a decade long debate on its legitimacy is particularly suprising given the fact that constitutional courts in Europe have much broader powers (Hahm, 2012, p. 7), and have had these powers since their inception (Kelsen, 1942).

morphed into constitutional law matters, with constitutional courts being recognized as significant political decision-makers (Pildes, 2004, p. 31).

At the same time, constitutions are linguistically underdetermined documents to such a degree that their interpretation necessarily includes extralegal considerations. Vague, ambiguous, and contested constitutional concepts often express moral positions and need interpretation (Goldford, 1990). Judicial interpretations of liberty, equality, integrity, legality, rule of law, etc., exist among the myriad of influential and inconspicuous interpretations of the same concepts in contemporary democracies. As a result, the interpretative activities of constitutional courts, it is often claimed, are influenced by one of the competing political positions regarding those basic concepts (Weiden, 2010).

In this part of the chapter, I'll discuss the phenomenons of the judicialization of politics and the politicization of the judiciary in order to provisionally identify the criteria for claiming that a judicial issue has been politicized or that a political issue has been judicialized.

2.1 Judicialising Politics

Constitutions and constitutional adjudication circumscribe political deliberation, resulting in majority parliamentary decisions. The tendency to defer to constitutions and constitutional courts for the solution of many political and moral issues has been diagnosed by Karl Loewenstein in his 1955 book *Reflections on the Value of Constitutions in Our Revolutionary Age*. In 1979, the same Loewenstein warned of the possibility of extreme judicialisation of political issues, subsuming it under the term *juristocracy* (Nogueira, 2020, p. 672–673).

According to Alec Stone Sweet, judicialization of politics is primarily judicialization of the law-making activity traditionally assigned to legislative bodies. Judicialization entails two aspects:

"(a) the production, by constitutional judges, of a formal normative discourse that serves to clarify, on an ongoing basis, the constitutional rules governing the exercise of legislative power, and (b) the reception of these rules, and of the terms of this discourse, by legislators" (Sweet, 2000, p. 195).

Judicialization thus entails judicial resolution of a contested political problem, including adopting the judicial resolution as one of the authoritative positions or the authoritative position regarding the political problem.

Constitutionalizing moral and political positions is already a form of removing political and moral issues from democratic decision-making and deliberation. Andrei Marmor convincingly argues that the "constitutional entrenchment of values, or conceptions of the right and the good, necessarily favors certain conceptions over others by essentially shielding some favored moral, political conceptions from the democratic decision-making process" (Marmor, 2007, p. 77). In other words, all political life within a constitutional democracy is supposed to revolve within the bounds of the constitutionally favored moral and political conceptions. In this sense, we talk about the *constitutionalisation of politics*—a situation or process in which some basic rules, values, rights, and other norms are excluded from political deliberation.

Judicial review is a step further in the constitutionalisation of politics by conferring the power to adjudicate between the conceptions of the right and the good to the highest courts or separate constitutional courts. Those who argue in favor of constitutional review most often claim "(1) that in a democratic society dedicated to the ideals of equality and mutual respect, we can come, by way of rational consensus, to substantive outcomes, expressed in terms of human rights, and that these outcomes should form the fundamental law of the given society, and (2) that democratic process is less reliable than the judicial one in identifying those rights and their precise content." (Jovanović, 2015, p. 67). Constitutional courts adjudicate competing conceptions of values by determining the content of the constitutional texts. In this way, political deliberation about the basic values of a political community is taken from the political representatives, and the power to have the final say on the content of those values is transferred to judges.

The pinnacle of translating political issues into legal issues is the ubiquity of constitutional courts with the power to challenge legislative acts in various domains. Already in 1994, the process of judicialization was described as a worldwide phenomenon (Vallinder, 1994). Vallinder defines judicialization as the expansion of judicial decision-making powers to issues traditionally the province of the legislative or executive branch of government and/or the adoption of judicial-making methods outside of the judiciary (Vallinder, 1994, p. 91). In a series of important contributions to the topic at the beginning of the century by Ron Hirschl treats the judicialization of politics as a crucial part of the trend of contemporary political systems to move towards a kind of juristocracy (Hirschl, 2004, p. 6). Accordingly, he gives a narrow definition of judicialization that entails transferring power from representative institutions to judiciaries.

In recent decades, courts, most notably the highest courts in a jurisdiction and/or constitutional courts, have been relied upon to "resolve a range of issues, varying from the scope of expression and religious liberties, equality rights, privacy, and reproductive freedoms, to public policies pertaining to criminal justice, property, trade and commerce, education, immigration, labor, and environmental protection" (Hirschl, 2011, p. 254). The same courts have decided political leaders' positions by constitutional procedures for the removal from office (Kim, 2014), banned political parties (Hogan, 2022; Bourne, 2018), decided on election outcomes, and the status of independence referenda (Jovanović, 2007). There is practically no prominent political controversy that won't be, at one point in time, framed as a constitutional issue to be resolved by constitutional courts (Hirschl, 2011, p. 255).[6]

The historical reason for the arrangement is most probably the specific position of the judiciary within the separation of powers.[7] If we are to judicial politics, we are expected to make the institution that deals with political matters as close to a regular court as possible. It is thought best to leave the job of protecting constitutions to traditional state bodies, unlike the political actors, expected to be independent and impartial, then to leave them to the whims of political actors and their goals. In other words, constitutional review inherits its normative underpinnings from the role of the judiciary within the separation

[6] Judicialization is not a one way street. In international politics it has already been noted that, after a long period of judicialization of international issues, there has been a tendency towards dejudicialization (Abebe and Ginsburg, 2019).

[7] It is also the covert argument used by many constitutional scholars to dismiss philosophical musings about the possibility of justifying judicial review of legislation. Hic Rhodus hic salta (Αὐτοῦ γὰρ καὶ Ῥόδος καὶ πήδημα).

of powers. Another reason for deferring to constitutional courts in deciding contested political issues is the authority of final judicial decisions. The finality of constitutional decision-making is, in most instances, a decisive argument in political struggles, even in highly polarising situations that endanger the unity of political communities.[8]

2.2 Politicising Constitutional Adjudication

To resolve constitutional issues, courts.

"examine the relevant provisions of the Constitution, their text and their context; the interplay between the different provisions; legal precedent relevant to the resolution of the problem (…); the domestic common law and public international law impacting on its possible solution; factual and historical considerations bearing on the problem; the significance and meaning of the language used in the relevant provisions; the content and the sweep of the ethos expressed in the structure of the Constitution" (Venter, 2005, p. 143–144).

Given the breadth of issues that enter into consideration, constitutional courts are, in many ways, necessarily political actors. The object of constitutional adjudication is political. 1. Constitutional courts review political acts and acts of public authorities based on the constitution that establishes and regulates public authority by instituting the political structure of a community and by limiting political behavior (Grimm, 2019, p. 308; Landfried, 2019, p. 4). 2. Their decisions have political consequences that often have society-wide effects for generations (Landfried, 2019, p. 4; Grimm, 2019, p. 308). The effects of constitutional adjudication Even in the Kelsenian model, whose adoption was arguably the single greatest change in legal systems worldwide in the last century, the decisions of constitutional courts invalidating legislation have political consequences (Ginsburg and Garoupa, 2011, p. 541). 3. Finally, judges engage in internal politics by adopting different and often conflicting interpretative doctrines or ideologies (Rosenfeld, 2019, p. 38).[9]

By politicization of constitutional justice Alec Stone Sweet means "(a) the move to activate constitutional review in order to alter legislative outcomes or the state of the constitutional law, and (b) the situation that constitutional judges find themselves as a result of this move." In both cases, Sweet is prone to understand judicialization and politicization in relation to the law-making function of the state. He insists that the two processes are interrelated through a sequence with the following form: constitutional conflict—> delegation to the constitutional court—> constitutional decision-making/rule-making—> judicialization (Sweet, 2000, p. 196).

By constitutional design of contemporary democracies, however, constitutional courts are independent and impartial bodies checking the other branches of power in

---

[8] In particular the decision of the Canadian Supreme Court from 1998 regarding Quebec 1998 2 SCR 217, Italian Constitutional Court regarding Veneto 118/2015, German Bundesverfassungsgericht regarding Baviera order 2 BvR 349/16, and Spanish Constitutional Court judgements 42/2014 and 117/2017 regarding Catalonia.

[9] Not to mention that Kelsen, as a result of the criticism that was directed at his idea of constitutional Courts by Carl Schmitt, that it is not possible to confine a constitutional court to the role of a negative legislator, and that a positive element is always present in constitutional adjudication (Kelsen, 1942; Ferejohn, 2002, p. 48).

relation to the Constitution. Their impartiality and independence are secured by a) the appointment and nomination process, b) adjudication detached from public opinion and political pressure, c) the prohibition of political ideology in judicial reasoning, d) lack of affiliation of justices with political parties, and other procedural and substantial doctrines. The measures for mitigating those undue influences of constitutional adjudication are permanent topics of dispute.

Many contemporary challenges question this impartiality and independence (Szente and Gàrdos-Orosz, 2019). The appointment and nomination process is plagued by the practice of court packing (Kosař and Šipulová, 2023) - a series of strategies aimed at changing a constitutional court's composition for achieving political aims. Fixed and non-renewable terms of office keep out political opinion and pressure, usually life appointments and ongoing training in judicial ethics. Judgments providing detailed reasons, public engagement and transparency, and the internal voting and procedure rules emphasizing dissenting opinions are thought to minimize the role of ideology in constitutional reasoning. Finally, in cases where constitutional change is even remotely possible, clear provisions on independence and impartiality are thought to provide a solid basis for eliminating illegitimate influences on constitutional adjudication.

But even with all the measures, formal and informal rules on the constitutional courts, and strict abidance by constitutional provisions, claims of political influences on the constitutional courts are omnipresent. Constitutional design pushes politics out of constitutional adjudication through the front door, and this same design opens a backdoor for politics to creep in. Sources of law used in constitutional reasoning are not just any legislative enactment to be changed or amended at will by a temporary legislative majority. Constitutional texts express the most general legal principles, values, and interests. To put it less dramatically, constitutions, being foundational legal documents, are abundant in ambiguity, vagueness, and, most importantly, contentedness. Insofar as the constitutional review is in a position to invalidate laws on substantive grounds, they do so by determining the meaning of constitutional provisions by adopting one of the several possible political conceptions of crucial constitutional concepts (Rosenfeld, 2004, p. 635–636). In other words, constitutional adjudication is not only political because of its object and effects. It is political insofar as the process in which judges reach decisions is also political in nature (Grimm, 2019, p. 309).

2.3 Some Realism About Constitutional Justice

At the core of the idea of politicization of the judiciary is the insight that judges never merely apply the law. They actively engage in political and moral issues in interpreting legal texts, becoming political actors.[10] And indeed, with some slight differences (Rosenfeld, 2004), signs of political influence on courts are overt (Garoupa and Grembi, 2013; Garlicki, 2019) or implicit, but they are most definitely existent. Constitutional courts adjudicate on ideology-based, identity-based, and interest-based disagreements,

[10] This is of course not the only reasons for the raise of prominence of courts in recent decades, but it's arguably a basis for it. The same Martin Shapiro claims that legislative inertia, for example, plays a prominent role in the increase of the importance of the judiciary (Nogueira, 2020, p. 676).

including but not confined to "abortion, affirmative action, the legitimacy of government redistribution or interference in the marketplace, the rights of criminal suspects, the precise meaning of religious toleration, minority cultural rights, the regulation of speech and spending in electoral campaigns…." (Jovanović, 2015, p. 72). Rights, interests, and identities are indeed protected by the letter of constitutional text, but the letter is not enough to decide cases. The normative content of the constitution is underdetermined by its linguistic content (Grimm, 2016, p. 205), leaving space for various influences on both the procedure and the outcomes of constitutional decision-making.[11] Richard Posner writes:

Because the materials of legalist decision making fail to generate acceptable answers to all the legal questions that American judges are required to decide, judges perforce have occasional—indeed rather frequent—recourse to other sources of judgment, including their own political opinions or policy judgments, even their idiosyncrasies (Posner, 2008, p. 9).

Certain interpretative rules and doctrines that are dominant within a jurisdiction influence the normative meaning of constitutional provisions. Sometimes, we question the originalist or (pseudo)originalist inclinations of the Supreme Court of the United States or the living document doctrine of the European Court of Human Rights. Yet, we rarely see a problem with the courts adjudicating according to an interpretative doctrine of its own or another's making. Other times, it might be influenced by its institutional position, allowing it to pass final judgment on matters like abortion and simultaneously discouraging it from tackling other issues like transgender rights. European constitutional courts are often not formally bound by past constitutional decisions and should, in principle, have more interpretative latitude than common law constitutional adjudicators (Rosenfeld, 2004, p. 637). Other times again, constitutional adjudication is determined by epistemic authorities that do not have the institutional position to influence constitutional decision-making. We do not see much of a problem when the constitutional court follows a court from another jurisdiction in solving a problem (Doyle, 2016) or when it makes ample use of legal scholarship or invokes the authority of prominent scholars to support its arguments.

However, we rarely think that political influences on constitutional adjudication can be legitimate. After all, as Dieter Grimm writes, "application of the law is a matter for the legal system, and in this process political motives are illegitimate" (Grimm, 2016, p. 204). Constitutional courts often make statements along the same lines, arguing that certain influences on constitutional adjudication are never justified, if they exist at all. For example, the South African Constitutional Court argues: "The legislative organ exercises a political discretion, taking into account the political preferences of the electorate which votes political decision-makers into office. Public opinion, therefore, legitimately plays a significant, sometimes even decisive, role in resolving a public issue such as the death penalty. The judicial process is entirely different." (Venter, 2005, p. 143–144).

[11] "It is possible that no reasonable doubts exist about the meaning of a norm with regard to a certain case. But cases like these usually do not reach the courts. Most constitutional trials arise from legitimate doubts about the meaning of constitutional provisions with regard to a concrete case." (Grimm, 2019, p. 314).

There is a strong expectation for the court to be a neutral actor and widespread doubts about its neutrality are often detrimental to the legitimacy of their decisions. Deciding on political issues is a balancing game for constitutional courts. If their decisions predictably side with one or another position in the political domain, the courts might develop a legitimacy problem regarding their specific decisions, potentially leading to a problem with the legitimacy of constitutional review in general. T It is commonly thought that constitutional courts deploy at least two strategies to address legitimacy issues. The first strategy is the defence of the decision on formalist grounds, as determined by the constitutional provisions and constitutional case law on the national or international level. Another way of mitigating problems of legitimacy is the anticipation of the reaction of the political public and trying to limit individual reactions or backlashes of the decisions.[12]

2.4 Interim Conclusion No. 1

The strategies will be discussed in the conclusion of the chapter. For now, it is enough to conclude that constitutional courts have been important actors in the judicialization of politics in the last century. Constitutional judicialization of politics in all contemporary political communities involves limiting politics by means of legal documents abounding in indeterminacies. To mitigate those indeterminacies, judges are influenced by non-legal, including political reasons in determining the meaning of constitutional texts. Conceptions of constitutional concepts adopted by the courts are often already entertained by political representatives. If those determinate conceptions crucially influence judicial interpretation, we can say that political representation determines constitutional adjudication.

3 The Influence of Representation on Constitutional Adjudication

On the one hand, it's commonplace in constitutional theory that constitutional courts are political:

"Once petitioned to control the constitutionality of a statute, the constitutional courts must take a decision and, in taking such decisions, it engages in behaviour whose effects are partly legislative... When they announce legally binding interpretations of statutory provisions, they rewrite or amend legislation, to the extent that the court's interpretation meaning – fully differs from that of the government and parliament. It has a limited and specialised lawmaking authority." (Sweet, 2000).

On the other, there is a strong expectation that democratic politics should be excluded from constitutional adjudication:

"Once in office, judges are immunized against politics. They are not subject to instructions and they cannot be removed or dismissed because of their decisions. Independence is justified because judges underlie different bonds, namely the constitution

[12] The two strategies with different terminology are discussed in: (Sweet, 2000, p. 200). The second strategy is particularly interesting from the perspective of the Dobbs decision of the US Supreme Court. Namely, the almost complete text of the judgement was leaked a couple of months before the publication of the judgement. It is speculated that it was released on purpose, to test the reactions of the public to the decision.

that they have to apply to the cases at hand. Their independence is not a personal privilege. It exists for law's sake. It is guaranteed to secure that judges can decide according to the law without fearing any disadvantage. Attempts to instrumentalize courts for political, religious, and economic interests are illegitimate."(Grimm, 2019, p. 311).

At best, the political character of constitutional adjudication is often considered specific. Michael Rosenfeld argues that constitutional courts engage in politics but not ordinary judicial politics. Once a law or an ordinance has been enacted, it is left to the courts that engage in judicial politics. What separates ordinary democratic politics from judicial politics is that judges stay within a peculiar legal language game, constituted by the legal setting and the perspective of those engaged in the language game (Rosenfeld, 2019, p. 42).

The differentiation between ordinary politics and judicial politics that Rosenfeld proposes is conceptually sound. Judges do indeed translate political issues into legal issues, confining themselves to legal discussions and resolutions of the problems before them. More than in other areas of law, the issues that are legally resolved in constitutional law are often *politically* controversial. The methodology of constitutional adjudication is, unlike democratic politics, expected to be limited by "existing legal doctrine, the relevant constitutional provisions, and authoritative judicial precedent" (Rosenfeld, 2019, p. 40). According to many constitutional theorists, these methodological specificities translating political issues into legal issues elevate constitutional courts above ordinary democratic politics.

However, translating ordinary politics into judicial politics doesn't magically eliminate ordinary politics from constitutional adjudication. For legal realists, this translation is simply politics by other means, a thin veil covering judges' true, usually ordinarily political, decision-making. This position has been descriptively developed in theories of models of judicial behaviour (Segal, 2011).

3.1 Judicial Behavior

Strategic models of judicial behavior in political science have long emphasized the influence of political context on judicial decision-making (Epstein and Weinshall, 2021). The behavior of judges is determined to a greater or smaller degree by political contingencies, like the situation in which one party dominates politics. In these cases, judges are less likely to defy the government. In situations with political fragmentation, judges are more likely to act according to their personal preferences with less regard for the views of political representatives (Aydin-Cakir, 2018, p. 1101–1102). However, the problem of political representation determining constitutional adjudication goes beyond the mere attitudes of judges.

Constitutional adjudication involves both a legal and a political component. The legal component is "the application of pre-existing rules or standards." In contrast, politics is the choice "one from among many plausible principles or policies for the purpose of settling a constitutional issue" (Rosenfeld, 2004, p. 637). Political representatives voice the interests and values of constituents. At times, the voiced interests and values are protected by the Constitution. Of course, different representatives vehemently disagree on the content of those interests and values. They entertain, so to speak, different conceptions of some core constitutional concepts.

Insofar as they are interested in their legitimacy, constitutional courts take note of different positions regarding the values and interests involved in constitutional adjudication. However, their position is not a simple observance of parliamentary debates. It is often claimed that the voiced representatives' positions crucially influence judicial decisions, especially in the long run. In many a case, according to those same claims, constitutional adjudication is influenced by the willingness or disposition of constitutional judges to interpret the constitution in a way that is favorable to the views of the political representatives (Grimm, 2016, p. 204), be it the representatives of the political majority, or those of a political minority.[13]

3.2 Instances of Perceived Political Influence

Examples of the influence of political representation on constitutional adjudication abound. The rule of law backsliding in Poland is considered by many to be a consequence of the influence of the ruling "Law and Order" Party on judges of the Polish Constitutional Court. On the one hand, Marcin Matczak explained his view of the situation using the house-building metaphor, in which the building inspector represents the investor. No matter how well-founded the neighbors' claims regarding the fact that the construction violates the plan (Constitution), the Inspector rejects the claims.[14] On the other hand, one of the judges of the Polish Constitutional Court framed the matter in terms of legitimate differences in constitutional interpretation. It happens that the ruling party favors a republican interpretation of the Polish Constitution and that the opposition parties favor a liberal one. According to the same constitutional court justice, the ruling parties and opposition parties have different views on the constitutional court's role. According to the ruling party's position, the Constitutional Court should have a conservative, restrained role. According to the other CC's role should be progressive or activist.[15] The Constitutional Court is, at the moment, simply siding with the majority view on how the Constitution should be interpreted.

In other cases, the relations between constitutional adjudication and political representation do not endanger the institutional construction of constitutional democracies. The decisions of the Supreme Court of the US are notoriously charged politically. The Dobbs decision in the US reversed Roe v. Wade and returned the right to abortion to the political arena of the US federal states. The right to abortion is not one of the liberties

[13] When we speak about result driven constitutional interpretation, we often take it to mean that the court is influenced in its decision-making by the political representatives forming the majority within a constitutional democracy. Hardly ever do we notice that the minority views might also be determinative of constitutional adjudication, or we notice, but find no problem with it. This is understandable. The classical argument for constitutional review invokes the possibility of a "tyranny of the majority" that is especially pronounced when identity based disagreements are at stake (Jovanović, 2015, p. 73).

[14] https://verfassungsblog.de/how-to-demolish-an-independent-judiciary-with-the-help-of-A-constitutional-court/

[15] https://verfassungsblog.de/a-critical-response/ The Polish case evolved into a full-blown legal crisis. The severity of the situation is perhaps best illustrated by the fact that some legal philosophers thought it appropriate to use the criminal law concept of self-defence in order to analyse the relations between the legislation and the judiciary.

guaranteed by the US Constitution; we all know the simpleton argument because only traditional rights are protected, and the Constitution doesn't refer to abortion. Samuel Alito, the author of the majority opinion and the leaker of the draft of the political opinion in Rome, delivered a more interesting informal part. He argued in favor of Dobbs opinion in the context of talks about religious freedom, claiming that this fundamental liberty is attacked by those who want to hold complete power. In doing so, he engaged in a political conversation with foreign leaders, claiming that their willingness to discuss US law was inappropriate and even that they paid the domestic price for doing so (Boris Johnson). Justice Alito's talk resounds the longstanding conservative worry that religion is under attack in the United States and mimics the positions of dominant portions of the Republican Party.

Of course, there are plenty of instances in which the lay and expert public perception had a strong inclination to consider constitutional court decisions to be determined by positions of political representatives. In the US, Bush v. Gore from 2000 and Citizens United v. Federal Election Commission (2010) are cited as common examples of ordinary politics determining judicial politics (Rosenfeld, 2019, p. 56–59). A similar but less commented tendency, with a strong inclination towards progressive politics under the guise of evolutionary interpretation, has been the topic of many criticisms of the European Court of Human Rights and other European courts following its practice (Pildes, 2019).

3.3 Indeterminacy of a Determinant

In these prominent cases and many others not so visible to the global public, we claim that the views of political representatives influenced constitutional adjudication. Until the advent of the illiberal democracies in Europe, that openly curtailed the independence of constitutional courts and packed them with loyal judges (Bugarič and Ginsburg, 2016),[16] the influence of political majorities on constitutional courts was mostly kept under the legal radar. In absence of overt practices aimed at influencing the adjudication of constitutional courts, it isn't easy to conclusively prove that political views determined the outcome of constitutional courts' interpretative and adjudicative activities. Notoriously, both the object and the outcome of constitutional adjudication are political in nature. It is far less obvious that the reasoning of constitutional justices is also political (Grimm, 2019). The reasons for this differ in different jurisdictions, but a formalist attitude regarding constitutional texts and public argumentation around the texts plays an important role in covering political influences with a legalistic veneer.

Historical and longitudinal studies on constitutional court adjudication have started painting a nuanced picture of the many political influences on constitutional courts (Friedman, 1990). Unfortunately, the studies have been, for the most part, confined to stable Western democracies (Epstein et al., 1998), with an emphasis on the United States. These studies seem to indicate that while the political preferences of constitutional justices are relatively stable, the entirety of the Supreme Court is prone to shifting its political positions with the changes of justices (Jessee et al., 2022).

---

[16] The most dramatic case of backlash against a model postcomunist court was probably Hungary (Sólyom, 2003).

The very decision on the constitutionality of a legislative act is a political position that sometimes matches the position of the political majority and sometimes matches the position of the political minority. In Poland, Hungary, and many a developing democracy, constitutional courts tended to decide on politically contested issues by "siding" with the representatives constituting legislative majorities (Preuß, 2019). In established constitutional democracies with a tradition of constitutional review and on the international level, the courts have decided to favor the positions of political minorities. In developing democracies, the ones that started their dubiously successful journey towards constitutional democracies, the courts have tended to "side" with the majority.[17]

It is difficult to prove conclusively that substantial political views regarding constitutional issues have determined constitutional adjudication. In singular cases that are decided, the best indication of the influence of politics on adjudication is the reports and behavior of judges who decided on the constitutional issue. In a series of decisions, political scientists and jurists have demonstrated a correlation between the political context and the decision-making of constitutional courts. Correlation, trivially, doesn't imply causation, and more empirical work is most certainly needed to settle the issue. However, the existing work on the topic makes it likely that constitutional adjudication is influenced by the positions and views of representative bodies and political representatives to a non-trivial degree.

From a philosophical perspective, we can, at best, argue about the criteria for claiming that political representation influenced constitutional adjudication. It is necessary that 1. The court decided on an issue that is a topic of political disagreement. 2. That the issue is not constitutionally settled, 3. The court's final decision corresponds to a position in the political debate, 4. The political position was a ground for the decision, in the sense that the decision couldn't have been made without the political position. Surely, the mere similarity of conceptions doesn't mean that political representatives influence the constitutional courts or that political representation determines constitutional interpretation. To claim the latter, much precise empirical work would be needed. However, empirical inquiries and these and other cases make it probable. Of course, your mileage may vary depending on your country of origin or involvement in comparative constitutional analysis.

3.4 Interim Conclusion No. 2

Available empirical data is far from conclusive, but it makes it probable that constitutional adjudication is influenced by the political positions entertained by political representatives in contemporary democracies. On the one hand, constitutional court decisions almost always side with one among many political positions. On the other

[17] These are, of course, just some general tendencies based on unstructured observation. Most of the literature argues that the political situation influences judicial decision making in the sense that a dominant party reduces the likelihood of courts ruling against the majority. In politically split situations, there is a tendency of courts to rule more assertively (Epstein and Knight, 1998). Recent research shows that there is room for nuance in these strategic accounts, depending on the constitutional matters that are decided by the court. (Aydin-Cakir, 2018).

hand, the under-determinacy of constitutional provisions makes it probable that constitutional judges' political preferences and ideologies play a significant role in steering the apparently legal methodology of constitutional decision-making.

4 Can Political Influence on Constitutional Adjudication Be Justified

So far, I have tried to establish that constitutional adjudication, at least in its decisional part, deals with the same political issues that popular representation deals with and that constitutional adjudication is influenced by popular representation. In this final part of the chapter, I'll discuss whether substantive views on the values and aims of the elected representatives can justifiably or legitimately influence constitutional decision-making.

Those who cherish constitutional review normally do so for at least one of the following reasons: (a) this institution is necessary for securing the supremacy of the constitution over ordinary legislation and/or (b) it is indispensable for protecting individual rights and freedom. Given that the very point of establishing constitutional adjudication within the judiciary or a discrete constitutional court was constraining the potentially unlimited power of political representatives, the answer to this question is *prima facie* negative.

This default position is challenged from two perspectives: the perspective of the abstract case against constitutional review and the perspective of the representative character of constitutional adjudication. Both challenges are not direct but emerge due to the views regarding constitutional review and the nature of constitutional adjudication.

4.1 Legitimacy of Judicial Review

The first critical perspective, adopted by Andrej Marmor, Jeremy Waldron, and others, argues that constitutional review is inherently flawed and that there is no real need for it in democratic political communities (Marmor, 2007; Waldron, 2006). In mounting cases against judicial review of legislation, Marmor and Waldron ask why courts should adjudicate on political matters.

Marmor argues that the constitutions already entrench certain conceptions and values, removing them from democratic deliberation. The problem becomes obvious when a country has an old constitution with a complicated change procedure. Interpretative flexibility makes the problem worse since more power to courts to interpret the constitution also means less power to democratic representatives (Marmor, 2007, p. 75–77). Waldron insists on the conditions that make legislative bodies a preferable locus of constitutional decision-making. Democratic institutions will, according to him, do a better job at decisionmaking if they are functional and based on universal suffrage, there is a set of judicial institutions, a commitment to minority and individual rights in a society, and disagreement about conceptions of rights among the members of the community (Waldron, 2006, p. 1360). The outcome of their discussion is that constitutional review is unjustified because it judicializes politics by adopting an undemocratic decision-making procedure about the content of constitutional concepts and values as well as other important societal issues, excluding deliberation on the part of political representatives.

Admittedly, the mentioned arguments are actually against judicial review in abstract. Normatively, their case against judicial review disregards the different kinds of political conflicts. For ideology and interest-based conflicts, a representative body might as well be in a better position to reach a final decision. However, identity-based conflicts are quite different. A majority decision in favor of the majority can not imaginably produce positive results for the minority population (Jovanović, 2015, p. 72–74). Empirically, it is problematic to identify both the societies that Waldron imagines when he talks about core cases[18] and to conceptualize the culture that would be a necessary prerequisite for making constitutional review superfluous (Jovanović, 2015, p. 77–78).

My question from the introduction to this chapter is somewhat different, but the abstract case against judicial review can be informative in answering it. Suppose there is no good reason for the courts to better adjudicate matters commonly discussed and decided by political representatives. Why is it considered illegitimate for constitutional courts to decide in line with the political positions of those representatives regarding fundamental constitutional concepts, values, and principles? If there is no need for constitutional adjudication and political representatives would just as well protect constitutional rights, why wouldn't constitutional judges openly defer to the conceptions of those rights held by political representatives? After all, we have seen that judges either are acquainted with the political views of representatives or can become acquainted with them and reason accordingly, as they often do. If the abstract case against judicial reviews is true, judges would be, in principle, justified in deferring to the positions of representatives regarding constitutional issues, at least in those cases in which there is a clear indication of the future results of the democratic procedure.

For the opponents of constitutional review, this might not be the optimal outcome, but it might be the second best thing given that political representatives are, for procedural, epistemic, and other reasons, in a better position to decide on contested constitutional issues.

4.2 Judges as Representatives

The second way to claim that political influences on constitutional adjudication are legitimate is to claim that constitutional judges are one kind of representative. Many conceptions of constitutional adjudication justify constitutional review by claiming that judges are a kind of representative. Robert Alexy argues that constitutional courts represent the people "argumentatively" (Alexy, 2016, p. 72; Alexy, 2005). Whatever the account of representation we hold, judges are non-elected representatives deciding on some of the same questions that elected representatives deliberate on in the public space. Mathias Kumm brings some much-needed nuance to the concept of representation and argues that there are at least four dimensions of representation - volitional, identitarian, argumentative, and vicarious (Kumm, 2019, p. 282), basing his ideas on the work of Hanna Pitkin (Pitkin, 1967). Volitional representation regards the relationship between

---

[18] Jovanović convicingly argues that the fact that a conutry might be considered a core case society acording to Waldron, doesn't mean that the rights of minorities will be protected. A lack of restraints on majority decisions leads to acts of tirany of the majority even in Switzerland, a core case country by any measure (Jovanović, 2015, p. 74-75).

the electorate and officials. In the case of constitutional courts, this link is very weak and is based on the fact that the election of judges is grounded in a constitutional or legislative act of the representatives of the people. Identiterian representation regards the "salient social traits" like race, gender, religion, and nationality of judges. Argumentative representation regards public reasoning that courts engage in that is "attuned to… Arguments that played a central role in the political process and that connects to beliefs held by those to whom the law is addressed" (Kumm, 2019, p. 287). Finally, vicarious representation regards the reactions of other institutions of the legal system to judicial decisions. In other words, for a decision to be vicariously representative, it must be implicitly endorsed by the legislative body (Kumm, 2019, p. 289–290).

But the problem with representation in contemporary democracies is that the representatives do not, strictly speaking, represent any single value, interest, or ideal of the constituents. This is so for two reasons. The first reason is that the representative mandate is free and not delegated. The chances of the electorate punishing the representative for not doing a good job in representing them are too far between. The second reason is that legislatures are "beholden to lobbyists and special interests or an executive branch effectively dependent on a handful of businesses and social elites" (Rosenfeld, 2019, p. 37). Volitional representation is almost completely absent in constitutional adjudication; identitarian representation is possible but not decisive; vicarious representation is prudent but unnecessary. Arguably, even in parliamentary representatives, all these kinds of representation are premised on theoretical notions of "social contract, popular sovereignty, and majoritarian democracy" that are normative idealizations, having little to no descriptive merit (without claiming that they do not have normative merit).

These normative positions mostly eschew some notorious facts about political representation in democratic polities:

"If one considers the bluntness of the electoral instrument with which democratic representation is determined, the ratio of representatives to those represented, the time span between elections, the limited nature of the restrictions placed upon the elected representatives, the difficulty with which legislators can be called to order by voters and the pressures of conformity to the injunctions given by party caucuses, one may seriously doubt the completeness of the representation rendered by elected legislators and executives even in a fully democratic system in which voters participate enthusiastically. The almost universal truth is that elected legislators and government executives are extremely difficult to dislodge or even to call to account between elections." (Venter, 2005, p. 145).

Still, it is one thing to claim that democratic representation is flawed in the forms practiced and wholly another issue to claim that constitutional justices are better representatives than elected officials. After all, with all the normative desiderata of constitutional democracies in place, representing a constituency in a constitutional court seems to be more of a bug than a feature.

Kumm, thus, argues that constitutional courts are mainly argumentatively representative in that they (a) adopt a kind of reasoning that is based on rules and principles but take into account the legitimacy of the policy that is brought into question (for example, by proportionality analysis), (b) use a style of opinion writing that engages with arguments and counterarguments, (c) allowing concurring and dissenting opinions (Kumm,

2019, p. 287–289). But even if we accept the idea that constitutional courts are representative in the sense Kumm describes, from the perspective of political representation in constitutional democracies, it remains an issue whether non-elected argumentative representatives represent the relevant views and interests then elected argumentative representatives. A positive answer to this question would mean that constitutional court judges do better in practical reasoning and argument presentation in a political community than the political representatives, parliaments, and their members.

Such a thin conception of representation seems to lead us to the conclusion that, while it might be flawed volitionally, in the identitarian sense, or vicariously, argumentative representation by political representatives in the parliament does a better job of mirroring both the style of the political debate and the practical reasoning (including flawed practical reasoning) then constitutional adjudication. In other words, democratic political representatives have an upper hand not only in volitional, identitarian, and vicarious representation but also in argumentative representation.

4.3 Justifying Influences on Constitutional Adjudication

A third mode of inquiry starts with (a) a hypothesis that constitutional courts can, some matters related to the constitution, be in a better position to decide constitutional issues than political representatives and (b) the notion that there are various influences on constitutional adjudication including the influence of the substantial political positions of political representatives. This allows us to set aside the issue of the legitimacy of the entirety of judicial review (at least temporarily) and the idea that judicial review has to be justified on the grounds that judges are a kind of representative and focus on whether influences on constitutional adjudication can be justified. Specifically, in this case, we are able to focus on the question of whether the influence of substantial views of political representatives in constitutional adjudication can be justified.

This mode of inquiry stems from constitutional scholars' common sense conclusion that "constitutionalization of politics… can have beneficial stabilizing effects so long as it is not extensive" (Rosenfeld, 2019, p. 44). What is crucial is the extent to which politics is constitutionalized, and this depends on constitutional content and political context. Striking down a law for procedural reasons related to the lack of quorum in the parliament that enacted the statute is less politically charged than deriving the right to abortion from the right to privacy (Rosenfeld, 2019, p. 46). Rosenfeld thus argues for a nuanced approach to the constitutionalization of politics with the scope of judicial politics by accessing the legitimacy of each judicial decision.

Given the nature of constitutional provisions and the general, ambiguous, vague, and essentially contested language they employ, it can be argued that political representatives are better positioned to decide on the meaning of constitutional texts on *legal grounds*, *popular or representative grounds* and *epistemic grounds.*

Legal justification would consider the normative underpinnings of constitutional democracies with their constitutionally mandated judicial review, separation of powers, and judicial independence. We go to great lengths, both in developed democracies and especially in perennially consolidating democracies (like Serbia), to make constitutional justices as detached as possible, both procedurally and substantially, from elected representatives and their potentially corruptive influences. In the US, even tour guides make a big deal out of the fact that, in spite of the geographical closeness of buildings in Washington, elected representatives do not even visit the building of the Supreme Court. In other words, In contemporary democracies, it would be difficult to find a legal system that endorses the influence of political representatives on constitutional courts.

Popular justification entails the claim that the substantive values and aims of the electorate that are represented by elected officials are particularly relevant for the adjudication of constitutional courts. I concluded the discussion on the representativeness of constitutional judges by claiming that judges are never in a better position to represent the actual electorate compared to political representatives. The position of political representatives in relation to the electorate makes it more probable that their articulation of views of the electorate regarding constitutional matters will be more in line with the actual positions of the public than those articulated by constitutional justices. Consequently, popular justification could lead us to the idea that absolute deference to the views of political representatives is justified.[19]

This leaves us with the possibility that the influence of political representation on constitutional justice can be justified on epistemic grounds. The *epistemic justification* entails the claim that political representatives hold special knowledge or a special position that suits them to know the substantive content of values and aims enshrined in the Constitution. But this thesis can hardly be defended. 1. The conceptions of constitutional values that the constituents hold are, as a rule, not very well defined, elaborated, or deliberated upon. 2. The conceptions of constitutional values that the representative holds are more elaborated but are, by the very nature of their position, partisan, biased, and one-sided. 3. Even under the cognitivist assumption that there is objective content to fundamental societal values, being elected for public office hardly makes one suitable to determine the objective content of those values. In fact, constitutional elaboration of constitutional values is epistemically better determined by law and constitutional law experts. While they might lack the quality of popular representativeness, the requirements to hold the office of constitutional justice in contemporary democracies make it so that it is far more likely that the constitutional court will produce a conception of a constitutional right or value that is legally sound, in line with the entirety of the legal system that the constitution is a part of.

4.4 Interim Conclusion No. 3

The influence of political representation on constitutional adjudication cannot be justified on legal grounds in contemporary democracies, nor can they be justified on epistemic grounds. Legally, constitutional judges are expected to be independent and neutral interpreters of the constitution. From the perspective of popular justification, political representatives have the upper hand in voicing the conceptions of crucial constitutional concepts that the constituents hold.

---

19 There is a lot to be said about the relation of constitutional justices to their own legitimacy. Or Bassok argues that the main source of legitimacy of Supreme Court Justices in the US until the advent of pooling, was in fact the opinions of political representatives (Bassok, 2013). Pooling has the advantage of being less tainted with the reformulation by political representatives, since it is quite obvious that the representatives do not simply mirror constituent preferences.

5 Conclusion: Safeguarding Popular Legitimacy by Giving Up the Formal Attire

The discussion led us to the following conclusion: 1. a) Political issues in contemporary democracies are judicialized in the sense that political actors defer to constitutional courts to adjudicate on many political issues that have traditionally been under the purview of political representatives. b) The indeterminate nature of constitutional text pointing to substantial political values makes it probable constitutional adjudication becomes politicized and that political representatives' political positions regarding constitutional issues influence constitutional courts' decisions. 2. Many instances of constitutional adjudication show significant political influence, with the views of political representatives serving as mostly tacit grounds for constitutional decisions. 3. Political representatives are in a better position to represent the views of the electorate regarding constitutional values, but they are not in a better position to develop legal conceptions of constitutional values, nor are they legally allowed to do so in contemporary democracies. There are no definite reasons for claiming that political representatives are in a better position to determine those issues than constitutional courts, especially in situations of high public polarisation regarding an issue.

But, if the decisions made by the courts are political, and if the judges are not in a better position than elected representatives to voice the constituents' opinions on the meaning of the constitutional texts, would this mean that there is no reason to have a constitutional review in the first place? Abstract arguments against constitutional review would seem to suggest that there is none. The answer to this second question by the literature also seems to be a resounding no. What courts do better than the political branches of government is they surround themselves and their opinions with a veil of formalism and legalism? The veil allows the justices to appear detached from common politics and their opinions detached from political debate.

Still, given the political character of the decisional aspects of the decisions in constitutional review, the public and elected officials continuously question the legitimacy of constitutional review. Being political actors in this sense, constitutional courts should permanently reassess their positions from the perspective of public opinion in order to secure their position as final adjudicators on constitutional matters. This makes it so that constitutional justices pay attention to the political positions of the political representatives, considering the legitimacy of constitutional review. Opinion polls have, however, made it possible to get to know the public opinion without reference to the positions of political representatives. Indeed, it has long been known that the constitutional courts pay close attention to their popular legitimacy by following opinion polls (Bassok, 2013).

There is, Martin Shapiro claims, a fundamental paradox in the working of courts. Courts occasionally make policy decisions. Constitutional courts make these same decisions regularly, making law in the process. In all modern judicial systems, these same courts are reluctant to recognize that they make law. Therefore, they vehemently deny that they make law and instead opt for denying that they make it, arguing that the case was decided entirely based on existing law (Shapiro, 1994, p. 155–156). Most of the time, the formal legalist veneer is considered to be in line with the care that judges and courts have for the popular legitimacy of their decisions. However, even among judges, some are more inclined to admit the influences openly. Brian Tamanaha goes to great lengths to list many instances of judges who have openly admitted that one of the roles of the judge is to make law (Tamanaha, 2009, p. 81–89).

On the most general level, there are two strategies in which constitutional adjudication can deal with the influence of political representation. The first strategy can be called *formalization.* The first strategy entails striping judicial opinions of all non-legal argumentation to present judicial decisions as chains of reasoning based on formalized legal and factual premises, leading inevitably to adjudicative conclusions. This approach might have many unintended consequences, but its main problem is that it makes the authority of the opinion almost entirely dependent on the court's legitimacy within a society. Rosenfeld argues that the main trait of constitutional adjudication is that its politics are not political in nature but legal. This is exemplified by the fact that political issues are successfully transformed into legal issues, with the style of judicial opinions being the main characteristic of this transformation. A formalist judicial style most obviously distinguishes legal from ordinary politics. The normative message of this position could reasonably be made to suggest that the courts should translate all political issues into legal issues in order to leave the impression that the politics they engage in are specific.

Needless to say, there is a problem with the formalist strategy: 1) First of all, complex decisions based on constitutional texts that are poor in communicative content are difficult to justify using legal reasons alone. 2) Both the political representatives and the public focus almost exclusively on the decision-making of the constitutional courts. If they tackle the legal reasoning behind the decision-making, they do so in a biased, partisan way. 3) The veil of formalism obscures substantial issues at stake in constitutional adjudication, leaving the impression of injustice. Virgílio Afonso da Silva argues in many cases there is a tendency to deliberate privately in constitutional courts, leading to a lack of popular legitimacy (da Silva, 2013). Still, even in courts that deliberate publicly, based on rules that allow for dissenting opinions, it is not evident that the decisions are based on publicly stated reasons (Grimm, 2019). Among this approach's many possible unintended consequences, one that stands out is the erosion of the possibility of popular legitimacy of individual judicial decisions. Extreme formalization turns opinions of constitutional courts into technical papers that are not understandable to the general public and that often are inscrutable for anyone outside of constitutional scholarship. This approach is dominant in contemporary constitutional courts.[20] The battle of conceptions within constitutional courts is politics disguised as law.

I'll call the second approach dialogization. It is commonly thought that we can distinguish the legal argumentation, or the public part of constitutional reasoning, from the decision-making of the constitutional courts. Constitutional reasoning is often legalistic and technical, in accordance with the judicial roots of the constitutional courts. This is even more the case in jurisdictions in which judicial review is done by ordinary courts. Reliance on judicial interpretative and evidential argumentation is considered crucial for the appearance of independence of the constitutional courts (as well as courts in

---

20 Martin Shapiro is probably the theorist that is most blunt about the mentioned issues. He argues: "This paradox means that although every court makes law in a few of the cases, judges must always deny they make law... There is nothing we can do about it, and there is nothing they can do about it... Such is the nature of courts… One may call this justificatory history, but I call it lying" (Shapiro, 1994). See also: (Yablon, 1990).

general). Judges have a special strategic incentive to make their argumentation as close to legal modes of argumentation as possible. The more legal argumentation is detached from political argumentation regarding fundamental constitutional values, the more one has the sense that the entirety of the reasons for adopting a political decision is constitutional and legal. Legal reasons and legal reasoning of constitutional courts is the main mode of legitimizing the decisions of those courts. The extreme formalization of judicial opinions of constitutional courts encroaches on the popular legitimacy of both the decisions and the courts. With a political object of inquiry and the political effects of the decisions, the technical legal jargon and technical legal reasoning to the untrained ear sounds like a dramatic departure from the judicial virtue of candor and honesty, like a game of make-believe that is completely detached from the society and politics that have been used as both the starting point and the end point of adjudication. Martin Shapiro is extremely blunt: "Courts and judges always lie. Lying is the nature of the judicial activity." (Shapiro, 1994, p. 156).

Dialogization mitigates the paradoxical nature of judicial activity by broadening the argumentation of constitutional courts to include the aspects of the political debate that are not strictly legal. Constitutional theory argues that political considerations are relevant in constitutional courts only as they can be formulated as legal questions. Rosenfeld calls this judicial politics, in which all issues are translated into issues of legal-interpretative doctrine and ideology. Grimm argues that in this peculiar kind of politics, judges should exclude everything that cannot be formulated as a legal argument (Grimm, 2019, p. 311). For a constitutional adjudication to count as legal, it has to be based on legal argumentation. A methodology of constitutional adjudication is considered legal if "what the judge adds to the text of the law in the process of interpretation has its basis in the text and can be derived from it in a reasonable argumentative manner" (Grimm, 2016, p. 205).

Constitutional justices have political preferences and even affiliations that influence their decision-making. However, Grimm strongly believes in what he calls "the neutralising effect of legal rationality" (Grimm, 2016, p. 208). At the same time, he claims that it is a prerequisite of judicial independence for the judges to "pay attention to the reaction their decisions elicit in society." (Grimm, 2016, p. 211). However, even this moderate level of legal formalism leaves much to be desired from the perspective of (a) the entirety of reasons that influence judicial decisions, and (b) increasing the potential for popular legitimacy of judicial decisions. In the first case, we are left wondering about the true reasons for the outcomes of constitutional adjudication. In the second case, if both the object and the outcome of a judicial decision have a political character, the reasoning that used the object to come to an outcome can hardly be made out to be entirely legal, eschewing all the political argument in its various forms for the sake of technical legal argumentation. A series of politically controversial decisions of a constitutional court that are supposedly argued on fully legal grounds strip away the possibility of judicial argumentation to convince anyone but the constitutional scholars within a jurisdiction.

Dialogization would thus entail that the courts embrace substantial arguments of the political representatives and the public to provide the most comprehensive and convincing reading of a constitutional document in relation to the adjudicated problem. For individual judges, it means a partial adherence to the virtue of judicial candor - defined as the "avoidance of deliberate falsehoods in judicial decisions" (Shapiro, 1987, p. 732). Judicial candor required by dialogization is not focused on the negative obligation of avoiding lies as much as it is focused on the positive obligation to include the positions conceptions of political representatives as arguments in judicial opinions. In this sense, it could be said that it is part of a broader conception of judicial candor defended by Richard H. Fallon that entails "forthright disclosures concerning vulnerabilities in, and possibly psychologically motivating influences on, their chains of formal legal reasoning" (Fallon Jr, 2017, p. 2267).

Arguably, dialogization would 1. Firmly situate constitutional adjudication in the political context that prompted it and keep the constitutional judiciary connected to the societal problems that it addresses, 2. Make judicial opinions more approachable (and interesting) to a wider public, 3. Promote the legal argumentation and reasoning of constitutional justices, 4. Increase the likelihood of popular legitimation of judicial decisions and the courts. Finally, the obligation of judicial candor regarding the substantive positions of political representatives 5. Would mean an explicit embracement of constitutional courts' dual – political and legal – institutional nature.

References

Abebe D, Ginsburg T (2019) The dejudicialization of international politics. Int Stud Quart 63:521–530
Alexy R (2005) Balancing, constitutional review, and representation. Int J Const Law 3:572–581
Alexy R (2016) Constitutional rights and constitutional review. In: Kenneth Einar Himma BS (ed) Fundamental rights: justification and interpretation. Eleven International Publishing
Aydin-Cakir A (2018) The impact of judicial preferences and political context on Constitutional Court decisions: evidence from Turkey, 16:1101–1120
Bassok O (2013) The supreme court's new source of legitimacy. J Const Law 16:153–198
Spaić B (2019) Institutional turn(s) in theories of legal interpretation. In: Duarte D, Moniz Lopes P, Silva Sampaio J (eds) Legal interpretation and scientific knowledge. Springer, Cham, pp 187–209. https://doi.org/10.1007/978-3-030-18671-5_8
Bourne AK (2018) Militant democracy and the banning of political parties in democratic states: why some do and why some don't. In Ellian A, Rijpkema B (eds) Militant democracy – political science, law and philosophy. philosophy and politics - critical explorations, vol 7. Springer, Cham, pp 23–46. https://doi.org/10.1007/978-3-319-97004-2_2
Bugarič B, Ginsburg T (2016) The assault on postcommunist courts. J Democr 27:69–82
da Silva VA (2013) Deciding without deliberating. Int J Const Law 11:557–584
Goldford DJ (1990) The political character of constitutional interpretation. Polity 23:255–281
Kyritsis D, Lakin S (eds) (2022) The methodology of constitutional theory. Hart Publishing
Doyle O (2016) Constitutional cases, foreign law and theoretical authority. Global Const 5:85–108
Epstein L, Hoekstra V, Segal AJ, Spaeth HJ (1998) Do political preferences change? A longitudinal study of U.S. Supreme Court justices. J Polit 60(3):801–818
Epstein L, Knight J (1998) The choices justices make. CQ Press, Washington, D.C.
Epstein L, Weinshall K (2021) The strategic analysis of judicial behavior. Cambridge University Press
Fallon RH Jr (2017) A theory of judicial candor. Colum L Rev 117:2265
Ferejohn J (2002) Judicializing politics, politicizing law. Law Contemp Probl 65:41
Venter F (2005) The politics of constitutional adjudication. ZaöRV 65:129–166

Friedman LM (1990) Opening the time capsule: a progress report on studies of courts over time. Law Soc Rev 24(2):229–240. Longitudinal Studies of Trial Courts
Garlicki L (2019) Constitutional court and politics: the polish crisis. In: Landfried C (ed) Judicial power: how constitutional courts affect political transformation. Cambridge University Press
Garoupa N, Grembi FG-PAV (2013) Judging under political pressure: an empirical analysis of constitutional review voting in the Spanish Constitutional Court. J Law Econ Organ 29:513–534
Ginsburg T, Garoupa N (2011) Building reputation in constitutional courts: political and judicial audiences. Ariz J Int Comp Law 28:539
Grimm D (2016) Constitutionalism: past, present, and future. Oxford University Press
Grimm D (2019) What exactly is political about constitutional adjudication? In: Landfried C (ed) Judicial power: how constitutional courts affect political transformation. Cambridge University Press
Hahm C (2012) Beyond "law vs. politics" in constitutional adjudication: lessons from South Korea. Int J Const Law 10:6–34
Hirschl R (2004) "Juristocracy" - political, not juridical. Good Soc 13:6–11
Hirschl R (2008) The judicialization of politics. In: Whittington KE, Kelemen RD, Caldeira GA (eds) The oxford handbook of law and politics. Oxford University Press
Hirschl R (2011) The judicialization of politics. Oxford University Press
Hogan J (2022) Analyzing the risk thresholds for banning political parties after NPD II. Ger Law J 23:97–116
Jessee S, Malhotra N, Sen M (2022) A decade-long longitudinal survey shows that the Supreme Court is now much more conservative than the public. Proc Natl Acad Sci U S A 119:e2120284119
Jovanović M (2007) Constitutionalizing secession in federalized states: a procedural approach. Eleven International Publishing
Jovanović M (2015) On the abstract case against constitutional review
Kelsen H (1942) Judicial review of legislation: a comparative study of the Austrian and the American constitution. J Polit 4(2):183–200
Kim YH (2014) Impeachment and presidential politics in new democracies. Democratization 21:519–553
Kosař D, Šipulová K (2023) Comparative court-packing. Int J Const Law
Kumm M (2019) On the representativeness of constitutional courts: how to strengthen the legitimacy of rights adjudicating courts without undermining their independence. In: Landfried C (ed) Judicial power: how constitutional courts affect political transformation. Cambridge University Press
Landfried C (2019) Introduction. In: Landfried C (ed) Judicial power: how constitutional courts affect political transformation. Cambridge University Press
Marmor A (2007) Are constitutions legitimate? Can J Law Jurisprud 20:69–94
Nogueira AJA (2020) State of the art research in the judicialization of politics. Beijing Law Rev 11:670–689
Pildes RH (2004) The constitutionalization of democratic politics. Harv Law Rev 118:25–154
Pildes RH (2019) The law of democracy and the European court of human rights. In: Landfried C (ed) Judicial power: how constitutional courts affect political transformation. Cambridge University Press
Pitkin HF (1967) The concept of representation. University of California Press
Posner RA (2008) How judges think. Harvard University Press
Preuß UK (2019) Judicial power in processes of transformation. In: Landfried C (ed) Judicial power: how constitutional courts affect political transformation. Cambridge University Press
Rosenfeld M (2019) Judicial politics versus ordinary politics: is the constitutional judge caught in the middle? In: Landfried C (ed) Judicial power: how constitutional courts affect political transformation. Cambridge University Press

Rosenfeld M (2004) Constitutional adjudication in Europe and the United States: paradoxes and contrasts. Int'l J Const L 2:633
Segal JA (2011) Judicial behavior. In: Goodin RE (ed) The oxford handbook of political science. Oxford University Press
Shapiro DL (1987) In defense of judicial candor. Harv Law Rev 100(4):731–750
Shapiro M (1994) Judges as liars. Harv JL Pub Pol'y 17:155
Sólyom L (2003) The role of constitutional courts in the transition to democracy. Int Sociol 18:133–161
Sweet AS (2000) Governing with judges: constitutional politics in Europe. Oxford University Press on Demand
Szente Z, Gàrdos-Orosz F (2019) New challenges to constitutional adjudication in Europe: a comparative perspective. Routledge
Tamanaha BZ (2009) The realism of judges past and present. Clev St L Rev 57:77
Vallinder T (1994) The judicialization of politics—a world-wide phenomenon: introduction. Int Polit Sci Rev 15:91–99
Waldron J (2006) The core of the case against judicial review. Yale Law J 115:1346
Weiden DL (2010) Judicial politicization, ideology, and activism at the high courts of the United States, Canada, and Australia. Polit Res Q 64:335–347
Yablon CM (1990) Are judges liars? A wittgensteinian critique of law's empire. Can J Law Jurisprud 3:123–138

Author Index

L. Pereira Coutinho (Ed.): ICPRCR 2022, IUSGENT 124, p. 139, 2025.
https://doi.org/10.1007/978-3-031-85983-0

MIX
Papier aus verantwortungsvollen Quellen
Paper from responsible sources
FSC® C105338

If you have any concerns about our products,
you can contact us on
ProductSafety@springernature.com

In case Publisher is established outside the EU,
the EU authorized representative is:
Springer Nature Customer Service Center GmbH
Europaplatz 3, 69115 Heidelberg, Germany

Printed by Libri Plureos GmbH
in Hamburg, Germany